# BRIAN McFARLANE

# STANLEY CUP FEVER

## 100 YEARS OF HOCKEY GREATNESS

Stoddart

First published in 1992 by
Stoddart Publishing Co. Limited
34 Lesmill Road
Toronto, Canada
M3B 2T6


**Canadian Cataloguing in Publication Data**

McFarlane, Brian, 1931–
    Stanley Cup fever : 100 years of hockey greatness

Includes index.
ISBN 0-7737-5554-3

1. Stanley Cup (Hockey) – History.    I. Title.

GV847.7.M43 1992        796.962'648        C92-095077-9


Cover Design and Typesetting: Brant Cowie/ArtPlus Limited

Cover Illustration: Al Wilson

Printed and bound in Canada

Some of the material in this book first appeared in 1978 in slightly different form as *Stanley Cup Fever*, published by Pagurian Press.

Stoddart Publishing gratefully acknowledges the support of the Canada Council, Ontario Ministry of Culture and Communications, Ontario Arts Council, and Ontario Publishing Centre in the development of writing and publishing in Canada.

This book is dedicated to the memory of my parents, Leslie and Amy McFarlane, who supported me in my love affair with the fascinating game of hockey, and to my five grandchildren: Keegan, Samantha, Aubrey, Kelly, and Max. Hopefully, some or all of the grandchildren will become players and enjoy the childhood games on ice as much as I once did.

# Contents

*Acknowledgments*   ix

*Preface*   xi

**1**   The Birth of the Cup   *1*

**2**   Discord and Dissension   *9*

**3**   Turn-of-the-Century Triumphs and Trials   *21*

**4**   The Fever Spreads   *36*

**5**   The Roaring Twenties   *49*

**6**   Cup Thrills of the Thirties   *68*

**7**   The Forties: Wartime Hockey and Postwar Growth   *90*

**8**   The Fabulous Fifties   *112*

**9**   The Swinging Sixties   *137*

**10**   The Savage Seventies   *162*

**11**   The High-flying Eighties   *192*

**12**   Into the Nineties   *231*

*Afterword*   *241*

*Statistics*   *245*

*Index*   *259*

# Acknowledgments

**T**HE AUTHOR WISHES TO THANK the following for their valuable assistance in the preparation of this history of the Stanley Cup: Leslie McFarlane for his inspiration and help in my earlier writing on the Cup, Joan McFarlane for her suggestions and expert proofreading of the finished material, Danielle Joel for her diligent research, student Sharon Morgan for obtaining many of the quotes herein, Michael Carroll as project editor, Darlene Money as copy editor, Jacquelyn Waller-Vintar as proofreader, and to my friends among the NHL Oldtimers whose recollections of games and series of long ago are deeply appreciated.

# Preface

**S**TORIES OF THE STANLEY CUP, one of the most coveted trophies in professional sport, have become an integral part of the game's heritage. Most of the stories centered on this century-old symbol of hockey superiority are not only fascinating but true.

Some of the best-known yarns border on the incredible. The renowned Ottawa Silver Seven captured the Stanley Cup in 1905. At the time the trophy was a silver bowl small enough to be carried under a man's arm. One of the Silver Seven carried it to a victory party in a local hotel and later, somewhat inebriated, decided to lug it home with him. As he and his teammates wended their noisy way homeward along the Rideau Canal, the player wondered aloud how far he could boot the Cup into the canal drop-kick style.

His teammates dared him to try. High in the air flew the Stanley Cup, landing somewhere in the snow and ice covering the surface of the canal. The players cheered their companion. Then everyone staggered home to bed, leaving the Cup resting in the blackness below.

The next day, club officials inquired about the Cup's whereabouts. The engraver was waiting to inscribe the names of the new champions. The players recalled their prank of the night before and rushed back to the canal. One of them, star forward

Harry Smith, retrieved the Cup, had it suitably engraved and then took it home for safekeeping.

The following season the Montreal Wanderers won the trophy and planned a celebration of their own. But the Stanley Cup was nowhere to be found. Finally, someone remembered Harry Smith and a search of his home turned up the Cup. Harry had stuffed it into a closet and forgotten about it.

In 1924 another victory party was held in Montreal, and once again the Cup was almost lost. The Montreal Canadiens whipped Calgary in two games, 6–1 and 3–0, the final game being played in Ottawa because there was no artificial ice in Montreal. On their return, the champions were invited to a postseason celebration at the home of team owner Leo Dandurand.

One carload of players headed for the party was forced to stop to repair a flat tire. While this work was being done, the Stanley Cup was placed on the curb. When the spare tire was in place, the players piled back into the car and roared off into the night. At Dandurand's home, the champagne was uncorked and Leo proposed a toast to the Cup. But there was no Cup. Someone mentioned the flat tire and said, "Gee, Mr. Dandurand, I think the Cup is a mile or so back down the road, sitting on the curb."

"Then get back there and find it!" roared Dandurand.

The players rushed back to the place where the tire repair had interrupted their journey. There stood the Cup, exactly where they'd left it.

When it wasn't being lost, misplaced, or ignored, the Cup was involved in other misadventures. In 1961, a Montreal hockey fan named Ken Kilander was in Chicago watching a playoff series between the Black Hawks and Montreal. When he saw his beloved Canadiens on the verge of being eliminated, Kilander rushed into the lobby of the Chicago Stadium and smashed open the glass showcase housing the Stanley Cup. Hoisting the trophy over his shoulder, he headed for the exit but was quickly apprehended by some startled ushers and held until police arrived. In court the next day he told a judge, "Your Honor, I was simply taking the Cup back to Montreal where it belongs."

In 1979, one of hockey's brightest stars couldn't resist the temptation to kidnap the Cup. Again, it all started with a victory party, where the Montreal Canadiens were celebrating their fourth consecutive Cup triumph. One stop of their pub tour of Montreal was at Toe Blake's tavern, another was at Henri Richard's. With beer and champagne flowing freely, nobody noticed Guy Lafleur slip away with the Stanley Cup and place it in the trunk of his car. Then he drove to the home of his parents in Thurso, Quebec.

When Guy placed the Cup on the front lawn of his childhood home, people came from miles around to admire it and have their photos taken beside it. Hours later, Guy looked out the window to see his son Martin filling the Cup with water from the garden hose. "Maybe it's time I took the Cup back to Montreal," he told his parents. "They must be pretty worried about it by now."

Guy was right. Montreal officials had been searching frantically for it for hours. When he turned it over, Guy was reprimanded. But the club found it difficult to stay angry with the Flower, especially after his 129-point season and ten playoff goals in 16 games.

When the New York Islanders won the Cup four straight years in the early eighties, a woman in the team's public relations department took it on promotional visits to schools on Long Island. "One day," she told me, "I took it into a classroom and the bowl fell off its base and bounced around the floor. All the kids went 'Oooh!' But listen, that bowl was soldered to the base very poorly. So I said, 'Geez, we better get this thing fixed.' I took it to a local auto-collision place, thinking they'd have some welding or soldering equipment.

"But the man I showed it to said, 'Sorry, lady, we're not gonna touch that thing. You crazy?'

"Then I took it to a jeweler, and he wouldn't touch it, either. Finally I called the NHL offices in New York and told someone the damn bowl had fallen off the base. He said, 'Aw, don't worry about it. Send it to us and we'll get it fixed.' So I did.

"But while I was toting it around I used to just throw it in the back of my little hatchback. I stopped for gas one time and the

xiv    STANLEY CUP FEVER

station attendant couldn't believe his eyes. 'Is that the Stanley Cup in there?' he asked.

"I said, 'It sure is. Want to touch it?'

"When I opened the hatchback, suddenly a bunch of gas jockeys and grease monkeys surrounded my car, all of them anxious to run their dirty fingers over the Cup. It made their day."

I asked her, "Did the kids in the schools ask some interesting questions about the Cup?"

"Oh, yes," she said. "The question they asked most was about the Cup's authenticity. Most of them thought it was a replica. I assured them there was only one Stanley Cup. This was it."

"Well, the kids on Long Island are pretty smart," I told her, "because the bowl on top of the Cup *is* a replica. Many years ago a silversmith in Montreal made an exact duplicate of the original, which was getting brittle with age. If you'd dropped the original on the floor it might have been damaged beyond repair. Incidentally, that first bowl is in the Hockey Hall of Fame in Toronto."

She said, "Interesting," in a way that made me think it wasn't — not to her, anyway. And I bristled a bit when she said, "Oh, I've had the Cup over to my house a few times. You know, to show it off to my friends at parties."

Obviously, this Long Island resident didn't understand the significance of this priceless trophy to people deeply involved in hockey, people smitten with a passion for the game. In my opinion, only winners of the Stanley Cup should be able to show it off at parties. They've earned the right. If Bryan Trottier took it home to bed with him, if Clark Gillies fed his dog from it, if Red Kelly's three-month-old son pooped in it during a photo session, if King Clancy kept it around one summer using it as a bill collector or ashtray, if it wound up at the bottom of Mario Lemieux's swimming pool — these postseason incidents involving the famous old Cup are understandable and perhaps even excusable. These men were Cup winners, champions. They earned the right — not to damage or abuse the Cup — but to enjoy its brief presence in their lives.

But when others get involved, like the Islander public relations woman, more stringent caretaking is necessary. The Cup should be treated like a precious child, not tossed casually into a hatchback or threatened by some mechanic's torch. The thought of the Stanley Cup bowl rolling around a classroom floor with small children in hot pursuit is enough to make a true hockey fan howl in protest. The old trophy, symbolic of one hundred years of hockey tradition, deserves more respect.

Over the years the Stanley Cup has grown in importance — and in size. As new champions were crowned, engravers ran out of space for team names. Many extra "collars" have been added, and the trophy has been rebuilt until today it is several times larger than the original silver bowl donated by Lord Stanley, who served as Canada's governor general a century ago.

Lord Stanley, who returned to England before the first Stanley Cup game was played, no doubt enjoyed receiving reports from the Dominion of early-day puckchasers fighting fiercely over his silver bowl — especially his Ottawa favorites. But he could never have envisioned the multimillions of dollars spent over the next ten decades by moguls and sportsmen all inspired by the same basic goal — to capture hockey's most coveted award, the Stanley Cup.

# The Birth of the Cup

**B**EFORE THE TURN of the century, hockey was played outdoors between snowbanks or in rinks designed for curling or pleasure skating. One outdoor arena in Kingston harbor even had a bandstand at center ice. In this odd rink, the rival goalies played the entire game without ever seeing each other, and attacking forwards had to make a choice — to go left or right when the bandstand loomed up in front of them.

In most arenas, a puck or an opponent could not be bounced off the boards because there were no high boards, just a narrow one-foot-high ledge around the ice surface. Players who skated too close to the low sideboards ran the risk of being knocked flat by curling brooms wielded by spectators. If the puck flew in among the spectators, it was caught and quickly thrown back with no need for a faceoff. If a player was bodychecked in among the fans, he might, with luck, land at the feet of a fair young maiden and linger awhile to beg her pardon. On less fortunate occasions, he might be propelled in among supporters of the opposing team, who'd pummel him before roughly tossing him back into the fray.

A team in the old days consisted of sometimes six, sometimes seven players, who were expected to play full tilt for two 30-minute halves. Each team carried a couple of substitutes, but these men saw action only if regulars were injured or became too exhausted to continue playing. Early players wore uniforms and spring skates but little padding and no gloves. Their sticks were extremely short by modern-day standards.

The goalie did not wear a mask or a chest protector. He would have scoffed at the very idea. When one enterprising netminder experimented with a crude iron mask in 1898, he was booed and jeered at by the spectators. Eventually one of the goal guardians borrowed some cricket pads to protect his shins from flying pucks, and other goalies followed suit. Ordinary gloves made their appearance. The pioneer goalie's jockstrap was a fur cap — the thicker the better — stuffed inside his pants.

The goal he protected consisted of a pair of four-foot-high poles embedded in the ice six feet apart. There was no crossbar, no goal line and no netting to catch the puck. A goal umpire, often selected from among the spectators prior to the game, stood on the ice behind the goal area and waved a handkerchief or small flag to signal a score. If, in the opinion of the players or the referee, the goal judges were inept or biased, they were quickly replaced by other volunteers.

*Early hockey game. Much was to change, including the goals and number of players. There are seven a side in this illustration.*

The goalie was expected to stay on his feet at all times. If he chose to, he could race up the ice and attempt to score, but few ever did. In 1905, a Montreal goalie named Fred Brophy made history by scoring a goal against Quebec. His astonishing feat far surpassed anything he'd done as a puckstopper that season, for his goals-against average was a woeful 8.2.

The defensemen — known as point and cover point — were stay-at-home types who cleared the puck down the ice by lifting it high into the air. The forwards carried the puck and tried to score from "combination play," which simply meant good passing, stickhandling, and shooting. A fourth forward was called a rover, and he dashed all over the ice.

In the old days the referee wore a derby hat and an overcoat and carried a handbell instead of a whistle. On faceoffs, he would place the puck carefully on the ice between the sticks of the opposing centers and shout, "Play!" as he leaped nimbly out of the way to avoid battered knuckles or knees.

The game was strictly amateur. Neither the players nor the officials were paid and the arena owners got most of the gate money. At 25 cents per ticket, it didn't amount to much. Later, when large arenas with real seats were built for hockey, the fans paid 50 cents to a dollar to watch a game in relative comfort. It didn't take the players long to figure out ways to divert some of the profits into their own pockets.

Today the Stanley Cup, the oldest professional sports trophy in North America, is a glittering symbol of the championship of the National Hockey League. It is competed for by million-dollar athletes engaged in a multimillion-dollar business. But a century ago, it was for simon-pure participants only. Some of those long-ago battles to win the Cup seem as remote in time as the Indian wars. Change has followed change until it would appear that the only thing hockey now has in common with hockey then is that the players wear skates, use sticks, and score goals. But the annual chase for the Stanley Cup has not changed; the fever to win it has survived everything. It has become a ritual of spring.

The Cup itself has changed from small silver bowl to mammoth trophy. In the mid-1960s, former NHL president Clarence Campbell was concerned that Lord Stanley's gift to hockey was getting old and brittle. Secretly, he had a Montreal silversmith fashion an exact duplicate. For months only a select few league officials knew about the substitution. The original Stanley Cup — the trophy that was once used as a flowerpot, abandoned on a street corner, tossed into the Rideau Canal, left forgotten in a clothes closet — no longer holds champagne for thirsty winners. It sits under glass in the Hockey Hall of Fame, and if it could talk what amazing stories it could tell.

*Carl Pederson, the Montreal silversmith who created a new Stanley Cup.* (Public Archives of Canada)

The conditions that have governed the Cup's destiny over a century of play have changed dramatically. It began as a challenge trophy to be fought over by amateur teams. The club that captured it was compelled to defend it when ordered to do so by the Stanley Cup trustees. Sometimes there were two or three Cup challenges in a season. The trophy's fame spread, and soon organized teams from centers large and small scrambled after it. Challenges came from places like Galt, Rat Portage (Kenora), Smiths Falls, and Queen's University in Ontario; from Sydney, New Glasgow, and Halifax in Nova Scotia; from Winnipeg, Edmonton, and Vancouver in western Canada; and even from Dawson City in the Yukon. The story of the Dawson City challenge, most hockey historians agree, is one of the most incredible odysseys in sports history.

Some of the early-day challenges were truly bizarre. The Dawson City players were forced to play two grueling games within hours of their arrival in Ottawa, even though they'd been on the road for almost a month with no opportunity to practice. Another team once played two goalies in the net — at the same time. In 1909 an Edmonton team composed almost entirely of ringers lost to the Montreal Wanderers in a Cup series; only one team member had played with the Alberta champions during the regular season. Once an Ottawa team was accused of flooding the ice with one or two inches of water prior to an important match, to slow down their fast-skating opponents. And a turn-of-the-century Stanley Cup game was never finished: the referee became so frustrated and angry with the feuding players that he took off his skates and went home!

As every Canadian knows — with the possible exception of schoolboys too busy playing hockey to get passing grades in history — for decades the reigning British monarch appointed a governor general to represent the royal presence in Canada. In recent years, the governor general has been a prominent Canadian, who is really appointed by the prime minister, but for a long time the post was filled by members of the British nobility. One such who came to reside at Government House — otherwise known as

Rideau Hall — in Ottawa was Sir Frederick Arthur Stanley, Baron Stanley of Preston.

Lord Stanley arrived in Ottawa in 1888 with a reputation as an ardent sportsman. In England he'd been involved in horse racing, soccer and cricket. But hockey on ice, as played by the skillful Ottawa players of the era, soon became his passion. His sons Arthur and Algernon became so enamored of the game that they equipped themselves with sticks and skates and, with their famous father's blessing, formed a team called the Rideau Hall Rebels. Lord Stanley even arranged for the players to use a large outdoor rink on Government House grounds. The Rebels helped popularize the sport by playing a handful of exhibition games around Ontario.

*Lord Stanley of Preston (1841–1908), Canada's sixth governor general. He never saw a Stanley Cup playoff game.*

Two years after Lord Stanley and his family returned to England in 1893, he took part in a memorable game on a large sheet of ice behind Buckingham Palace. A royal hockey team was formed during the cold winter of 1895 and a challenge issued to a team skippered by the former governor general. Lord Stanley had four members of his family playing alongside him; Arthur and Algernon were the best players on the ice, and their Canadian hockey experience gave them a big advantage. The Stanleys scored numerous goals against the Royals while allowing just one. The royal team included such luminaries as the Prince of Wales, later to become King Edward VII, and the Duke of York, who became King George V.

This wasn't the first time royalty had taken up the game. In the hard winter of 1853, guests at Windsor Palace donned skates for a game of shinny, or hockey. Sides were chosen, sticks found, and the bung from a barrel acquired to replace the rubber ball, which bounced too much to suit the players. While Queen Victoria stood on the sidelines offering encouragement, officers of the guard whipped the wooden bung at the goalies, one of whom was Albert, the prince consort. After the contest, the players were rewarded with a well-spiced rum punch.

It is a pity that Lord Stanley never witnessed a Stanley Cup playoff game. He returned to England just when the fervor over hockey began to build in Canada. Before his departure, wishing to contribute something tangible to the sport he had embraced, he prepared a letter to be read by his aide, Lord Kilcoursie, at a banquet for the Ottawa hockey club at the conclusion of the 1892 season. The letter is part of hockey's history.

I have for some time been thinking it would be a good idea if there were a challenge cup which could be held from year to year by the leading hockey team in Canada. There does not appear to be any outward or visible sign of the championship at present. Considering the interest that hockey matches now elicit and the importance of having the games fairly played under generally recognized rules, I am willing to give a cup that shall be annually held by the winning club.

> I am not quite certain that the present regulations governing the matches give entire satisfaction. It would be worth considering whether they could not be arranged so that each team would play once at home and once at the place where their opponents hail from.

When Lord Kilcoursie read the letter, the Ottawa players saluted its author with three rousing cheers. Lord Kilcoursie was cheered, as well, for many thought the idea for a championship trophy was originally his. Kilcoursie, after all, was not only an ardent fan and occasional referee, but a popular member of the Rideau Hall Rebels, a player of considerable skill.

When Lord Stanley learned that his offer of a championship trophy had been gratefully accepted, he contacted a friend in England and asked him to visit the best silversmith in London and purchase a small silver bowl with an interior finish of gold, set on an ebony base. The cost was ten guineas or $48.67 in Canadian funds. On the bowl's arrival at Government House, it was promptly christened the Stanley Cup.

A vital provision, with Lord Stanley's departure imminent, was the appointment of a pair of trustees to administer the trophy. The men appointed were P. D. Ross and John Sweetland. Sweetland, age 57, was sheriff of Ottawa. Ross, then in his early 30s, was at the beginning of a long and brilliant career that would see him become publisher of the *Ottawa Journal* and one of the most highly respected Canadians of his time. Ross and Sweetland knew the game of hockey and were men of enormous integrity and of forceful personality, who took their duties seriously. It is fortunate that they were because much controversy and many dramatic challenges lay ahead.

# 2 Discord and Dissension

**I**N 1893, THE FIRST YEAR the Stanley Cup was up for competition, the trustees faced a difficult decision. The Ottawa hockey club had won the championship of the loosely formed Ontario Hockey Association in the preceding year, and the temptation must have been strong to make Ottawa the first Cup winners. Lord Stanley would have approved, for he was a big fan of the Ottawa players.

"That is not going to happen," stated Sweetland and Ross, the Cup trustees. "Forget about the past. The Stanley Cup is a challenge trophy, and as such it must be won on the ice. If Ottawa wants the Cup, let them win it in competition." Having made their decision, the trustees stuck to it.

When the 1893 Amateur Hockey Association season opened in January, the Ottawa club lost its opening game to the lowly Montreal Victorias. The defeat turned out to be disastrous for Ottawa, for at season's end they finished one game behind the Montreal Amateur Athletic Association club. The Stanley Cup trustees decided that Montreal's record of seven wins and one defeat (a loss to Ottawa) made it "the leading hockey team in Canada" and quietly shipped the Stanley Cup to Montreal, even though there had been no playoff for the trophy. One might think that the Montrealers would quickly have claimed the Cup, fearful

*The Montreal Amateur Athletic Association, winners of the first Stanley Cup in 1893.* (Public Archives of Canada)

perhaps that the trustees might change their minds. But no! The MAAA players almost refused to accept the trophy. It seems the hockey team — one of several sports clubs under the umbrella of the MAAA — felt slighted when Sheriff Sweetland arrived in town unannounced and presented the Cup to officers of the MAAA, not to the hockey captain, who was out of town. The players wanted to send the cup right back to Ottawa. But directors of the MAAA, afraid of offending Lord Stanley, hushed up the dispute and retained possession of the shiny new trophy.

When Montreal defeated Ottawa 7–1 in one of the key games of the short eight-game season in 1893, more than 4,000 fans witnessed the game in Montreal. Reporters covering the game showed their bias. One Ottawa correspondent wrote: "There was a very regrettable feature of the match. It was the many mean fouls of the Montrealers. They continually tripped and interfered with the Ottawa forwards, a fact which the referee did not seem to notice while he paid particular attention to the Ottawa men who were warned for trivial offenses." The reporter also mentioned that Lord Stanley would present a cup to the winners of a Montreal–Ottawa championship match *if* the game was played in Ottawa. Obviously the Montrealers, as league champions, didn't relish another game with second-place Ottawa, especially on the latter's home ice. So they politely declined and later accepted Lord

Stanley's silverware without having to battle for it on the ice. As a result, the first Stanley Cup game was not played until March 1894, ten months after Lord Stanley was succeeded as governor general by the Earl of Aberdeen, a curling enthusiast.

There were five teams in the Amateur Hockey Association in 1894 — Ottawa, Quebec, and three teams from Montreal: the AAA, the Victorias, and the Crystals. The Crystals were as fragile as their name suggested and lost all eight games. The other clubs wound up in a unique four-way tie — each with five wins and three defeats. At a meeting on March 10, the league ordered play-offs, but a long wrangle erupted over the site of the playoff games. Quebec officials, weary of arguing, withdrew from the meeting and went home. Their season was finished. When Ottawa agreed to Montreal as the site of the playoffs, the league granted Ottawa a bye and ordered a game between Montreal AAA and Montreal Victorias. This match was the first semifinal in Stanley Cup history.

The game was played in Montreal's Victoria rink on St. Patrick's Day before an estimated crowd of two to three thousand spectators. In places the ice was covered with water but was hard enough to permit the fastest skating seen all season. At the end of an hour's play, the score was tied 2–2. After 15 minutes of overtime Billy Barlow became the first playoff hero when he scored the winning goal, his second of the night. The *Montreal Gazette* reported that "Barlow undoubtedly did the most. He is a very fast skater and an accurate shot. Had it not been for him, the Victorias must have won."

On March 22, in the same arena, Montreal edged Ottawa 3–1 in the deciding game for the Stanley Cup, the first such match in history. The Victoria rink was packed with 5,000 fans, and although the ice was soft, some brilliant hockey was played. Morel, the Ottawa goalie, was described as "a marvel of coolness between the Ottawa posts and stopper of many hot shots." Rough and foul play were frequent, the defenses of both teams indulging in tripping and slashing. Weldy Young of Ottawa, who had refereed the earlier playoff game between Montreal and the Vics, was injured in the second half, and although he finished the game, collapsed at the end of it.

After the game the Montreal players were carried off the ice on the shoulders of their fans. Once again most of the praise and applause went to Billy Barlow, the 125-pound forward, who had come through with a pair of goals. Barlow was the first famous Stanley Cup scoring star.

During the 1895 hockey season, Lord Stanley's successor, the Earl of Aberdeen, developed a fondness for hockey. He was often recruited to drop pucks at ceremonial faceoffs and to shake hands with winning teams. His wife, Lady Aberdeen, kept a diary and penned the following comments on the game:

> Went this evening with all of our party to witness one of the championship hockey matches between Ottawa and Montreal. The latter expected to win but were beaten 5 to 1. The game appears to be a most fascinating one and the men get wildly excited about it. But there can be no doubt as to its roughness.

> If the players get too keen and lose their tempers, as they are apt to do, the possession of the stick and the closeness to one another gives the occasion for many a nasty hit. Tonight one man was playing with his nose badly broken. The game had to be stopped twice, once because a man got hit in the mouth and the other because one of the captains was knocked down unconscious and had to be carried out. When he recovered consciousness he came out and played again.

> There are many men and boys who reside here in Ottawa who practically live for hockey. It must be said that it is beautiful to see the perfection of skating that is involved in the playing of the game — the men simply run on the ice as if they were on the ground.

If Lady Aberdeen thought the Ottawa fans and players were emotional about hockey, she would have been appalled at the midseason uproar that took place in Quebec City during the 1895 season. After a wild game from which Ottawa emerged with a 3–2 victory, Quebec fans were so incensed over a referee's call that they chased him out of the rink. They caught him as he was hailing a horse-drawn rig to take him to the railway station and hauled him back to the arena, demanding that he call the game a draw. Fortunately, police intervened and saved him from a bad mauling. The league executive blamed the home team, not the fans, for the rough treatment accorded the frightened official, and suspended Quebec for the balance of the season.

The incident was an extreme example of what was common behavior toward referees. It is a wonder league officials could find anyone willing to serve. Referees were subject to constant criticism, if not assault, and were often vilified in the press. A *Montreal Gazette* critic wrote of one early-day referee:

> The Ottawas may thank their stars that they had a referee who was so easily rattled. If they had picked out a guiding light from the celestial regions they could not have picked a better choice than Mr. Barlow. He looked rattled all through the game and his decisions proved it. He had a remarkable quick eye every time there was an offside when the puck was in Ottawa territory and was possessed with a wonderful forgetfulness in the offside when matters were vice versa. To put it in straight plain English, the Crystals were filched of the match.

After a Montreal loss in 1899, two of the players blasted referee Fred Chittick in the press. "Altogether referee Chittick was very severe on anything resembling Montreal and his tongue wagged too frequently," said one. Another added, "Chittick's condition was such that he was not capable of refereeing the game." It was clear the players thought that Chittick performed his duties while intoxicated. Chittick's reply was a lawsuit, claiming defamation of character. When the players publicly apologized, he withdrew the suit.

The sports pages of the day often reserved space for candid comments on the officiating:

There is little wonder at Waterloo objecting to Mr. King as referee for their game the other night. He is a tinhorn sport of the first water and should not be allowed in decent hockey circles. (*Toronto Telegram*)

The referee was unfitted to the game and should stick to bowling. But then, the next step before death is refereeing. (*Ottawa Citizen*)

Gord Lewis may be a good goalkeeper but he knows nothing about refereeing a match. (*Ottawa Citizen*)

Part-time referee Fred Chittick may have been a disaster in the eyes of many players and fans, but the Ottawa goaltender — who once refused to play in a big game because management wouldn't give him enough complimentary tickets — was recruited to handle a Stanley Cup game in 1895 between Montreal and some college lads from Queen's University.

Fans were stunned when the trustees announced the match because the Montreal Victorias (6–2) had displaced Montreal (4–4) as league champions, and the Vics justly felt they should have been selected to face the college boys. The trustees muttered something about having arranged the game before the Vics nailed down the championship and not being prepared to make last-minute changes. Montreal beat Queen's by a 5–1 score, but the names engraved on the Stanley Cup were those of the champion Victorias. It was another bizarre incident in Stanley Cup play.

Viewed by modern eyes, early-day Stanley Cup team lineups have one strange feature. Not a French Canadian player in the group, not even on the Quebec City roster! It seems incredible now, but their day was yet to come. When it did come, French Canadians added some dazzling achievements to the hockey record book.

Early Stanley Cup records indicate that the best organized teams and leagues were concentrated in the Montreal–Quebec–Ottawa corridor, where the most famous clubs were located. But the game was spreading fast into towns and cities everywhere. It swept through Ontario and out into the growing West. It grabbed the attention of players and fans in the northeastern United States and Minnesota. Promoters enticed Canadian teams to play exhibition games in big cities like New York, Pittsburgh, Chicago, and St. Louis. And they played on artificial ice, years before it became a vital part of Canadian hockey.

In Manitoba, where the Manitoba Hockey Association had been organized in 1891, Winnipeg iced two strong clubs. Each cast a covetous eye on the Stanley Cup. Sensibly, they joined forces as the Winnipeg Victorias and issued a challenge to the Montreal Victorias. The influence of Queen Victoria, who reigned until 1901, was powerful in that era. In midseason, the Winnipeg team dug up enough money to finance the train trip east — about $50 per player — and showed up in Montreal ready to do battle.

Perhaps the Montreal club regarded the challenge too lightly, wondering what Westerners, most of whom indulge in curling, could know about big-time hockey. They soon found out. Winnipeg recorded an astounding shutout, the first in Cup history. The man who recorded it was Whitey Merritt, a goalkeeper ingenious enough to protect his legs with borrowed cricket pads. The official score was 2–0 for the visitors. Montrealers screamed in fury when referee Alex Martin of Toronto called back a goal by Montreal's Hartland McDougall. Sportswriters blasted Martin; one said he had shown himself to be "utterly ignorant of the rules."

A *Winnipeg Free Press* reporter wrote:

A royal welcome was extended the champions on their return to Winnipeg a few days later. Long before the train from the East arrived, a steady stream of citizens assembled at the CPR depot. Suddenly there was a cry of "Here she comes!" Then the iron horse appeared, a Union Jack fluttering in front of its headlight and the cowcatcher adorned with hockey sticks and brooms, emblematic of the clean sweep in Montreal.

All eyes turned to the rear sleeper from which the champions emerged, to be taken in charge by their enthusiastic friends. They were handed high hats adorned with the club colors, which gave them a truly distinguished appearance. To the tune of "See the Conquering Heroes Come," played by the Dragoon Band, the heroes were escorted in cabs up Main Street. A great many rigs and hundreds of citizens followed on foot. The Stanley Cup, coveted by every team in the Dominion, occupied a prominent place in the leading cab and was the center of admiring eyes.

At the hotel, another immense crowd had gathered. When Mayor Johnston rose to speak, he was greeted by shouts of several thousand proud citizens. He spoke of the good to be derived from the pursuit of manly sports and expressed the hope that the peerless seven would long be spared to defend the title they so nobly won.

There were loud calls for Mr. Armytage, who, upon rising, was greeted with great cheers. The worthy captain took but a few minutes to thank his large audience for their enthusiastic welcome and stated that he hoped the Stanley Cup would long remain a prominent feature in the city of Winnipeg.

At the conclusion of the speech making, the team and the ubiquitous newspapermen adjourned to the smoking room where the capacious trophy was filled to the brim with champagne.

Many were the trophies and souvenirs exhibited by the boys, pieces of ribbon worn on the memorable occasion being eagerly sought after by enthusiastic friends. Chief interest centered on the game puck, which has been embellished almost out of recognition. On the face of it is a silver shield with the names Whitey, Higgy, Army, Roddy, Tote, and Dan. On the reverse side is a similar shield, surmounted with the figure of a buffalo, with the inscription: *Montreal, February 14, 1896. Score 2–0.*

Unable to shake off the sting of defeat at the hands of their western counterparts, the Montreal Vics issued a challenge, which was accepted. They journeyed to Winnipeg in December 1896, determined to bring the Cup back East. The game, played on

December 30, was a sellout with tickets selling for as much as $12.

Winnipeggers were ecstatic when the home team whacked in three quick goals. They were silenced somewhat when Montreal replied with two goals against Merritt and they were morose when Montreal tied the score in the second half and then edged ahead on a goal by Drinkwater. They were joyous when Winnipeg pet Danny Bain tied the score, but their victory hopes were dashed when Montreal's Ernie McLea stormed down the ice and whipped in the winning goal in a 6–5 triumph. The Stanley Cup had been restored to the East. Winnipeg fans — after a period of mourning — insisted the game was the greatest one ever played.

Back home at the Victoria rink in Montreal, the champions were feted in an unusual manner. A brass band played as they paraded onto the ice and marched to a platform where the club directors were seated. Also on the platform was the Stanley Cup, on a stand constructed of hockey sticks and beautifully decorated by the wives of club members. After several congratulatory speeches and three cheers for the Vics, everyone retired to the club room for a luncheon and drinks.

Earlier that December of 1896, before the 1897 season, the Stanley Cup trustees ordered the Montreal Vics to defend the Cup against an upstart team from Ottawa, the Capitals. The challenge was advertised as a two-game series, but the first game was so one-sided — Montreal winning by 12 or 13 goals — that no one bothered to keep track of the goal scorers. The Capitals are remembered for being the first team ever to concede a Cup match, for they didn't show up for game two. One humiliation was quite enough.

There were no challenges for the Cup during the 1897 season. Perhaps the Montreal Vics, with a sparkling 7–1 record in league play, frightened off all potential challengers. It was a similar story in 1898, when the Vics sailed through the schedule unbeaten. Their 8–0 record forced other teams with Cup ambitions to think twice about trying to wrest Lord Stanley's basin away from them.

In four seasons the Vics won 28 games, lost four, and outscored opponents 177–103. But the dynasty came to an end in 1899. Playing in a new league — the Canadian Amateur Hockey Association — and in a new 4,000-seat arena that opened on New Year's Eve 1898, they were displaced by a new Montreal team, the Shamrocks. A 1–0 victory over the Vics on March 1 enabled the Shamrocks to finish with a 7–1 record. The Vics finished 6–2.

The Shamrocks boasted the league's top scorer in Harry Trihey, who scored 19 goals in seven games. Trihey set a record with ten goals in a game against Quebec. The Vics countered with a new star, 18-year-old Russell Bowie, who weighed all of 120 pounds. Bowie played for the next ten years, scoring 234 goals in 80 league games, but with the Vics' glory years behind them, he never played on a Stanley Cup winning team.

It was during this 1899 season that goal nets made their first appearance in hockey. Frank Nelson, a Montreal fan, came up with the idea while watching fishermen cast their big nets in Australian waters. He discussed the idea of attaching nets to goal posts with W. A. Hewitt, who was then sports editor of the *Montreal Herald*. Hewitt persuaded a couple of Montreal teams to give the nets a thorough trial. Some goalies complained that their freedom to move in and around the goal area was hampered by

*Montreal Shamrocks, the Stanley Cup champions in 1899.* (Public Archives of Canada)

the netting; others thought the nets were a wonderful idea. Goal judges, who for years had stood on the ice dodging errant shots, were particularly enthusiastic. Hewitt went on to become sports editor of the *Toronto Star* and a hockey referee, then secretary of the Ontario Hockey Association for many years. In later years his son, Foster, and his grandson, Bill, shared his love for the game and became noted hockey broadcasters.

In Ottawa, one correspondent in the *Citizen* pleaded with hockey officials to introduce goal nets:

> Goal nets might save the life of a luckless man who, in a moment of weakness, submits to being a goal umpire. No brush can paint nor pen describe the feeling of an umpire when an infuriated mob is waiting to annihilate him. When the surging mob thirsts for gore, the goal umpire's in particular, and threatens to tear one limb from limb, it is then an umpire's thoughts turn to home and mother.

> An umpire never feels quite so insignificant as when a small boy, backed by his gang, pokes a sharp stick in his back and dubs him "a big stiff from the city" or some such choice phrase. An umpire longs to take said youth by the neck but he has the gang behind him and is only awaiting the poor man's exit. Then he will present him with a rare collection of bricks, thrown one at a time. Yes, have the goal nets by all means.

In January 1900, goal nets were formally adopted as standard game equipment, the first hockey innovation of the twentieth century.

The final year of the 1800s would not have been complete without another extraordinary playoff conflict. It happened during a two-out-of-three series in Montreal between those old opponents, the Montreal Vics and the Winnipeg Vics. This time Winnipeg introduced a new rover, Tony Gingras, who was talented and tough. In the first game, Gingras scored the only goal for the visitors, which stood until the dying moments of the game, when Bob McDougall tied it up and Graham Drinkwater blasted home the winner with seconds to play.

The biggest crowd in history — 8,000 fans — packed the new arena three nights later for game two. Winnipeg was without star forward Dan Bain, who had suffered a serious eye injury in the opening match. Montreal was leading 3–2 with three minutes to play when Bob McDougall slashed Tony Gingras across the knee. Gingras was carried off to the dressing room in great pain, and referee J. A. Findlay gave McDougall a two-minute penalty. "Not enough!" screamed the Winnipeg players. "McDougall should be thrown out!"

A wild argument ensued. When Findlay had heard enough, he said, "That's it, gentlemen. I'm through for the night." With that, he took off his skates and went home. League officials jumped in a horse-drawn sleigh and took off in pursuit. Eventually the frustrated referee was persuaded to return. He gave the Winnipeg players 15 minutes to return to the ice, and when they didn't show up, he awarded the game to Montreal. It was alleged that some of the Winnipeg players were already relaxing in a nearby tavern, but referee Findlay said he entered the dressing room, counted the players, and they were all there. It was a bizarre ending to an important game and the first time a Stanley Cup match went unfinished.

After the game, Winnipeg officials claimed that Gingras's leg was paralyzed for several hours, and that Bain's career was over as he was almost certain to lose the sight in one eye. Bain recovered and played for three more seasons.

The Montreal Vics relinquished the Cup two weeks later when they were beaten 1–0 by the Shamrocks in the final league match. The Cup trustees, anxious to get one more challenge played before the ice melted, ordered the Shamrocks to defend against some eager college boys from Queen's. It was no contest, the Shamrocks winning 6–2. As hockey moved into the twentieth century, the Stanley Cup occupied a prominent position on the mantelpiece of the Shamrock Hockey Club.

# 3 Turn-of-the-Century Triumphs and Trials

**A** **NEW CENTURY ARRIVED,** and with the booming popularity of hockey new clubs and leagues sprang up everywhere. Each Canadian community had its local club and hometown stars. When it became all-important to trounce teams from nearby communities, all kinds of enticements were offered to attract good players. The most effective lure was employment — a job with good pay, little work, and plenty of time off to play hockey. Often the jobs were supplemented with generous cash handouts, which were of necessity under-the-table deals because professionalism was frowned upon. A common practice was to slip a wad of bills into a player's street shoes while he was performing on the ice.

Professionalism came to hockey gradually, veiled for a long time to the point of hypocrisy. Gradually, team promoters realized that while job offers were fine, promises of fancy cash salaries for a season's work made recruiting top players a whole lot easier.

Amateurism was doomed, in fact, as early as 1903, when the International Professional League was organized in the United

States. It was the first openly professional league, and it attracted many top Canadian players who were willing to discard their amateur status for hard cash. Canadian teams began to come across, too — but discreetly, the money still changing hands under the table.

All these financial shenanigans began to affect the challenge games for the Stanley Cup. It had never been actually spelled out that the Cup, awarded to "the leading hockey club," was solely for amateurs; this was taken for granted. With each passing season, it became more obvious that amateurism was slipping into limbo.

In 1900, with goal nets officially in use, the Montreal Shamrocks defended the Cup against the customary invasion from Winnipeg and retained it by winning the rubber match of a three-game series. The Winnipeg Vics used unusual sticks and skates in the series. The stick blades were shaved, so that the upper part of the blade was quite thin while the lower part was the usual thickness. The visitors wore light aluminum blades on their boots, an invention of a champion speedskater named McCulloch.

In the third game, the score was tied at four with little more than a minute to play. Winnipeg's Danny Bain suffered a severe leg injury and was carried off the ice. When play resumed, the referee faced the puck directly in front of the Winnipeg goal. A lucky poke at it by a Shamrock forward sent it into the net, touching off a wild celebration by Shamrock supporters.

The Shamrocks wound up their season with a two-game series, total goals to count, against a lightly regarded team from Halifax, the Crescents. The Shamrocks won by lopsided scores of 10–1 and 11–0. A Montreal hockey official said, "The Crescents were handicapped by excessive padding: ponderous knee pads, shin guards, and shoulder cushions. A cumbersome weighty make of boot and skate also mitigated against them."

In January 1901, the pesky Vics from Winnipeg took the long journey back to Montreal for yet another crack at the Cup. This time they wrestled it away from the Shamrocks after two close matches. Dan Bain was the series hero, scoring the winner in overtime in game one and, two days later, collecting both Winnipeg goals in a 2–1 victory over the Shamrocks.

Ottawa breezed through the season without losing a game and might have captured the Cup had it not been carted off to Winnipeg. Because of the lateness of the season, Ottawa decided not to challenge for it.

Winnipeg was the site of a fascinating two-out-of-three-game Stanley Cup series in 1902. For the first time, a Toronto team, the Wellingtons, challenged for the Cup. The Iron Dukes, as they were known, failed to lift the Cup, losing 2–1 and 5–3, but they put up a gallant fight and fans journeyed from many parts of western Canada to witness the thrilling matches. After the final match, the *Winnipeg Tribune* reported: "It was well there were none present affected by heart disease, for if there had been, several cases of sudden death would have been reported. The games will long be remembered as two of the most brilliant of any played in competition for the world's championship."

One goal was scored in a rather peculiar manner. In a scrimmage near the Vic net, the puck broke cleanly in two. Chummy Hill of the Wellingtons grabbed one piece, raced in on Brown, the Vics' goalie, and scored. Goalie Brown said afterward he thought the play had stopped with the breaking of the puck and was taken by surprise. There were other oddities in the series. A huge Newfoundland dog jumped onto the ice during halftime and refused to go away even when two burly sweepers tried to escort him off by the ears. At one point, the puck lodged in the rafters over the ice. The players each had a shot at it with their sticks, and the one who dislodged it brought forth enthusiastic applause. Later on, the puck flew into the crowd and was lost; there was a long delay until another puck was secured.

Although the hour of play made the match late by Toronto time, hundreds of inquiries as to its progress were received at all the Toronto morning newspaper offices. Fortunately, arrangements were made to announce the result of the match to the whole city by means of the giant whistle on the Toronto Street Railway powerhouse. Many fans held their breath after two hoarse blasts were heard, hoping that there would be no third. The fatal third came, but though the Wellingtons were defeated they made good their promise to be worthy challengers for the Cup.

Two months later, Winnipeg had visitors from Montreal. A powerful but small Montreal Vics team — the so-called Little Men of Iron — brought the Cup east again after a historic series that saw spectators pay as much as $25 for a seat. The ice was so soft in game one that the players were drenched with water before the game was five minutes old.

The arena was packed for game two despite a raging blizzard that blocked all avenues leading to it. The ice was soon covered with snow that fell through cracks in the roof and more snow blew in through large ventilators.

Game three, won by Montreal 2–1, was one of the most exciting matches ever seen in Winnipeg. Big Bill Nicholson, the 300-pound Montreal goalie, was credited with saving the game for the easterners. Bill McFarlane, the referee who ruled with an iron fist, said he'd like to become even more involved in Stanley Cup play the following season. "I'll probably turn out with the Vics as a player next year," he told reporters.

Irritated at seeing its winter schedule interrupted by Stanley Cup challenges, the Canadian Amateur Hockey League issued a little challenge of its own. It defied the Stanley Cup trustees and ordered its clubs to play no challenge games until the end of the regular season. This was calculated to show the Stanley Cup trustees once and for all who was in the driver's seat. The trustees shrugged and stood firm. Winnipeg could always be relied upon to come up with another Cup challenge; they never gave up. And when Winnipeg asked for another chance, the trustees calmly ordered Montreal to defend against the Westerners — in midseason.

Montreal won the first game of the three-game series 8–1. Fans were surprised to see the visitors skate through the pregame warm-up wearing long dressing gowns over their uniforms. Most of the spectators left early, stating it was the poorest exhibition of playoff hockey they'd ever seen. In game two, the teams were all tied up in overtime on a Saturday night, when midnight arrived, and with it the Sabbath, which was more righteously observed then than now. The mayor of Westmount had no desire to earn a place in history as the first Canadian mayor to give Sunday hockey his official blessing. He stepped in and ordered the game to cease at the stroke of twelve o'clock. The match was a sensational spectacle but marred by tiresome delays. Whenever a player had his wind knocked out, both teams would rush to their dressing rooms and get a quick rubdown.

Winnipeg won the third game by a 4–2 score, and officials decided a fourth game would be necessary to declare a champion. The Montreal manager, even though his team stood to earn $3,000 from the series gate receipts, said his team might give the Stanley Cup back to the trustees if they won it. "There is just too much bother with these challenges," he declared.

But when his club emerged from the fourth game with a 4–1 victory — and it was pointed out that 18,000 fans had paid to see the four-game series — he was happy to grab his team's share of the gate — and the Cup. There was no more talk about handing it back.

Back in Winnipeg, the Bell Telephone Company placed ten extra operators on duty on the night of the final game. Thirty thousand calls flooded in, all of the callers seeking information on the game in Montreal.

Montreal didn't hold the trophy very long. Ottawa and the Montreal Victorias tied for the league title in 1903 with 6–2 records and played off for the right to succeed Montreal as Cup champions. The teams fought to a 1–1 tie in game one, but Ottawa, led by Frank McGee's three-goal performance, shut out the Vics 8–0 in the second game, played on ice covered by pools of water two to three inches deep.

Just two days later, on the traditional soft ice of March, the new champions faced a western challenge from the Rat Portage Thistles. Ottawa swept the two-game series by scores of 6–2 and 4–2. The Thistles were just kids; only one of them had reached his 21st birthday. Ice conditions were so bad that on one occasion the puck slipped through a hole in the ice and disappeared. One of the players went fishing for it with this stick but to no avail.

Interest in hockey in Rat Portage in those days was at such a peak that a judge in a nearby town called for a trial to begin at 2:00 a.m. so that he could finish his court business in time to catch the morning train to Rat Portage — and see the next day's hockey game.

By 1904, there was so much dissension in the Canadian Amateur Hockey League that a rival circuit, the Federal League, sprang up and initiated a hockey war among the eastern clubs. The Stanley Cup trustees were in a quandary after Ottawa suddenly resigned from the CAHL over the issue of the midnight curfew in the Montreal suburb of Westmount. Ottawa had arrived there late for a game with the Victorias and had been leading by 4–1 when midnight came and the game was stopped. Ottawa refused to replay the game when ordered by the league to do so. A showdown resulted and Ottawa walked out — taking the Stanley Cup with them.

During the 1904 season, and before they bolted from the AAHL, Ottawa defended the Cup in a best-of-three series with the Winnipeg Rowing Club. It was before this series that a line was drawn along the ice from one post to the other to help the goal umpire determine whether the puck entered the net. Ottawa easily won the first game by a 9–1 score, lost the second match 6– 2, and kept the Cup with a 2–0 shutout in game three.

One month later, Ottawa met the Ontario Hockey Association champions, the Toronto Marlboros, in a two-game series. With Ottawa superstar Frank McGee at his best, scoring three goals in the first game and five in the second, Ottawa won by scores of 6–3 and 11–2.

A week later came another challenge, this time from a Montreal team called the Wanderers, newly crowned champions of the upstart Federal League and boasting a 6–0 record. The first game, played in Montreal with an inch of water on the ice, ended in a 5–5 tie. The Wanderers refused to play overtime because they were thoroughly fed up with the work of "Doc" Kearns, the referee.

The Cup trustees sighed and ordered the two-game series to start all over again — with both games to be played in Ottawa. The Wanderers howled, but the trustees decreed that the Cup defenders had always had the right to open on home ice. Fuming, the Montreal club withdrew its challenge.

The Ottawa club, eager to improve on their splendid record in Cup competition, then accepted a challenge from Brandon, the Western champions. Brandon was no match for Frank McGee and his mates. McGee chalked up another five goals in leading Ottawa to a 6–3 triumph in game one and added three more in game two, a 9–3 rout of the visitors. It was in one of these games that Lester Patrick, Brandon's great point man, replaced Morrison, his team's goalie, in the net. Patrick made one save in his brief appearance. Nearly a quarter of a century later, he would be a replacement goalie in a pivotal game for the Stanley Cup — this time for the New York Rangers.

In 1904, one of the most bizarre stories in Stanley Cup play unfolded. A challenge came all the way from Dawson City, a gold-mining town in the far-off Yukon Territory. The great Klondike gold rush of 1898 had drawn goldseekers from all over the world. Some of them — not many — struck it rich. Among these was

*The plucky team from the North — the Dawson City Nuggets in 1905.*

Colonel Joe Boyle, adventurer and hockey fan from Woodstock, Ontario. Boyle earned his title of "Colonel" while running boatloads of prospectors through the perilous Whitehorse River rapids. He wound up owning a power company, sawmills, and just about everything else in Dawson City. He was known as the King of the Klondike and his career was just getting into high gear.

Dawson City had a few hockey players. One of them — Weldy Young — had played on one of Ottawa's greatest teams. In Dawson City, there was even a fine indoor arena. But the local team had no opposition, and Boyle, on a trip back east, met with the Stanley Cup trustees and submitted a challenge. At first the trustees just smiled, then they were swayed by Boyle's charm, energy, and enthusiasm. "Think of it, gentlemen," he said. "A team traveling 4,000 miles to Ottawa in the dead of winter to play a Stanley Cup series. It's a hockey promoter's dream." The trustees enjoyed listening to Boyle's blarney, and the bid from the Klondikers was accepted.

The story of the Dawson City challenge has been told before — hundreds of times — but no history of the Stanley Cup would be complete without it. It remains the strangest and most colorful saga in the annals of hockey. The epic story of the team's courageous expedition to Ottawa had everything but a happy ending.

The Dawson City Nuggets set out for Whitehorse, 320 miles away, on December 19, 1904. Some walked the distance, covering 30 and 40 miles per day; some used bicycles, until they broke down in the snow, one or two traveled by dogsled. From Whitehorse they took the train to Skagway on the Alaska Coast. Delayed by storms, they missed the boat to Vancouver and a few days later they traveled by boat to Seattle, Washington. From Seattle they took a train to Vancouver and then another train to Ottawa. When they finally pulled into Ottawa's Union Station, they had been on the road for 23 days and had had no chance to practice.

Colonel Boyle immediately requested a two-day postponement of the series so that his boys could find their skating legs again, but Ottawa said no. The series had to be played immediately, with the first game scheduled for the following night.

The Dawson City goalie, Albert Forrest, originally from Three Rivers, Quebec, set a record the moment he stepped between the poles. At 17, he was the youngest goalie in Cup history.

The visitors, out of condition, lost the opener of the three-game series 9–2. But they took some comfort from the fact that the legendary "One-Eyed" Frank McGee had scored just one goal. One Klondiker was overheard to say, "McGee didn't look so hot," a misjudgment that may have given rise to the hockey maxim, "Never run down a player in public, or he'll make you eat your words." McGee heard about the slight, pulled up his hockey socks, and whacked 14 goals past poor Forrest and the amazed Nuggets in game two. The blond center scored three goals in 90 seconds, four more in a span of two minutes and 20 seconds, and eight goals consecutively. These records still stand, not only for Stanley Cup competition, but for professional hockey in any era.

Despite the humiliation of giving up a record number of goals, young Forrest was praised by Ottawa sportswriters, "But for him," one of them wrote, "the score would have been double what it was. He was a marvel and made many sensational stops."

Three weeks later, the Ottawa team, known as the Senators or the Silver Seven, faced another challenge from the Rat Portage Thistles, this time with star forward Tom Phillips in the visitor's lineup. Phillips had been lured away from Toronto where he'd starred on the Marlboro team that challenged Ottawa for the Cup in 1904.

Phillips was a whirlwind in game one, scoring five times and leading the Westerners to a stunning 9–3 upset. In the second game, Ottawa played roughhouse hockey and every one of the Rat Portage boys was injured after receiving butt ends, cross-checks and body slams. Ottawa won 4–2. Late in the contest, Billy McGimsie collapsed in front of the Thistles' goal and drew a five-minute penalty for obstructing the goal line. In an unprecedented move, the Thistles played two men in goal throughout the game, which made scoring slightly more difficult for the Ottawa players. After the game, Rat Portage officials accused Ottawa arena attendants of flooding the ice with an inch of water in order to slow down the fast-moving Thistles.

"There was absolutely no need for the flood of water," said the outraged officials. "The temperature was well above freezing all day. It was just another dirty Ottawa trick."

The third game, played on harder ice, was equally as rough as the others, and a *Toronto Star* correspondent reported:

> In the first half, played under Manitoba rules, there was a judge of play, a sort of second referee. His presence on the ice had a good moral influence and the Ottawas were under restraint a bit. In the second half, however, they made up for lost time, and hacked and jabbed their opponents until they were a sight to behold. McGee, Pulford and Gilmour were the chief offenders although Moore and Smith laid out their men when it was necessary. Mr. Grant, the referee, wore a hard hat for protection and let everything go. Even the Ottawa and Montreal newspapermen gasped at his decisions. When Rat Portage seemed sure to score several times he blew his whistle for offsides. Both the sixth and seventh goals for Ottawa were deliberately offside. Cross-checking and jabbing in the face were frequent Ottawa tactics.
>
> Three times the challenging Thistles were in the lead and 91 seconds before time ran out the score was a tie. With only a minute and a half left to play, McGee landed the puck between the legs of goaltender Geroux and the Senators went ahead. Then what a scene! The 4,000 spectators who thronged the rink went wild. Never had such an outburst of enthusiasm followed a hockey match. Men swarmed on the ice and hugged the victors and it was with difficulty that the ice was cleared for the remaining half minute of play.

Before another game played that season, between Quebec and Montreal for the championship of the CAHL, fans couldn't wait for the ticket sellers to arrive and the turnstiles to open. They stormed the arena, broke down the doors and windows, and swept inside, occupying all the best seats. Everyone got in free.

The Stanley Cup passed out of the hands of the Ottawa Silver Seven during the 1906 season but not before they had fashioned a remarkable three-year dynasty, winning 17 Cup matches and losing only three. Ottawa and the Montreal Wanderers deserted the Federal League and joined a new circuit in 1906 named the Eastern Canada Hockey League. A new trophy, the Arena Cup, was introduced for presentation to the winners of the ECHL. One star player called it "just another piece of silverware. It'll never have the meaning of the Stanley Cup." Fred Brophy, the wandering goalie, distinguished himself by scoring another goal for Montreal late in the season.

Both Ottawa and the Wanderers made successful debuts in the new league and finished in a dead heat atop the standings with records of 9–1. A playoff between the two powerhouses would decide not only the league title but the fate of the Stanley Cup as well. During the season, Ottawa had successfully defended the trophy twice, first against some students from Queen's University, and later against a team from the nearby town of Smiths Falls, champions of the fading Federal League. Queen's was hopeless against the Silver Seven, losing 16–7 and 12–7. Fans were more excited over a dressing-room punchout between two Ottawa players regarding the choice of team captain than they were over the results on the ice.

Smiths Falls fell 6–5 and 8–2, with Frank McGee scoring nine goals against them in the two games. Percy Lesueur, the brilliant young goaltender for Smiths Falls, gave Ottawa fits during the series. He was embarking on a career that would take him all the way to the Hockey Hall of Fame.

Now the stage was set for one of the wildest and most talked-about confrontations of all time — the two-game, total-point clash between the Silver Seven and the Wanderers. When the puck was dropped for the opener in Montreal, however, the game proved to be lacking in drama. The Wanderers had brought Lester Patrick eastward, and on home ice they manhandled Ottawa 9–1. Hague, the Ottawa goaltender, was roasted by the Ottawa fans for his lackluster play in the massacre. Before the second game, in

Ottawa, he was replaced by young Lesueur, hurriedly picked up from Smiths Falls.

Perhaps the Ottawa fans had an inkling of a dramatic Ottawa comeback, because more than 5,000 fought their way into Dey's Arena for the return match. Eight goals behind, Ottawa came out flying. Their great left-winger, Harry Smith, banged home five goals, his brother Alf scored once, and so did Rat Westwick. One-Eyed Frank McGee potted a pair and the game was tied 8–8. The crowd went wild. Even the governor general, Lord Grey, forgot that he was supposed to remain neutral. He grabbed Harry Smith and pumped his hand.

But the game was tied, not over. Lester Patrick rose to the occasion and gave his wilting teammates a memorable pep talk, then set a personal example with attacks on Lesueur that resulted in two Wanderer goals. The crowd went silent. The end had come. Ottawa's brilliant Cup reign was over. The Wanderers, 12–10 winners, swept up the Cup and took it back to Montreal.

In 1907 the Eastern Canada League permitted professionals and amateurs to play together. Teams even listed the names of their amateurs and pros, which resulted in much snickering around the league. The press refused to believe that several players on the amateur list were even remotely simon-pure.

A team from New Glasgow, Nova Scotia, wanted a crack at the Wanderers — and the Cup — but the trustees were inclined to ignore the bid. "They are simply too weak," they concluded. But the Wanderers threatened to pull out of the league if the games weren't scheduled, and the two-game series was played late in December, before the start of the regular season. The trustees were right — New Glasgow was weak. Lester Patrick scored back-to-back hat tricks in the Wanderers' 10–3 and 7–2 victories.

In January 1907, the Wanderers looked after some unfinished business from the previous season. Time and ice had run out in the spring of 1906, and there had been no East-West championship for the Cup. So Rat Portage, now known as Kenora, western champs in 1906, came east the following January to meet the Wanderers. They borrowed Art Ross from Brandon for the series, and his sparkling rushes paced Kenora to 4–2 and 8–6 victories over the shocked Montrealers. Before the season ended, the two clubs would meet again.

In the same year, the Federal League was disrupted by a charge of murder against a hockey player. Owen "Bud" McCourt, a Cornwall star, died in hospital after a game against the Ottawa Vics. Police accused Charlie Masson of the Vics of causing McCourt's death. It was the only time in hockey history that a player has been hauled off to jail and charged with such a serious offense.

During the game, McCourt, who led the league in scoring and averaged two goals per game, was chopped down with a stick during a melee. In a matter of hours he died of a fractured skull and Masson was arrested for murder. The charge was later reduced to manslaughter. In court, Masson was acquitted when witnesses could not say with certainty that his stick had been the murder weapon.

The Victorias were so shaken by the McCourt fatality that they quit hockey for the season, even though the league title was within their grasp. "I never want to see another hockey game," said one of the Vics. "Poor Charlie Masson. The game was frightfully rough and he kept telling us to play clean or not to play at all."

The Wanderers, meanwhile, after posting a perfect 10–0 record in league play and averaging more than ten goals per game, desperately wanted to regain the Stanley Cup before the tulips bloomed. They journeyed west for a series with the Kenora Thistles, but a couple of major controversies erupted. First, William Foran, a Cup trustee, said the Kenora rink was too small for a Cup series and ordered the matches to be held in Winnipeg. He also decreed that two players Kenora had imported from Ottawa, Alf Smith and Rat Westwick, were ineligible for the series. His decisions triggered arguments, protests, and counterprotests. One Kenora official was so incensed that he carried the Stanley Cup to the end of a dock and threatened to throw it into the Lake of the Woods.

Ultimately, with ice turning to slush, compromises were reached. Smith and Westwick played in the games that were moved from Kenora to Winnipeg. The Wanderers breezed to a 7–2 victory in the first game, lost the second 6–5, and won the series with most goals, 12–8. In his postgame report to his Montreal paper, a reporter wrote: "I wonder if old Lord Stanley of Preston ever thinks of all the trouble and excitement his famous trophy has caused in Canada."

In 1908, the Wanderers toppled several patsies who posed as legitimate Cup opponents. They took little pride or pleasure in walloping the Ottawa Vics 9–3 and 13–1 in a January series. Ernie Russell scored four goals in game one and six in game two. The Ottawa club was a mediocre team representing the Federal League and was involved only because the two leading clubs, Montagnards and Cornwall, had folded.

The Wanderers then hosted the Winnipeg Maple Leafs, champions of the Manitoba League, in a March series. The Westerners were outclassed in both games, losing 11–5 and 9–3.

A mere two days later, another Maple Leaf team, this one from Toronto and just as lightly regarded as the one from the West, almost stole the Cup from the cocky Wanderers. The Toronto Maple Leafs, champions of the new Ontario Professional League with a 10–2 record, were given a one-game shot at the Cup. The Wanderers turned down Toronto's pleas for a two-game series, claiming they were tired after playing 22 games during the season. The Wanderers arrogantly predicted they would double the score on the Toronto team and many bets were made as a result of that boast. The Maple Leafs, led by Newsy Lalonde, a bright new star, almost upset the champions but lost 6–4. One of the Leaf goals was scored by Lalonde from a center-ice faceoff. The Montreal goalie and a couple of his teammates were at the sideboards talking to supporters who offered them bonuses if they'd keep their promise to double the score. While that was happening, Lalonde won the faceoff and slapped the puck into the empty net from center ice.

A year later, professionalism, outright or thinly disguised, had come to stay when the Eastern League attempted to introduce legislation that would forbid players from jumping from team to team. Montreal and the Victorias, two clubs that encouraged such movement — Montreal had just lured Art Ross and Riley Hern of the Wanderers into their fold — opposed the motion. Both clubs resigned, leaving the Eastern League with four fully professional teams — Ottawa, Quebec, Wanderers, and Shamrocks.

Acquiring "ringers" to strengthen a team was another problem. The Edmonton club thumbed its nose at critics of the practice. For the 1909 Stanley Cup series, Edmonton packed a team with stars; only one player had been with them in the weeks prior to their Cup matches with the Wanderers. Even so, they lost on total goals, 13–10. After their defeat, most of the Edmonton players rejoined their former clubs.

At the close of the 1909 season, the trustees ordered the Wanderers to hand over the Cup to Ottawa. Ottawa had earned it, they ruled, because the Senators had captured the Eastern League championship with a 10–2 record. They had also scored a record-high 117 goals, an average of almost 12 per game.

In the first decade of the twentieth century, leagues and franchises rose and fell, amateurism all but disappeared, and contracts were made and broken as skilled performers transferred their allegiance even in midseason if the money was right. A different era was arriving with the decade that opened in 1910 — the Money Era. The new emphasis brought about major changes in the game. Some say it came close to ruining it.

# 4 The Fever Spreads

**I**N **NORTHERN ONTARIO** in 1905 and 1906, a mining boom began with the great Cobalt silver stampede. Like the Yukon gold rush of 1898, it drew fortune hunters from afar. In the harsh winter months, the miners looked to hockey for entertainment.

Three towns within a ten-mile radius — Haileybury, Cobalt, and New Liskeard — formed the Temiskaming Mines League. As local rivalries intensified, good jobs and incredible cash offers attracted many of the best hockey players in the world. Some didn't stay long. They'd appear mysteriously, score a few goals, pick up their cash — sometimes as much as a thousand dollars for a few days' work — and go back where they came from.

The Timmins brothers, a couple of Mattawa storekeepers who became millionaires from their silver holdings, wanted nothing but the best brand of hockey for their adopted town of Haileybury. And they were willing to pay for it. Rival mining magnates in Cobalt and New Liskeard tried to keep pace.

There was also Renfrew, a community on the Ottawa River. It was the hometown of M. J. O'Brien, a man who had made a considerable fortune out of railroading, lumbering, and mining. He and his son Ambrose, both of them enthusiastic hockey fans, decided that Renfrew should have a world-class hockey team. The easiest way to get one was to buy it.

Good players, who in the past had been accustomed to pulling a few dollars from the toes of their shoes after a game, suddenly discovered there was big money in hockey. The O'Briens signed Lester and Frank Patrick at $3,000 each. They wooed Cyclone Taylor, Newsy Lalonde, and other big stars with similar offers. On a per-game basis, Cyclone Taylor, as a member of the Renfrew Millionaires, was earning far more than baseball's biggest star, Ty Cobb.

The actions of the O'Briens and the Timmins brothers triggered a hockey war at the beginning of the new decade. The Eastern Canada League folded and gave way to the Canadian Hockey Association, formed for the express purpose of freezing out Renfrew and the Wanderers. The Canadian Hockey Association included Ottawa, Shamrocks, Nationals, Quebec, and All-Montreal, a new franchise. When the Wanderers and Renfrew sought admission to the new circuit, their applications were promptly denied.

Undeterred, the mining men got together and formed a new league — the National Hockey Association, forerunner of the National Hockey League. The founding teams were the Wanderers, Renfrew, Cobalt, and Haileybury. Mr. Hare, a Cobalt executive, felt that Montreal should be doubly represented in the league and purchased a franchise to be named Les Canadiens. His plan was to turn over the club to a group of Montreal sportsmen

*The Renfrew Millionaires in 1910, featuring such greats as Cyclone Taylor, Newsy Lalonde, and the Patrick brothers.* (Public Archives of Canada)

as soon as possible. But most of the financial support for the new circuit came from the O'Briens, the exception being the Wanderers.

The new league had a wild, colorful initial season, especially in the north country where players shifted from one club to another in bewildering fashion. Wagering on the outcome of any game reached astronomical figures. Some rinks were hastily erected and safety standards were lax. But they were always jammed. One night the roof of the Cobalt arena caved in, but no one was injured. During another game in that arena, so much money was tossed onto the ice that big Billy Nicholson, Haileybury's 300-pound goalie, waddled out and found a wash-tub. He scooped up the money, shoveled it under the tub, and sat on it for safekeeping.

Much to the disappointment of the O'Briens, the Wanderers captured the NHA title in 1910 with a record of 11–1. Despite their star-studded lineup, the Renfrew Millionaires, also known as the Creamery Kings, did not jell and finished with a record of 8–3–1.

In mid-January, the Canadian Hockey Association was on the verge of folding. The NHA stepped in and plucked the best franchises, Ottawa and the Shamrocks, for their own league. Tears were shed by the remaining teams, All-Montreal, Quebec, and the Nationals, when their hockey world crashed down around them. Ottawa, holders of the Stanley Cup until the Wanderers took possession at the end of the NHA season, defended it against a Galt, Ontario, team on January 5 and 7, winning both games easily. Two weeks later, they defended against Edmonton and once more rolled up mighty scores, 8–4 and 13–7.

When the Wanderers claimed the Cup as league champions, they were tested in a single game by a team from Berlin (later Kitchener, Ontario), which held the title in the Ontario Professional League. Ernie Russell, with four goals, led the Wanderers to a 7–3 victory to close a rather turbulent season.

Hockey men observed that recent Stanley Cup games had lost much of their appeal. Fans weren't interested in games featuring teams from Berlin, Smiths Falls, and Galt. Unless they felt a challenger really belonged in select Stanley Cup society, they preferred to stay home. Club owners were finally discovering that unrestricted bidding for players was poor business and some teams were bound to go bankrupt. First the mining men pulled out. They had learned a valuable lesson — mere money would not buy a Stanley Cup. It was time to regroup. Quebec joined the NHA and took over the Haileybury and Cobalt franchises, dashing forever Northern Ontario's hopes of ever witnessing a Stanley Cup victory celebration.

The new-look NHA of 1911 was composed of Ottawa, Renfrew, Canadiens, Wanderers, and Quebec. The schedule was increased to 16 games and a salary cap put on the member clubs. No team could spend more than $5,000 in total for its players. With a maximum of ten men on a team, no player could expect to earn much more than $500. Some players grumbled about the salary cap and the fact they had less freedom to change teams because of stricter contracts. There was even talk of a players' revolt or a strike, but nothing came of it.

Ottawa led the league in 1911 with 13 wins and only three defeats. At the end of the season, the Senators barely worked up a sweat in a couple of unremarkable Cup series. First came a challenge from Galt, champions of the Ontario Pro League. Galt had eliminated tiny Port Hope, Ontario, in a playoff game leading up to the challenge. On a sea of slush in Ottawa, Galt fell 7–4 to the Senators.

Three days later, Port Arthur — winners of a Western playoff against Prince Albert — took their chances with Ottawa and were crushed 13–4. The Senators' Marty Walsh provided most of the excitement, notching ten goals and coming close to Frank McGee's 1905 record of 14.

The next season brought another big change — six-man hockey — when the old position of rover was abolished. Many people didn't like the move. Frank and Lester Patrick, two of the most respected men in the game, were busy forming the Pacific Coast Hockey League and said they would have nothing to do with this weird notion. The Patricks placed teams in New Westminster, Vancouver — which had seating for 10,000 fans — and Victoria. The new rinks in the latter two cities were the first in Canada to have artificial ice.

In Renfrew, Ambrose O'Brien had had enough of — and spent enough on — hockey and gave up his dream of a Stanley Cup for the creamery town. His players were supposed to be divided by lot among the other teams, but the more aggressive owners ignored this directive and signed some of O'Brien's stars, anyway. George Kennedy, a wrestling promoter whose real name was Kendall, owner of Les Canadiens, got a break when he was given a monopoly on French Canadian players.

Quebec, led by Joe Malone, moved up and won the NHA championship in 1912 despite an unimpressive record of 10–8. New Westminster was the best team on the West Coast with a 9–6 mark.

The Cup trustees continued to recognize challenges — no matter how weak — from all parts of Canada. In 1912 it was Moncton's turn. The Maritime champions were involved in the first series played under six-man rules and were defeated 9–3 and 8–0 by Quebec.

During this period, hockey seasons got longer, with schedules beginning in later December and ending in March. For the 1912–13 season, the NHA added two Toronto clubs, the Blueshirts and the Tecumsehs. Hockey's popularity on the West Coast prompted the Patricks to keep raiding Eastern clubs for playing talent, and the NHA lost many stars. The Patricks clamored for a Stanley Cup series between the winners of the East and the Pacific Coast League champs. "Let's make it more than a two-game series," suggested Lester Patrick, thinking of the gate receipts. However, the Quebec Bulldogs, winners of 16 out of 20 league games and at the top of the NHA once again, were reluctant to risk the Cup against the West. The trustees backed them up. Quebec did agree to an exhibition series with Victoria, the Coast champions — but only after the NHA champs had completed a Cup series with the winners of the Maritime Pro League.

As it turned out, Joe Malone might have been able to handle the Sydney, Nova Scotia, challenge all by himself. He scored nine times for the Bulldogs in a 14–3 rout in game one. Perhaps it was boredom that kept Phantom Joe out of the second game. Without Malone to harass them, the Sydney club looked a little more like professionals, but they still lost 6–2.

The Quebec Bulldogs immediately journeyed west for the exhibition series they had promised Victoria. The Pacific Coast champions surprised the Bulldogs, winning two of the three games played. After the series, Lester Patrick said, "Next time let's make such a series mean something. Let's make it a series for the Stanley Cup."

By the 1913–14 season, league scorers had begun to keep track of assists, goalkeepers who deliberately fell down to smother shots were subject to a two-dollar fine, and Art Ross of the Wanderers threatened to start a players' association if he didn't get a pay hike. Thanks to Ross, who got his raise, salaries inched upward until the average was $1,000 per season. The NHA and the Pacific Coast League edged toward an agreement for annual Stanley Cup playoffs on the basis of a three-out-of-five series, Western and Eastern rules to alternate.

Then World War I broke out, creating havoc with team rosters as hundred of young men of hockey-playing age donned another kind of uniform. The NHA hockey season ended with Montreal and Toronto in a first-place tie, each with 13 wins and seven losses. In the two-game playoff, Toronto lost the first game 2–0 in Montreal. Back home, playing on their new artificial ice surface, the Blueshirts registered a 6–0 shutout. As champions they were handed the Stanley Cup.

Then from out of the West came Victoria, the Pacific Coast League winners, seeking battle with the Blueshirts. Victoria neglected to file a formal Cup challenge with the trustees, assuming that if they defeated Toronto, the cup would be theirs. This proved to be a big mistake, for the trustees insisted that without a challenge the Cup was not in contention. Had Victoria won the series there would have been a great uproar. But Toronto won 5–2, 6–6 in overtime, and 2–1.

The oversight was remedied in the spring of 1915, when the East–West agreement went into effect, creating a best-of-three series for the Stanley Cup. Ottawa and the Wanderers, with identical 14–6 records, played off for the 1914–15 NHA championship in the East, the Senators winning the two-game, total-goals series, 4–1. Vancouver rolled to the Pacific Coast League title with 13 wins and four defeats in the 18-game schedule. Vancouver's final match with Victoria was canceled.

The Ottawa Senators traveled west to meet the Vancouver Millionaires in the first Stanley Cup series ever witnessed by fans living west of Winnipeg. Vancouver wanted to use Lester Patrick of Victoria in the series as a substitute for the injured Griffis, but Ottawa howled in protest. Frank Patrick, manager, coach, and player with Vancouver, bowed to the visitors and said quietly, "We're good enough to win this series with or without my brother."

He was right. Vancouver won the opener 6–2 under Western rules, then took the second game 8–3 with Eastern rules governing the play. The final match was no contest, Vancouver romping to a 12–3 win. Barney Stanley scored four goals while Mickey MacKay and Frank Nighbor each scored three. The Stanley Cup, for the first time, remained in the West, and those who'd witnessed the shellacking of Ottawa predicted it would remain there for years to come.

On the Coast, the Patrick brothers were stocking two new teams, Portland and Seattle, but the war had made good players scarce. The Patricks stepped up their raids on the old established clubs of the East. Several players from the 1915 Toronto club wound up in Seattle. Eastern clubs fought back and lured players like Frank Nighbor and Bert Lindsay back from the West.

Away from the battleground, trustee Foran announced that if Seattle and Portland won the Pacific Coast League crown, they would be eligible for the Stanley Cup playoffs. That was not what Lord Stanley had had in mind when he presented the trophy. It was to be presented to "the leading hockey team in Canada" at a time when all teams were amateur. For years, professional teams had scrambled after it and few had complained when amateurism died out. But now two American clubs were reaching for the Cup and some Canadians were alarmed at the thought of losing it across the border.

"The Stanley Cup," declared trustee Foran, "represents more than the championship of Canada. It's really the symbol of the championship of the world." When he put it that way, most of the squawkers were silenced, only a few complaining about the eligibility of American-based teams to win it.

And it didn't take long for an American team to come to the fore. In 1915–16, the Portland Rosebuds emerged as Coast League champs with a 13–5 record. Montreal Canadiens were the class of the NHA, winning 16 and losing seven. One game was tied. Canadiens were favored in the Stanley Cup series with Portland, for not only did they have home ice advantage, they faced a team that had finished its schedule three weeks earlier. But despite their layoff and the long trip east, the Rosebuds skated rings around Montreal in game one and captured it 2–0. Canadiens fought back with two straight victories, Portland won game four, and thanks largely to Georges Vezina's great work in goal, the Canadiens squeezed out a 2–1 victory in the deciding match. Each player on the winning team received $238 as his share of the playoff receipts. The losers pocketed $207.

The war was affecting hockey, just as it was all endeavors. So many players were in the armed forces in 1916 that an all-army team, the 228th Battalion, entered a club in the NHA and even experimented with khaki uniforms. The 228th was packed with stars and dominated the first half of the split schedule. Other clubs protested, claiming the soldier boys were getting more than service pay and arranging transfers so that good stickhandlers showed up where their on-ice talents were considered to be more important than the normal duties of a serviceman. When the 228th was ordered overseas in February 1917, leaving several games unplayed, league executives engaged in a row with Toronto owner Eddie Livingstone over the manner in which the schedule should be completed. As a result, Toronto was dropped from the league and the Toronto players moved to other teams.

Canadiens and Ottawa, as winners of the first and second halves of the split schedule, were deadlocked with 8–2 records. A two-game playoff series, total goals to count, was arranged to decide the championship. Canadiens won the first game 5–2 but lost star forward Newsy Lalonde for game two; he was suspended after he clubbed Ottawa star Frank Nighbor on the head, opening a huge gash over the Ottawa player's eye. Ottawa fought back with a 4–2 victory but lost the round seven goals to six.

A week later the Canadiens were in Seattle, eager to take on the Western champions. An added incentive for Montreal to win was the desire to keep the Stanley Cup in Canada. The Pacific Coast League was now three-quarters American: Victoria had moved to Spokane, adopting the unusual name Canaries, and joining Seattle and Portland as American teams. Vancouver was the only Canadian representative in the West. Seattle had won the league title with 16 wins and eight defeats and were favored to beat the Eastern champs.

Canadiens upset Seattle 8–4 in the opener with Didier Pitre scoring four goals. Seattle squared the series with a 6–1 victory in a game in which the Canadiens' Newsy Lalonde took five penalties. He even threw a butt end at referee George Irvine, whereupon judge of play Mickey Ion pitched into Lalonde and chased him off the ice, later adding a fine of $25. Lalonde was fortunate to escape a suspension.

A Seattle reporter was shocked at the rough play. He wrote:

During the contest Harry Mummery threw himself into Jack Walker with such force that the frail forward of Seattle had to be stretched out and then carried off the ice. Mummery and Rickey swung their sticks on one another's head so hard that the raps could be heard up in the gods and Rickey and Couture staged a bout that would have furnished a lively reel for the movies. Perhaps ice hockey should be added as a supplementary course in the U.S. army, for it would make the soldiers fit for the most ruthless kind of warfare.

Seattle's Bernie Morris was the star of game three, scoring three times against Georges Vezina in a 4–1 win. Seattle followed up with a convincing 9–1 rout in game four, with Morris scoring six times for the Metropolitans. Morris scored 14 goals in the series, an average of more than three per game. For the first time in history the Stanley Cup crossed the border out of Canada. "It could have been worse," wrote one Canadian reporter. "It could have been won by a bunch of Canaries."

Late in 1917, at a November 26 meeting in Montreal, the National Hockey Association was dissolved and its directors set up shop again as the National Hockey League, with the same basic constitution. Frank Calder, former NHA secretary, was elected president. Actually, the NHL was created as a means of getting rid of Eddie Livingstone, owner of the Toronto team. The other owners simply could not get along with Livingstone. "Eddie still has his franchise," one of the owners said with a chuckle. "He just hasn't got a league to play in." The new league was formed with the understanding that the Toronto Arenas would replace Livingstone's franchise in Toronto.

Professional hockey in the East was in trouble in 1917. Crowds were falling off, partly due to wartime conditions, partly because the NHA had been a shoddy league, badly run, and with management that showed little regard for the fans. In some places amateur hockey was more popular than the so-called big-time variety.

In its initial season the National Hockey League suffered two blows. The first was the disbanding of the Quebec Bulldogs. The Quebec players were drafted by the remaining teams — Ottawa, the Wanderers, the Canadiens, and Toronto. The Wanderers, with first choice in the draft, somehow ignored superstar Joe Malone, who went to the Canadiens. Malone was a superb performer in a Canadiens' uniform, scoring 44 goals in 22 games. (He missed two games, making his record even more remarkable.) On percentage, no player has equaled his mark, which was achieved against two of hockey's greatest goaltenders, Harry Holmes of Toronto and Clint Benedict of Ottawa.

The second setback was a disastrous fire that destroyed the Wanderers' arena early in the season. The once-mighty team was finished. A group from Hamilton offered to take the franchise but Wanderers' owner Sam Lichtenhein said no, and his proud team became part of history. Trivia buffs know the Wanderers as the only team to win just one game in the NHL (10–9 over Toronto in their home opener). Their record was 1–3 when they left the NHL forever.

The NHL was thus reduced to three teams in its opening season. The Canadiens won the first half with ten wins in 14 games. Toronto won the shorter second half with a 5–3 record. Toronto then won the two-game playoff by a 10–7 margin.

In the West, the Patricks initiated a playoff system to determine the Pacific Coast champions. First-place Seattle (11–7) met second-place Vancouver (9–9) in a two-game series. The opener, played in Vancouver, finished in a 2–2 tie. In game two in Seattle, Vancouver goalie Hugh Lehman was unbeatable when the Millionaires upset the Metropolitans with a 1–0 shutout.

Vancouver then showed up in Toronto for the Stanley Cup series with two of hockey's most popular and entertaining stars in the lineup — Mickey MacKay and Cyclone Taylor. Taylor was making his first trip east since playing for the Renfrew club seven years earlier. He scored twice against the Arenas in the opener, but Toronto won the game 5–3. MacKay scored three times and Taylor twice in game two, won by Vancouver 6–4 under Western rules. In game three, Taylor came through with a pair of goals for the third straight game, but it wasn't enough as Toronto skated to a 6–3 win. Game four went to Vancouver 8–1, with MacKay and Taylor playing starring roles. Taylor chipped in his usual two goals.

Set up by MacKay in the fifth and deciding game, he produced only one. It was not quite enough. Alf Skinner tied the score at 1–1, and Toronto appeared to be a little fresher than Vancouver in the final few minutes when Corbett Denneny of Toronto scored the winner. The Stanley Cup came back to the East, and back to Canada.

Postseries complaints centered on the playoff rules. It didn't seem to make sense to have one major league playing with six-man teams and the other playing with seven.

The war ended in November 1918, but the NHL was still on a precarious footing. Eddie Livingstone was threatening lawsuits and trying to reactivate the NHA. Attendance figures were a concern, and teams were anxious for players serving in the armed forces to return. Hopefully, they would not have lost their skating legs.

Canadiens (7–3 in the first half of the season) and Ottawa (7–1 in the second) met in a new kind of series — a best-of-seven affair for the NHL championship. Although Ottawa goaltender Clint Benedict, under the new rules, could now sprawl on the ice without fear of penalty or fine, he could not win the series for Ottawa. Canadiens captured it in five games. Montreal's Newsy Lalonde scored five goals in game three, a game in which Harold Darragh of the Senators was bashed over the head by a stick swung by Bert Corbeau. In the fourth game in Ottawa, Corbeau spent much of his time dodging rotten fruit tossed at him by Ottawa fans.

On the Coast, a two-game playoff for league honors was won by Seattle over Vancouver. Canadiens, meanwhile, had been waiting for two weeks to meet the winners for the Cup. The Eastern champs showed the effects of the layoff when they lost the opener 7–0 under Western rules. They fought back under Eastern rules to win the second game 4–2, with Lalonde scoring four goals. Seattle's Frank Foyston scored four times in game three, a 7–2 romp for the Metropolitans.

Pacific Coast fans said game four was the greatest ever seen in the West. The teams played one hour and 40 minutes of overtime before officials ended the game and declared it a scoreless draw.

In game five players on both sides appeared to be skating in slow motion. Fans assumed the teams — Montreal especially — were exhausted after the long overtime in the preceding match. Some Canadiens staggered off the bench and fell down on the ice. When Montreal's hardest hitter, Joe Hall, collapsed, he was carried off semiconscious and rushed to the hospital. The Canadiens held on for a 4–3 win in overtime, and spectators wondered how they'd ever finished the game. Most of them, it was learned, had the dreaded influenza virus and as least five were confined to bed for the next few days. The influenza epidemic of 1919 claimed millions of victims around the world. Joe Hall, the sturdiest of the Canadiens, suffered the most, and five days later, on April 5, he died.

The trustees had no choice but to abandon the series. For the second and hopefully the last time in Stanley Cup history, a season ended without fresh engravings on the Stanley Cup.

# 5 The Roaring Twenties

**I**N SPITE OF ITS SHAKY START, the NHL was organized just in time to share in the golden age of sport, the postwar era that saw every spectator sport boom to unbelievable heights of popularity. Tex Rickard achieved the impossible when he promoted the million-dollar gate in prizefighting. The heroics of Babe Ruth packed them in at the baseball parks. Newspapers that once gave a few select sports a mere half page now found space for almost every sport. Radio reached millions of stay-at-home fans who thrilled to the vivid descriptions of World Series games, championship fights, horse racing events and the Stanley Cup playoffs. Many of them became curious enough to go to the ballpark, the football stadium, and the hockey arena to see for themselves what all the excitement was about.

Sport became big business. Hockey, popular in Canada but still a minor attraction in international terms, shared in the general expansion. But this was only achieved when the professional game was stabilized, and bigger and more comfortable arenas were built, complete with that marvelous invention, artificial ice.

Ottawa, with its natural ice, encountered problems in spite of having one of the greatest teams ever assembled. In 1920, the Senators, with steady Clint Benedict in goal and with other stars like Jack Darragh, Frank Nighbor, Cy Denneny, and Harry

"Punch" Broadbent, were the class of the NHL and won both halves of the 1919–20 schedule, 9–3, and 10–2.

On the Coast, Seattle (12–10) met Vancouver (11–11) in a playoff for the Pacific Coast League title. Seattle captured the two-game series on the round, seven goals to three, and traveled east to meet the Senators.

More than 3,000 fans greeted the Metropolitans when they arrived at Union Station in Ottawa. Since both clubs wore similar uniforms, Ottawa switched to white jerseys for the best-of-five series. After three games in Ottawa played in slush, the series was transferred to artificial ice in Toronto. Game three, won by Seattle, was the first penalty-free game in Cup history.

When Seattle won game four to tie the series at two games apiece, Lou Marsh wrote in the *Toronto Star*: "If that combination of collar and elbow wrestling, African golf, American billiards, animated checkers and fancy ice skating is hockey, then I'm a Hottentot with a ring in my nose. It was cut and dried for Seattle to win so that a fifth game might be played."

The Senators, perhaps stung by the suggestion they'd played dead, rolled to a 6–1 victory in the deciding game to claim their first Stanley Cup since 1911. Jack Darragh scored half the Ottawa goals with a hat trick.

IN 1920–21, the Senators won five straight games early in the season and finished on top at the halfway point with a mark of 8–2. But they stumbled badly in the second half, losing seven in a row and allowing Toronto St. Pats (10–4) to capture the second-half crown. The Senators roared back to life in the Eastern playoffs, blanking Toronto 5–0 and 2– 0.

Before the deciding game, the St. Pats players dropped a bombshell. They refused to go onto the ice until they'd been given a cash bonus. The officials were stunned at the demands of the "greedy mercenaries." After 15 minutes of wrangling, the players appeared, having been promised the bonus. A *Toronto Star* editor expressed his fury: "This high-handed action has given the players a black eye with the public. No one begrudges the pros all the money they can get, but this last-minute strike stuff is not the proper procedure. Perhaps the ringleader of the strike may find himself out on his ear next season. It is coming to him."

When Ottawa went west for the Stanley Cup matches, they recruited Sprague Cleghorn from Toronto to bolster their chances. Strangely, neither the Cup trustees nor the Vancouver officials objected.

The first game of the series in Vancouver drew a record crowd of 11,000 fans, and the rest of the matches were almost equally well attended. Once again the Senators were slightly stronger than the Western champs, although the games were very close and the teams finished with an equal number of goals — 12. For the deciding game, more than 2,000 fans were left clamoring at the gates, unable to get in. They would have been bitterly disappointed had they found a place, and witnessed Ottawa take the fifth game by a 2–1 score. The game ended in a free-for-all with all players on the ice throwing punches. Eddie Gerard and Sprague Cleghorn of Ottawa and Lloyd Cook of Vancouver were thrown out of the match and fined $25 each. Jack Darragh scored the winning goal and, following the game, announced his retirement.

IN 1921–22, the NHL abandoned its split schedule and announced a 24-game season. This was the year Leo Dandurand and Joe Cattarinich bought the Canadiens franchise for $11,000 and began a rebuilding program that would make hockey history. It took a few years, but Dandurand, one of the best-liked sportsmen in the game, had the patience and the managerial skill to do the job to perfection.

In the spring of 1922, Ottawa (14–8–2) won the league title over Toronto (13–10–1), thanks in part to the record-breaking performance of Punch Broadbent, who scored in 16 consecutive games, and in part to the introduction of two flashy rookies, Frank "King"Clancy and Frank Boucher.

Under the new playoff structure, the first- and second-place finishers met in a home-and-home series for the NHL title. Toronto's Corbett Denneny sank the Senators' hopes for a third consecutive Stanley Cup by scoring the winning goal in a 5–4 opening-game victory. The second game, played in the familiar late-season slush at Dey's Arena in Ottawa, was scoreless.

A new league took shape on the Prairies for the 1921–22 season, the Western Canada Hockey League. Charter members were the Saskatoon Sheiks, the Regina Capitals, the Calgary Tigers, and the Edmonton Eskimos. Edmonton and Regina finished in a tie for league honors with 14–9–1 records. In a replay of an earlier tie game between the two clubs, Edmonton won 11–2. The loss placed Regina in a second-place tie with Calgary, and the teams met in a playoff series, won by Regina 2–1. Regina then met Edmonton again and, after an opening-game tie, captured the first championship of the new league with a 2–1 victory in the deciding match.

The Regina club journeyed to Vancouver where they met the Pacific Coast League champions in a home-and-home series to determine the Stanley Cup finalists. Regina stunned Vancouver with a 2–1 victory in game one, but they wilted back on home ice, losing 4–0. While Regina's Amby Moran was taking his postgame frustrations out on the referee by belting him around the dressing room and incurring a $100 fine, the Vancouver boys were packing up and rushing off to catch the eastbound train for Toronto.

Toronto fans were surprised when Vancouver won the first game under Eastern rules 4–3. Their surprise turned to utter confusion when they showed up for game two and tried to decipher the Western rules, which necessitated a multitude of markings on the ice.

Under NHL rules, the ice was marked off with a 40-foot no-offside area in center ice. The local amateurs who'd used the arena all season had lined off a 20-foot no-offside area for defensemen in front of each goal. Coast rules required a division of the surface into three equal sections, so more lines were added. The result was eight lines painted across the ice, ten if one counts the penalty shot line 36 feet out from each net. "Why, the bloomin' ice surface looks like a football gridiron," moaned Charlie Querrie, manager of the St. Pats.

The newly instigated penalty-shot rule under Western regulations added to Eastern confusion. A player tripped from behind while on a breakaway was to be awarded a free shot. But any one of his teammates was allowed to take it. And if he was fouled while skating in from the wing, the shot was to be taken from that angle, not straight on as happens today. "If any Westerner beats my goalie, John Ross Roach, from 36 feet," declared Charlie Querrie, "I'll eat the puck and the goal pads, too."

Toronto won game two in overtime despite the mystifying rules, and the teams split the next two games. The series became so rough that Inspector Bond of the Toronto Police Department visited both dressing rooms and pointed out the thin line between five minutes in the box and 30 days in jail. "I'll back the paddy wagon up and haul you all away if you don't behave," he threatened.

When Toronto clinched the Stanley Cup with a 5–1 triumph in game five, Lou Marsh wrote in the *Star*:

> The Millionaires team turned out like an auction room watch — looks well, but won't stand the wear and tear. The Irish squad just whaled the Coasters 5–1 in the deciding game and the result was absolutely the biggest surprise we ever had in this chunk of the old hemisphere. Vancouver can have no excuses. There are no alibis. When they were whaled Saturday night at their own game of seven-man hockey they practically quit cold after the first period. That stood out like a carbuncle on a fat man's neck. They did not quit last night.

> With nothing to worry Toronto, with John Ross Roach, the Port Perry Woodpecker, guarding the cash register, Noble, Dye and Denneny absolutely played their best hockey of the season. Dye, the lazy one, scored four times and acted like someone had sifted red pepper into his flannels. He was absolutely a wild man, always up for passes, yelling like a Comanche Indian.

> Just cancel that order for the town band and tell the Mayor of Vancouver that he needn't sit up anymore composing his ode of "Welcome to the Victorious Warriors." There ain't going to be no welcome for the Pacific Coast champions in that city by the western ocean.

**I**N MONTREAL in the early twenties, Leo Dandurand was trying to build his Canadiens into a mighty club. One of his best moves was to acquire a tiny superstar, a French Canadian prospect named Aurel Joliat. Joliat came east from Saskatoon in exchange for a fading great, Newsy Lalonde. A frail young man who never weighed more than 135 pounds, Joliat was a brilliant stickhandler and a veritable phantom who could elude the hardest-hitting defensemen. From the first of his 16 seasons with the Canadiens, he was among the top goalgetters.

Joliat helped Montreal to a 13–9–2 record in his rookie season, but his team couldn't match Ottawa's 14–9–1 mark. When the two teams played off for the NHL title in 1923, lines half a mile long formed outside the Mount Royal Arena for the series opener. It was butchery on ice. Montreal's tough guys, Sprague Cleghorn and Billy Couture, clubbed Lionel Hitchman and Cy Denneny to the ice with their sticks. Sportswriter Baz O'Meara wrote: "Cleghorn should have been given a jail term."

The attacks were so vicious that even Dandurand was shocked and lost all respect for his own players. He immediately suspended his two stars and fined them $200 apiece. Dandurand blamed referee Lou Marsh of Toronto for the fiasco. He said, "The last time Marsh refereed here he went back to Toronto and said that there had been missiles thrown and I was responsible for it, whilst in Ottawa for the past two years, they have been throwing lemons, metal pipes, and rubber boots and nothing has been said. While here, Marsh struck a spectator and he threw his bell at a fan in Toronto." Ottawa shut out the Canadiens 2–0.

The *Toronto Star* called for fans to cease throwing objects on the ice and cited the case of Montreal fans, who were apprehended for throwing beer bottles. The more fiendish in the group broke the necks of the bottles before heaving them, so as to maximize any damage inflicted. One hockey official suggested a novel punishment for players who used the butt end. There would be a five-minute penalty the first time. If it happened a second time, the culprit would be required to place a big soft rubber crutch cap over the butt of his stick and leave it there for the rest of the season. One wag carried the idea a little further. A cross-checker, he suggested, would therefore be forced to use a stick with a padded shaft and a slasher would finish the season wielding a mop.

Cleghorn and Couture pleaded with Dandurand to lift the suspension and allow them to play in the return game, but the manager refused to reconsider.

Hitchman and Denneny were barely able to suit up for the game, and it's no wonder; Denneny could hardly see or breathe through all the bandages that covered his head. Joe Malone played a sensational game for Montreal and set up two goals that tied the Senators on the round 2–2. Denneny shook off the effects of his concussion long enough to score the winning goal for Ottawa.

Before the 1922–23 season, the position of rover was finally eliminated in the west and seven–man hockey became a thing of the past. The Pacific Coast League and the Western Canada League worked out an interlocking schedule, the Coast circuit opened its season in mid-November — almost summer by previous standards — and the Vancouver Millionaires changed their name to Maroons. The Maroons topped the Pacific Coast League standings with 17 wins, 12 losses, and a tie. In a two-game playoff series with Victoria, Vancouver took the round five goals to three.

Edmonton, first-place finisher in the WCHL, eliminated Regina in a thrilling two-game series, then journeyed to the West Coast to await the winners of the Vancouver–Ottawa matchup.

The underdog Ottawa Senators hopped off the train from the east, stretched their legs, went rabbit hunting in the afternoon, and donned their blades in the evening to administer an artistic trimming of the Maroons 1–0. Vancouver fans were surprised at the Ottawa effort, having heard of the 4–0 shellacking the Senators had taken from Calgary in an exhibition game on their way west. Vancouver fought back to win game two by 4–1, and Ottawa's Frank Nighbor scored the winner for Ottawa in game three.

Goalie Clint Benedict was almost the whole story in game four, won by Ottawa 5–1. The Senator netminder kicked out pucks from all angles — hard ones, easy ones, bouncers, and bullets. Young King Clancy sparkled after Eddie Gerard was sidelined with a shoulder injury. Clancy was referred to as the "find of the season" by Vancouver observers.

Ottawa was in dreadful shape physically for the final series with Edmonton; injuries left their bench almost bare. They had a lone sub, Lionel Hitchman, whose broken nose was smothered in plaster. Eddie Gerard played despite a shoulder injury that would have kept most players in hospital. Cy Denneny and Hitchman scored the game's only goals, and King Clancy made history when he played every position for his team, including that of goaltender. In that era goalies served their own penalty time, so when Benedict was penalized, Clancy took over for him and recorded a two-minute shutout.

In game two Ottawa's battered lineup displayed its famous defensive strategy to thoroughly frustrate the Eskimos. Punch Broadbent broke away for an Ottawa goal, and the Senators won the Cup.

*Hall-of-Famer King Clancy, shown here in the uniform of his beloved Toronto Maple Leafs.*
(Turofsky)

A sizable crowd of Vancouver and Edmonton well-wishers turned out to see the Cup champions off when they boarded the train for home. On their arrival in Ottawa a tremendous crowd greeted them, and they were acclaimed by their admirers as they paraded in automobiles through the streets of the capital.

**FOR THE 1923–24 SEASON** Ottawa had a new 10,000-seat arena, complete with a shimmering artificial ice surface. The Senators' great captain Eddie Gerard retired, but most of the championship team was still intact. Montreal introduced a flashy rookie, Howie Morenz, and the two bad boys, Sprague Cleghorn and Billy Couture, were back in the good graces of manager Dandurand. Ottawa breezed to the league title with 16 wins and eight ties in the 24-game schedule, but they had a lot of trouble with Montreal in the two-game playoff. The Canadiens won the first game 1–0 on slush in Montreal. Back in Ottawa, more than 10,000 fans turned out to cheer their favorites, only to be bitterly disappointed when the defending Cup champions fell 4–2. Morenz showed blinding speed, scoring twice, and Aurel Joliat played one of the greatest games of his career, arousing the fans to a frenzy with his stickhandling.

On the Coast, Seattle, Victoria, and Vancouver waged the usual close battle, with Seattle winning the title with a 14–16–1 mark. All three Pacific Coast League teams finished with losing records at the close of the interlocking schedule with the Prairie teams. Seattle lost 11 of 16 games against WCHL clubs and still finished on top of its own circuit. Seattle and second-place Vancouver battled to a 2–2 tie in the first game of the playoffs, but Vancouver squeezed out a 2–1 overtime win on home ice to win the round. The two WCHL playoff games between Calgary and Regina were just as close, with Calgary winning on the round, four goals to two.

Calgary then advanced against Vancouver, even though both teams knew they would be heading east for Stanley Cup battles with Montreal, thanks to a strange agreement made with the NHL several months earlier. The final Western series was merely to determine which team would get the bye into the finals. At first Montreal flatly refused to countenance playing off against two challengers from Western Canada. Montreal finally gave in but only after an agreement that they pay transportation costs of just one team.

The series between Calgary and Vancouver was spread out over most of the West. One game was played in Vancouver, another in Calgary, and the third in Winnipeg. With each game, the two clubs moved closer to Montreal. When Calgary won the third game in Winnipeg to earn the bye, fans were so disappointed at the poor display of hockey that they hissed at the players as they left the ice.

Eastern fans turned up their noses at the idea of three teams in a final playoff for the Stanley Cup, and only diehard hockey supporters showed up when the Canadiens hosted Vancouver. The *Toronto Star* called it a "nonsensical semifinal series" played under the "kick, bite, and scratch rules which prevail in the West."

The sports editor of *Le Canada*, a Montreal paper of that era, left his readers confused when he wrote about the Canadiens' 1–0 victory in game one. They couldn't tell whether he was impressed or not when he wrote: "The game was at once thrilling and brilliant, but on the other hand, did not furnish an exhibition of hockey as fine as we have seen in the closing matches of the NHL season. As a spectacle no one could have asked for anything better but the hockey played was not first class."

The Canadiens eliminated Vancouver with a 2–1 victory in the second game. Billy Boucher scored both Montreal goals. The referee, Art Ross, encountered some difficulties with the Western rules. Playing two men short, Montreal began to rag the puck and Ross allowed them to do it — that is, until the entire Vancouver team skated over to him and informed him of his mistake.

What about those Western rules? How much did they differ from the Eastern variety? A lot of fans of the era required an explanation. The most prominent departures from Eastern rules were the antidefensive play rules, kicking of the puck, and penalty-shot rules. Western ice was divided into three equal sections and the defending team was permitted to have only four players, including the goalie, inside the first line. In other words, two players always had to be in the center area when the team was defending, making a six-man defense impossible. Kicking the puck was permitted anywhere except that a goal could not be scored in this manner. There was no forward passing and consequently no loafing offside near center ice. If an attacking player was deliberately fouled with a trip, a cross-check, et cetera, when he had a good chance to score, the referee could award a penalty shot. These shots were to be taken from spots marked on the ice about 40 feet from the nets, one in the center of the rink and one at each side midway between center ice and the sideboards.

Montreal's Howie Morenz excelled under any rules and scored three goals in the opener of the final playoff series with Calgary. It was a brutal affair. Morris, Morenz, and Couture were all knocked unconscious by blows to the head, and Dr. Smirle Lawson was called on to stitch them up. "I never want to see such a rough game again," said Lawson. "It was vicious. Why, Cully Wilson used to be called a bad man around Toronto — Cully is a lily-white angel compared to some of those birds."

The second match was played in Ottawa, where the hard artificial ice produced a furious pace. Rookie Morenz was seriously injured when he was flattened by a terrific body check delivered by Red Dutton. Morenz suffered torn ligaments in his shoulder and chest. He, Boucher, and Joliat scored in the Canadiens' 3–0 victory. All the Calgary attacks were turned aside by Montreal goaltender Georges Vezina, known as the Chicoutimi Cucumber, who faced all shots with the placid demeanor of an archbishop.

**BEFORE THE FIRST PUCK** was dropped to open the 1924–25 season, major changes took place in the game. For $15,000 Jimmy Strachan received a franchise for a second club in Montreal, which he named the Maroons. Home arena for the team was the new Montreal Forum, the first Montreal rink with artificial ice. Another franchise, managed by former player and referee Art Ross, was granted to Boston. Other American cities sought membership in the league, but their applications were put on hold. The schedule was increased from 24 to 30 games, and a new playoff system introduced.

The most sought-after player in hockey was forward Harry Watson, star of the Canadian Olympic team, which scored 110 goals and allowed only three at the 1924 Games. Watson was a torrid scorer in the tournament, averaging seven goals per game. But he turned down all pro offers.

In Hamilton, Percy Thompson had grabbed some top amateurs from the Sudbury Wolves, and his moves paid off when the Tigers moved from last place to soar to the regular season championship with a mark of 19–10–1. They finished one point in front of Toronto. Under the new playoff system Hamilton earned a bye, while Toronto and Montreal were ordered to meet in a semifinal series. But the Tigers, led by Red Green, had a complaint. Their contracts called for 24 games, not 30. They wanted more money and suggested $200 per man.

At this distance the request seems reasonable enough, but the NHL owners saw it as a challenge to be met head-on. The principle at stake, the right to strike, was a big one. NHL president Frank Calder ordered Hamilton to play and forget this nonsense of more pay. The Tigers refused and went on strike. Calder suspended them and fined each player $200. Foolishly, he also said that fourth-place Ottawa would replace Hamilton in the playoffs and get the bye. When the press roasted Calder, he changed his mind and stated that Toronto and Montreal would play off for the NHL title, the winner to advance against Victoria, the Western champions.

Goalie Georges Vezina was in wonderful form for the Canadiens in the two-game playoff with Toronto. He gave up two goals in the first game but registered a shutout in game two and Montreal won the round 5–2. Howie Morenz scored three of the five goals.

In the West, meanwhile, the Patrick brothers were having trouble keeping their Pacific Coast League together. When Seattle folded, Vancouver and Victoria joined the Western Canada

League. Calgary finished on top (17–11), and waited for second-place Saskatoon, called the Crescents, to meet third-place Victoria. Victoria eliminated Saskatoon and upset Calgary in the finals. The teams tied 1–1 in game one, and Victoria's star goalie, Harry Holmes, shut out Calgary 2– 0 in the second game.

The opening game of the Stanley Cup series, played in the West, went to Victoria 5–2. Victoria skated Montreal into the ice, and forward Jack Walker of the Cougars scored a pair of goals. Game two, played in Vancouver before more than 11,000 fans, saw Walker score two more goals in leading Victoria to a 3–1 victory. Montreal struggled back with a 4–2 win, but Victoria simply flew at Montreal in game four and won it 6–1. Walker was the star of the playoffs in the West with eight goals in eight games. For the first time, the Stanley Cup rested with Lester Patrick's Victoria Cougars. It would stay a few months and then move on, never to return. Throughout the series, crowds in Montreal stood on street corners in Montreal until 2:00 a.m., waiting to hear telegraphic game updates from the West.

**T**HE HAMILTON players' strike was historic, for it paved the way toward making the NHL truly international. Percy Thompson, who a few years earlier had paid $5,000 for the franchise when it was based in Quebec, sold the Tigers to Bill Dwyer, a New York sportsman, for $75,000. The striking players were reinstated by president Calder but not until each of them apologized to him personally for being so rebellious. They were ordered to report to New York and play for Dwyer's team, the Americans. Over the years, most of the stars in New York were seen only on the uniforms, for their jerseys looked like Old Glory had exploded. Still, the Americans drew 17,000 fans on opening night and New York finally had big-league hockey.

With Boston and New York already in the fold, the NHL was inclined to view further American applications with favor. Pittsburgh, long a hotbed of hockey because of its "amateur" Yellow Jackets, was also awarded a franchise.

The Senators' great Clint Benedict moved to the Maroons, but a capable replacement was Alex Connell, who recorded 15 shutouts and a 1.2 goals-against average in 36 games. Rookie Nels Stewart broke in with the Maroons and captured the scoring title with 34 goals. Hockey lost popular Georges Vezina, father of 22 children, who died late in the season of tuberculosis. A huge funeral was held for the great goaltender in his hometown of Chicoutimi. Vezina was a favorite everywhere he played, and within a year the NHL introduced a goaltenders' trophy in his memory.

Bright ideas abounded. A man named George Beeston claimed to have invented a bounceless puck, and Joe Munro of Ottawa invented an air-padded hockey stick grip. If a man was butt-ended, the air cushion in the knob would protect him from injury. In New York, promoter Tex Rickard planned to build a huge open-air stadium somewhere on Long Island, complete with artificial ice, so that NHL teams could play there in the summertime. It would be an ideal venue, he said, for future Stanley Cup matches.

Ottawa lost only two games during the first half of the schedule and wound up in first place at season's end with a 24–8–4 mark. The league's newest teams, the Maroons and Pittsburgh, finished second and third. In the playoffs, the Maroons eliminated the Yellow Jackets in two games, six goals to four. The Maroons went on to upset Ottawa in two games. The teams tied the opener 1–1, and Benedict shut out his old mates in game two, 1–0.

In the West, a lad named Eddie Shore created a stir with Edmonton, which edged Saskatoon for the championship of the Western Hockey League. But Victoria, the third-place finisher, knocked off both Saskatoon and Edmonton to advance to the Stanley Cup finals.

After 45 games and 30,000 miles of travel, the weary Victoria club came east but were easily outclassed by the Maroons, and lost in four games. Clint Benedict earned shutouts in three of them, and Nels Stewart, otherwise known as "Old Poison," handled most of the scoring. An awkward stickhandler and slow afoot, Stewart had remarkable reflexes and a deadly wrist shot. As a goal scorer, he was often called a "garbage collector" — as if that mattered to Maroon fans! He was responsible for six goals in the series, two of them in the final game — a 2–0 shutout. The annual East-West playoff for the Stanley Cup, with  its long train rides and double set of rules, ended with that game, because the Western League folded.

The Maroons, coached by Eddie Gerard, were all from Ontario. Dunc Munro, their captain, had by 1926 established a unique record for leadership. He had captained the Canadian junior champions, the University of Toronto team, the world's senior champions, the Canadian Olympic team champions, and the world's professional champions. Like most players, Munro was superstitious. He claimed that the Maroon victory was partially due to his father, Dunc Munro, Sr., who rubbed each player's back with a lucky rabbit's foot just before game time.

**W**HEN THE WESTERN LEAGUE folded in 1926, many star players moved east and joined teams in the NHL, which now included the New York Rangers, the Detroit Cougars, and the Chicago Black Hawks. The league embraced ten clubs in eight cities and was divided into two divisions. The Montreal Canadiens, the Maroons, the Ottawa Senators, and the Toronto Maple Leafs played in the Canadian Division; the New York Rangers, the Americans, the Pittsburgh Yellow Jackets, the Boston Bruins, the Chicago Black Hawks, and the Detroit Cougars played in the American.

Conn Smythe, a college coach in Toronto, was hired to manage the Rangers, but he had a falling-out with his New York bosses and was replaced by Lester Patrick before the season began. Smythe wasn't gone long. He resurfaced in Toronto, borrowed money, and bought the St. Pats franchise, which was rumored to be sought by American interests in Chicago and Philadelphia. Smythe changed the team's name to Maple Leafs and set about fulfilling his dream of building a mammoth new arena for his franchise.

With all this expansion and consolidation in 1926–27, the NHL established a basic format for the Stanley Cup playoffs. At the end of the regular schedule, which had been stretched to 44 games,

Ottawa was on top of the Canadian Division with 64 points, while the Rangers finished first in the American Division with 56 points. The Canadiens and the Maroons, as second- and third-place finishers in Canada, would play a two-game series for the right to meet Ottawa. Boston and Chicago would meet in a similar American Division series for the right to advance against the Rangers. The final series for the Stanley Cup would be a three-of-five meeting between the champions of each division.

The Canadiens ousted the Maroons by two goals to one in a low-scoring, thrilling series, with Howie Morenz delivering the lone goal of the second game in overtime. Ottawa overpowered the Canadiens in the follow-up series, five goals to one. In the American Division semifinals Boston outscored Chicago ten goals to five and then knocked out the Rangers three goals to one.

The final series between Ottawa and Boston opened in Boston and ended in a scoreless tie after 20 minutes of overtime. In game two, Eddie Shore, the Bruins' great defenseman, took five costly penalties, and Ottawa won by a 3–1 score. Game three in Ottawa finished 1–1 after a period of overtime, and Ottawa captured the Stanley Cup with a 3–1 victory in game four. The Ottawa players mobbed their diminutive goaltender, Alex Connell, who had given up just four goals in six playoff games for a 0.67 goals-against average. But the game ended on a sour note. Half a dozen fights broke out, and NHL president Calder handed out several fines and suspensions. The most severe was to Boston's Billy Couture, who had attacked referee Gerry Laflamme, knocking him down. Calder expelled Couture from the NHL for life and fined him $100. Five years later, Couture was reinstated, too late to resume his career in pro hockey.

Despite their successful season, the Senators were having trouble keeping up to the other teams financially, and there was grave concern about their future.

IN THE SPRING OF 1928, Howie Morenz led the Canadian Division in scoring for the second year in a row. Hockey was booming in Montreal because of the rivalry between the Habs and the Maroons. The Canadiens were the idols of the French-speaking crowd, while the Maroons represented the English; both factions got together every week to form long lines at the box office. That year the Maroons defeated Ottawa three goals to one in a semifinal battle and then eliminated the first-place Canadiens in a stirring series, three goals to two. In the American Division, after disposing of Pittsburgh, the Rangers eliminated Boston five goals to two, with Frank Boucher in a starring role.

The stage was set for an epic Stanley Cup final between the Rangers and the Maroons. With the Rangers forced out of Madison Square Garden because of other bookings, all games were played in Montreal. The Maroons shut out New York 2–0 in the opener.

In the second game, Ranger coach Lester Patrick, then 44 years old, performed his legendary feat as a substitute goalie in an effort to save his club from defeat. Lorne Chabot, the Rangers' only netminder, had been struck over the eye by a shot and could not continue. Maroon manager Eddie Gerard refused to let the

*Coach Lester Patrick achieved everlasting fame when he tended goal at age 44 in a Stanley Cup game.*
(Bill Galloway)

Rangers use Alex Connell, Ottawa's nifty netminder, who happened to be in the crowd. And no wonder. Connell had just finished a 15-shutout season — six of them in a row to set a record that has yet to be beaten. Patrick felt he had no choice; he would have to don the pads himself. For a man long retired from the game and never a goalie by profession, he did amazingly well, turning aside 18 shots until Nels Stewart beat him for a goal. The game went into overtime, and when the Rangers' Frank Boucher scored the winning goal, Patrick was mobbed by his players. He had created one of the most stirring stories in Cup history.

This kind of courage and leadership inspired the Rangers. After losing game three, with Joe Miller, a substitute goalie, in the nets, they came back with victories in games four and five to win the Stanley Cup.

Ranger fans, bitterly disappointed because they were unable to attend any games in the memorable series, nevertheless outdid themselves in a welcome-home party for the new champions. After a noisy parade to city hall, Mayor Jimmy Walker embraced the silver-haired Patrick, coach and emergency goaltender extraordinaire, who had brought New York its first Stanley Cup.

IN 1928–29, the Boston Bruins, with rookie goalie Tiny Thompson backstopping brilliantly, surged to the top of the American Division, while the Canadiens were the class of the Canadian Division. The Habs lost only seven games all season, thanks largely to netminder George Hainsworth, who racked up an incredible 22 shutouts and a 0.98 goals-against average. Toronto's Ace Bailey captured the NHL scoring crown with 22 goals and ten assists for 32 points.

The league introduced a playoff variation that year that called for the division leaders to meet in a best-of-five series, while the second-place clubs in each division met in another series and the third-place finishers played each other, as well. It didn't seem to make sense for the two top clubs to meet in the first round, but that was what the league brass decided.

The series between the Bruins and the Canadiens provided outstanding goaltending, with Thompson besting Hainsworth. Boston won three straight games by scores of 1–0, 1–0, and 3–2. Meanwhile, the Rangers knocked off the Americans in two games. Harry Connors foolishly punched the Rangers' Frank Boucher in the jaw, drawing a five-minute penalty in game two that led to Butch Keeling's goal — the only one of the series. In the other series, Toronto ousted Detroit seven goals to two on the round.

The Rangers advanced to the finals by beating Toronto in two straight games, and for the first time in history two U.S. clubs engaged in a best-of-three-game series for the Cup. The Bruins' Tiny Thompson, on home ice, shut out the Rangers 2–0 in game one, and his teammate Bill Carson was the hero in game two, scoring the winning goal in a 2–1 victory. Said Bruin superstar Eddie Shore, when the Bruins returned to Boston carrying the Stanley Cup, "It seems like a fitting way to end the decade."

# 6 Cup Thrills of the Thirties

IN THE THIRTIES, professional hockey, like every other business, suffered through the worst depression of modern time.
Franchises changed hands and some of the old clubs, notably
the famous Ottawa Senators and the New York Americans, faded
from the scene. Even the Montreal Canadiens had box office
problems and wound up one season with a profit of only $3,500
after winning the Stanley Cup. In Toronto, Conn Smythe ran into
Depression problems before his 12,000-seat sports palace, Maple
Leaf Gardens, was even finished. At one point, he and his able
assistant, Frank Selke, persuaded workmen to accept stock in the
venture in lieu of money. As a result, his new arena opened in the
fall of 1931 in spectacular fashion. It has been a near-sellout oper-
ation ever since.

During the 1929–30 season, veteran goaltender Clint Benedict
introduced a face mask for goaltenders, a leather contraption that
left only the eyes exposed. He wore it a few times, then, after getting belted in the nose during a game, decided it was time to
retire. It would be almost 30 years before the goalie face mask
reappeared.

Prior to the 1929–30 season, a change in the playoff format had
been announced. A two-game, total goals-to-count series replaced
the best-of-three series introduced two years earlier between the

winner of the second-place teams and the winner of the third-place teams.

A bizarre game was played in New York in 1930 between the Rangers and Pittsburgh. Lester Patrick had persuaded the league to allow the game to be governed by Western rules. Unfortunately, the players didn't know — or had forgotten — these rules and the referee was in the dark, as well. According to referee Lou Marsh, the game degenerated into a glorious game of pond hockey. "The players kicked the puck and batted it baseball-style," he said. "One even grabbed it and tried to throw it into the net. They did everything but tee it up and drive it down the fairway. If the NHL ever adopted that code, the game would be ruined in a month." How did the New York fans like the experiment? "Oh, they loved it," said Marsh. "That's the crazy thing. They said it speeded up the game."

The opening of the decade saw the Boston Bruins, Stanley Cup holders, again dominating the American Division of the NHL. In 1929–30, the Bruins lost only five games in the regular season. Cooney Weiland led the league with 43 goals and 30 assists for 73 points, and his teammate Dit Clapper wasn't far behind. The Bruins had one record 14-game winning streak and wound up 30 points ahead of second-place Chicago. In the Canadian Division, the Maroons and Canadiens were tied in points at the end of the season, but with two more wins than the Habs, the Maroons won first place. It was recognition the Maroons didn't need or want because it meant they had to meet Boston in the first round of the playoffs. Sure enough, the Bruins wiped them out in four games. The Canadiens eliminated Chicago in two games, with Montreal's Howie Morenz scoring the goal that won the series in overtime. The Rangers eliminated Ottawa, six goals to three.

The Canadiens moved on to push the Rangers aside with two straight wins in the semifinal series. Little-known Gus Rivers scored the winner for the Habs in game one after a record 68 minutes and 52 seconds of overtime.

With a regular season and playoff record of 41–4–1, Boston entered the finals against the Canadiens highly favored to win.

But they were unable to cope with the Canadiens' blinding speed and passed out of the Stanley Cup picture in two straight games. Ironically, it was winger Nick Wasnie who emerged as the hero in the finals, scoring a goal and an assist in each game. During the regular season, Wasnie had been roundly jeered by Montreal fans for his poor play.

A New York writer, Lawrence Perry, attributed the Montreal victory to "the thundering enthusiasm of the crowd of 13,000 in the Montreal Forum. Men like Morenz, Mantha, Joliat, Mondou, Leduc, and Lepine, whose souls tingle with Gallic temperament, are at their best with the crowd behind them. They rushed the Bruins off their feet."

After the season, a fan wrote W. A. Hewitt, sports editor of the *Toronto Star*, about the length of the playoffs and the number of games required to determine a champion: "About the hockey championship. I am making the suggestion to NHL president Calder that on account of the Canadiens winning the Stanley Cup and the Bruins winning the league title, it would only be in keeping if he was to leave them play it off again. Another series of from seven to eleven games between the two could be dragged out until the baseball season opens, and would probably draw what little dough the hockey fans have left, if any."

IN OCTOBER 1930, the Pittsburgh hockey team was transferred to Philadelphia and became the Quakers. Dick Irvin took over as coach in Chicago and King Clancy, Ottawa's top player, was sold to the Leafs when the Senators ran into financial difficulties. Leaf owner Conn Smythe raised the money for Clancy — a reported $35,000 — at the racetrack. He bet a bundle on one of his own horses, a 100–1 longshot named Rare Jewel, and won.

In 1930–31, the Canadiens (26–10–8) finished first in the Canadian Division with 60 points. Boston (28–10–6) was the top team in the American Division with 62 points. The Bruins–Canadiens series went five games, and the final game required 19 minutes of overtime before the Canadiens won it on Larochelle's goal. Chicago ousted Toronto on the round, four goals to three, and the Rangers bounced the Maroons 5–1 in the first game and 3–0 in the second.

The final series between the Canadiens and the Black Hawks opened in Chicago, the first time a final series game had ever been played there. Bruised and battered after their grueling series with Boston, the Canadiens eked out a 2–1 victory in game one and lost by a similar score in game two when Johnny Gottselig scored in overtime. The 18,000 fans in attendance rose en masse to salute the Hawks and sent up cheer after cheer, even after both teams had left the ice.

The teams moved to the Montreal Forum for the final three games. In game three the Black Hawks came from behind to tie the score, and after almost a full hour of overtime, Cy Wentworth scored the winning goal. Fans noticed that coach Dick Irvin changed his lines precisely every three minutes during the series. Still sadly crippled through injuries, the Canadiens fought back to square the series, coming back from a two-goal deficit to win 4–2.

From the opening whistle in game five, the Hawks were attacked by a swarm of red-shirted Habs. Johnny Gagnon scored in the second period and Howie Morenz followed up with a spectacular goal — his first in ten playoff games — to give the Canadiens a 2–0 lead. Coins, programs, and overshoes were tossed on the ice, and Morenz took a sprawl when his skate hit a coin. A drunken fan threw a full bottle of gin at referee Bobby Hewitson, missing his head by inches. The fan was arrested and fined $50. The Canadiens were able to hang on for the shutout. After the traditional postgame celebration, they grabbed Chicago goaltender Charlie Gardiner and hoisted him to their shoulders, an unexpected but fitting tribute to one of the best playoff performances by a goaltender they'd ever seen.

The season ended with two clubs dropping out of the NHL — Philadelphia, with only four wins in 44 games, and Ottawa. Once a great power in hockey and a Stanley Cup winner on nine occasions, Ottawa had won just ten games and sought a one-year leave of absence. Eight clubs remained for the new season, four in each division.

*Two hockey
immortals —
Conn Smythe
(left) and Dick
Irvin.* (Turofsky)

**THE 1931–32 SEASON** was the Year of the Leafs. Conn Smythe opened his Maple Leaf Gardens on November 12 with nearly 14,000 cash customers in the building. When the Leafs got off to a slow start, Smythe fired coach Art Duncan and replaced him with Dick Irvin, who had been dismissed by the Black Hawks.

Some team owners were concerned that the American Hockey League champions would be allowed to challenge for the Stanley Cup. NHL president Frank Calder said the league would forfeit the Cup if that ever happened and accept another trophy in its place, one "worth more than $1,000" and donated by a wealthy unnamed sportsman. Cup trustees Foran and Ross, however, said they'd give consideration to any Stanley Cup challenge and render a fair decision as to its merits. When Calder stated emphatically that the NHL would refuse to meet the American League champions for the Cup, the trustees at first adopted an equally tough stance, declaring there would be no Stanley Cup games in 1932. After huddling with Calder, however, the trustees announced that the American League challenge would be postponed for a year. Little more was ever heard about this matter.

The Canadiens finished on top of the Canadian Division, four points ahead of the much improved Leafs, and were favored to win their third straight Stanley Cup when they met the Rangers,

American Division titleholders. The teams split the first two games, played in Montreal. In the next two games, played in New York, the Rangers outskated the Canadiens and captured the series three games to one. In Series B between Toronto and Chicago, the Leafs lost the opener 1–0, then roared back with a 6–1 win on home ice and ousted the Hawks 6–2. In the third playoff series, the Maroons eliminated Detroit 3–1.

Series D between the Maroons and the Leafs was a thriller. After the teams tied 1–1 in game one, the Leafs' Hap Day scored a dramatic goal late in game two to tie the score at two. Then Bob Gracie scored the winner in overtime to send the Leafs into the finals.

Toronto's Busher Jackson was the individual star in the opening game of the final series, played in New York before 16,000 fans. He collected three goals in a 6–4 win. The second game was played in Boston because a circus was booked at Madison Square Garden. Toronto's Kid Line — Jackson, Conacher, and Primeau — dominated the game and accounted for four of the Toronto goals in a 6–2 victory. Back at Maple Leaf Gardens, the Leafs scored half a dozen goals for the third straight time and won the Cup. Some referred to the finals as the "tennis series," since the game scores were 6–4, 6–2, and 6–4. Ranger goalie John Ross Roach took a roasting for allowing 18 goals in three games. Millions of fans followed the series, as they had followed the Leafs during the regular season, on radio. Foster Hewitt, the voice of hockey from his gondola high above the Gardens' ice surface, was quickly building up an enormous following. Winning coach Dick Irvin had little time for celebration. He rushed back home to Regina where his son was seriously ill. The lad recovered, grew up, and earned considerable hockey fame of his own — as a commentator on *Hockey Night in Canada.*

In the off-season, alarmed at the rising costs of hockey, the NHL declared that no club could have on its roster more than 14 players, exclusive of goaltenders, and that the total salaries for these players must not exceed $70,000. When the league ruled that no player could earn more than $7,500 per season, there were loud protests from the men on the ice, and several holdouts followed, but eventually all signed up for another season.

**T**HE ECONOMY MOVES instituted by the league prompted Ottawa to jump back in for the 1932–33 season, and several players leased to other clubs were forced to return to the Senators. The Depression continued to haunt the game. Attendance plummeted around the league, even though tickets were available in most arenas for as little as 50 cents, and the best rinkside seats could be purchased for three dollars. Only 4,000 fans turned out in Chicago to see the champion Leafs play the Black Hawks early in the season, and only 2,000 showed up at the Detroit Olympia for a game between the hometown Falcons and the Americans.

Toronto (24–18–6) won the Canadian Division title, while in the American Division, Boston and Detroit finished with identical 25–14–8 marks. The Bruins were awarded the division championship because they had scored more goals than Detroit — 124 to 111.

League rules still required the two top teams in each division to meet in a first-round playoff series, and the opening games in Boston between the Leafs and the Bruins were thrillers. Boston took the opener 2–1, and the Leafs came back to capture game two, which was scoreless until Busher Jackson's overtime goal. Eddie Shore's dramatic overtime goal following an end-to-end rush gave the Bruins a 2–1 triumph in game three. Toronto took game four 5–3. The deciding game on April 3 was one of the most memorable in NHL history. Six overtime periods were required before the Leafs' diminutive Ken Doraty clicked for the winning goal at almost two o'clock in the morning. Toronto won the marathon 1–0 and captured the series three games to two.

The Detroit Falcons eliminated the Montreal Maroons and the New York Rangers ousted the Montreal Canadiens from further play. The Rangers moved on to defeat Detroit six goals to three on the round.

The Leafs, after their early-morning overtime win over Boston, were required to be in New York the following day for the opening game of the final series. They had nothing left against the Rangers, who swept to the Stanley Cup in four games. The fourth game required overtime, but the Leafs' Levinsky and Thoms were penalized early in the overtime period. While they were in the box, Bill Cook scored on Lorne Chabot to win the Cup for the Rangers.

**B**EFORE THE 1933–34 SEASON the Detroit Falcons changed their name to Red Wings. The Ottawa management decided to try once more to keep their franchise alive. Boston's Eddie Shore was a holdout and missed the Bruins' opener. When he finally signed, some skeptics said the Bruins had found a way to pay him more than the maximum allowable salary of $7,500.

In mid-December, Shore was the central figure in one of hockey's great tragedies, the career-ending injury to Leaf star Ace Bailey. During a game in Boston, Shore upended Bailey when he crashed into him from behind. The Leaf forward flew backward, striking his head on the ice and suffering a fractured skull. Toronto tough guy Red Horner hovered over Bailey for a moment, then skated up to Shore. After some hot words, he lashed out and flattened the Bruin with one solid punch so that he, too, struck his head on the ice and was out cold. Shore wasn't seriously injured, but Bailey wavered between life and death for the next few days. Two delicate operations were required to remove a blood clot from his brain. In time he recovered, but his hockey career was over.

Shore was suspended for only 16 games, despite demands from several league governors that he be barred for the rest of the season. The Bruins, perhaps fearing a lawsuit, donated the proceeds from one of their league games to Bailey, but the amount turned over to him was less than $7,000. Later, a benefit game was held in Toronto between the Leafs and an NHL all-star team, with the proceeds — about $20,000 — also going to the Leaf star. The highlight of that evening was a simple handshake at center ice between Bailey and Shore. Bailey wasn't one to hold a grudge. On

March 6, in Boston, they shook hands once more when Bailey was invited to face-off the puck before a Boston home game. Bailey went on to become a college coach with the University of Toronto and also served as a penalty timekeeper at Maple Leaf Gardens for 47 years.

Toronto (26–13–9) captured the Canadian Division title and faced Detroit (24–14–10), the American Division champs, in the opening round of the 1934 playoffs. Detroit got off to a fast start, winning the first two games on Toronto ice. Toronto fought back with two victories in Detroit. In the deciding game at Maple Leaf Gardens, Ebbie Goodfellow scored the game's only goal to give the Red Wings their first NHL title since they entered the league eight years earlier.

The Canadiens–Black Hawks series was won by Chicago on the round, four goals to three. In game two at the Chicago Stadium, an oddity took place between the end of the third period and overtime. Instead of lining up immediately for the overtime period as the rules required, the Canadiens rushed to their dressing room. League president Frank Calder, who was at the game, ordered them back onto the ice, but by the time they returned, the Habs had enjoyed a good rest.

Goalie Dave Kerr of Montreal starred when the Maroons met the Rangers in Series C. The Maroons won the round two goals to one. In Series D, Chicago eliminated the Maroons in two straight games.

The first game of the final series between Chicago and Detroit, played at the Olympia in Detroit, was decided when Paul Thompson scored in overtime for the Black Hawks. Chicago also won game two. For game three, 18,000 fans jammed the Chicago Stadium, eager to see their favorites win the Cup. But goalie Chuck Gardiner, the Hawks' always reliable netminder, allowed Doug Young's dribbler to find the back of his net, and that goal proved to be the winner in a 5–2 Detroit victory. Chicago's Mush March wore the hero's mantle in game four when he beat Red Wing goalie Wilf Cude for the only goal of the game. Black Hawk netminder Chuck Gardiner played brilliantly in every game and lost only once in eight playoff starts.

As part of the postgame celebrations, Chicago's Roger Jenkins made good on a vow he'd made to Gardiner and wheeled him around downtown Chicago in a wheelbarrow. But Gardiner's joy ended abruptly two months later. At home in Winnipeg he suffered a brain hemorrhage and collapsed. Three days later he died, at the peak of his career but assured of an honored place in the Hockey Hall of Fame.

**T**RADITIONALLY, player salaries in sport rise from season to season. In the NHL during the early thirties, however, salaries were going down. For the 1934–35 season, a salary cap of $62,500 was placed on teams, and the league's general managers were ordered not to pay more than $7,000 to any individual player.

Tommy Gorman didn't have to worry about negotiating with the Stanley Cup winners, all of whom probably deserved fatter paychecks. Gorman was bounced as the Black Hawks' manager, despite the Stanley Cup victory he'd helped engineer. He was replaced by Clem Loughlin. Gorman promptly joined the Montreal Maroons as manager and took big Lionel Conacher with him.

The New York Americans were struggling to make ends meet. Owner Bill Dwyer denied reports that his players were on the verge of a mutiny because their salaries weren't being paid on schedule.

The Ottawa Senators sold many of their best players and were granted permission to move to St. Louis, where they were called the Eagles. Before long the Eagles began playing like old crows and their supporters stayed away. Two of the St. Louis stars, Syd Howe and Scotty Bowman, were purchased by Jack Adams in Detroit. Before he left, Bowman made history by becoming the first NHLer to score a goal on a penalty shot.

Chicago tried to gain strength by acquiring the great Howie Morenz from the Canadiens, but Morenz was uncomfortable in a Chicago uniform and scored only eight goals. Lorne Chabot, acquired from Toronto, replaced the deceased Gardiner and won the Vezina Trophy as a Black Hawk.

The Leafs' Big Train, Charlie Conacher, led all goal scorers that season with 36, and even played in goal for three minutes one night when netminder George Hainsworth was struck by a puck and went to the Leaf dressing room. Not bothering to don the big pads, Conacher said, "Just gimme his goal stick and I'll shut 'em out." He did, too, to the delight of his many fans.

At the end of the season, Frank Boucher of the Rangers, winner of the Lady Byng Trophy for gentlemanly play for a record seven times in eight seasons, was told to keep the cup. Lady Byng thought he had earned permanent possession of it, and since she was willing to donate a second one, the league governors agreed.

Toronto (30–14–4) won the Canadian Division with 62 points, while Boston finished on top of the American Division with 58 points. Series A between the Leafs and the Bruins began at the Boston Garden. In game one, Boston's Dit Clapper scored the only goal after 33 minutes and 26 seconds of overtime. The Leafs won game two 2–0, helping George Hainsworth to a shutout by outshooting the Bruins 41–16. Hainsworth, back on home ice, recorded his second straight shutout, blanking Boston 3–0. He remained hot and allowed only one goal in the deciding game, won by the Leafs 2–1.

In Series B between the Maroons and the Black Hawks, neither team could score until "Baldy" Northcott beat Lorne Chabot in overtime in game two, eliminating the Hawks by that single goal on the round.

The opening game between the Rangers and the Canadiens in Series C featured a donnybrook at Madison Square Garden. The Habs' Nelson Crutchfield tangled with Bill Cook and cracked the Ranger forward over the head with his stick. Bleeding profusely, Cook slumped to the ice and both benches emptied. A handful of New York's finest jumped into the melee, and when order was restored, Crutchfield was sent to the penalty box for the remaining 22 minutes of the game. And with no substitute allowed! Cook returned from the medical room, his head covered in bandages and wearing a helmet, just in time to score the winning goal against Wilf Cude, the beleaguered Habs' goaltender. In game two, the teams skated to a 4–4 tie. At the final whistle, Crutchfield and Cook patted each other on the back and shook hands. The Rangers advanced by winning on the round, six goals to five.

In Series D, the Maroons ousted the Rangers by winning the opening game 2–1 and skating to a 3–3 tie with the New Yorkers in game two.

For the first time in a decade, two Canadian teams — Montreal and Toronto — met in the Stanley Cup finals. It turned out to be a battle between two outstanding goaltenders, Alex Connell of Montreal and George Hainsworth of Toronto. The Maroons took the first two games by 3–2 and 3–1 scores, silencing fans at Maple Leaf Gardens. Back on home ice in Montreal, the Maroons captured the Stanley Cup with a 4–1 victory. Baldy Northcott and Cy Wentworth banged in goals during a 12-second span in the second period and dashed all Toronto hopes of a comeback. Alex Connell had turned back the famous Kid Line and other stars like Clancy, Horner, and Day.

**BY THE MID-THIRTIES,** hockey team owners and managers had already discovered that money alone wouldn't buy a Stanley Cup. But farsighted thinking would help. Most felt the key to success lay in a strong farm system, and wise hockey men were looking far ahead, developing potential stars in the minor leagues and scouting teenage skaters in every town that boasted a rink. Detroit, which drew thousands of fans from across the river in Windsor, Ontario, had become a hockey hot spot. Jack Adams reached far and wide for players. There was Normie Smith in goal, Syd Howe, Marty Barry, and a brilliant rookie from Sudbury, Larry Aurie, on the forward line, plus hard-hitting Bucko McDonald on defense. These were some of the Red Wings who were destined to win Detroit's first Stanley Cup in the spring of 1936.

The 1935–36 season began without the St. Louis franchise, which had folded. The St. Louis players were drafted by the other

NHL clubs, and Boston got a huge bargain when they selected center Bill Cowley for a fee of $2,250. Much less able players were drafted ahead of Cowley and went for up to $4,000. The Montreal Canadiens signed a young player named Toe Blake, who was said to have great potential. A former Hab star, Howie Morenz, went from the Black Hawks to the Rangers in a trade but still failed to show much of his old-time form.

With Montreal and Toronto in a heated battle for first place in the Canadian Division, Leaf owner Conn Smythe lost his composure one night and created a hockey "first" by invading the penalty box to lecture the penalized Canadien player, Sylvio Mantha. Referee Mike Rodden intervened; so did league president Frank Calder and Canadiens' governor Ernie Savard. Never before had a penalty box housed a player, two NHL governors, a referee, and the league president.

The Montreal Maroons captured the Canadian Division title, edging Toronto 54–52 in points, while Detroit won the American Division with 56 points. Boston, Chicago, and New York all finished with 50 points as American Division runners-up, a most unusual situation.

The most dramatic game of the playoffs, and one of the most talked about in NHL history, occurred when Detroit played the Montreal Maroons in Series A. On March 24 and on into the early-morning hours of March 25, millions of radio listeners, and thousands of ticket holders at the Montreal Forum sacrificed a good night's sleep as the scoreless game went into six periods of overtime. The weary players were staggering into 177 minutes of hockey when "Mud" Bruneteau, a rookie with only two goals and no assists in 23 games, scored the winner against the Maroons' goalie, Lorne Chabot. It was 2:25 a.m. when Bruneteau ended the longest game in history.

Detroit netminder Norm Smith collected his second straight shutout two nights later when the Red Wings won 3–0, and the series ended with the Red Wings winning their third straight game 2–1 back on home ice.

The Boston–Toronto series began with the Bruins' Tiny Thompson shutting out the Leafs 3–0. But Toronto surprised

Boston with a strong comeback in game two and emerged with an 8–3 victory. The Leafs credited King Clancy's quick wit and sharp tongue with the victory. When Boston's Eddie Shore vehemently protested a Leaf goal by Red Horner, claiming Horner was in the crease, Clancy sidled up to Shore and said, "It was a lousy call, Eddie. The guy robbed you for sure. Don't let him get away with it." Whereupon the irate Shore shot the puck at the referee, hitting him on the backside. Shore was banished for two minutes, but en route to the box he picked up the puck and threw it into the crowd, for which he was sentenced to an additional ten minutes. While Shore fumed in the box, the Leafs rapped in three goals, a big part of their series-winning margin, eight goals to six. Meanwhile, the New York Americans, in the playoffs for the first time since 1929, upset the oddsmakers by ousting Chicago on the round, seven goals to five.

The Americans and the Leafs split a pair of games in the follow-up best-of-three series. King Clancy was the star and scored the winner in the final game, a 3–1 Leaf triumph.

In the final series for the Stanley Cup, Detroit was too fast for Toronto in the first two games, winning by scores of 3–1 and 9–4. The Red Wings were leading 3–0 in game three and preparing to sip champagne from the Cup when suddenly the Leafs roared back with three third-period goals to tie the score. Then, after half a minute of overtime, Toronto's Buzz Boll clicked for the game winner to prolong the series.

When the Leafs tried to ignite a similar comeback in game four, also played in Toronto, the spark was missing, and the Red Wings rolled to a 3–1 victory. Since the Cup was won on foreign ice, there was little interest in a presentation ceremony at Maple Leaf Gardens. The Red Wings congregated back at their downtown hotel where Detroit owner Jim Norris accepted the Cup from NHL president Frank Calder.

It had been four years since a Canadian club had won the Stanley Cup. Five more years would pass before a Canadian club would win it again. It was beginning to appear that the powerful

American teams had taken over Canada's national game where it counted — at the annual Stanley Cup presentation.

**F**OR THE 1936–37 NHL SEASON, the New York Americans were barely able to function. The franchise had been taken over by the league and the club was up for sale. The Montreal Canadiens, last-place finishers in 1936, sought help and found some when they traded with the Rangers for Howie Morenz. Morenz was reunited with his old linemates, Aurel Joliat and Johnny Gagnon, and had 20 points midway through the season. But one night he caught his skate in a rut, crashed into the boards, and snapped a bone in his leg. On March 8, the hockey world was stunned to hear of his death in hospital of a heart attack. Thousands attended a special service at the Montreal Forum for this great star, the most dynamic player of his era.

In New York, the Rangers' remarkable line of Bill Cook, Frank Boucher, and Bun Cook was disbanded when Bun Cook was sold

*Latter-day Canadien great Bernie Geoffrion and his wife Marlene look at a photo of Boom Boom's famous father-in-law Howie Morenz.*
(David Bier)

to Boston. Joe Primeau's retirement from the Leafs ended the glory days of the high-flying Kid Line of Conacher, Primeau, and Jackson. King Clancy retired from the Leafs early in the season, and rookie Walter "Turk" Broda took over from George Hainsworth in the Toronto goal. The Leafs also introduced a future star in Sylvanus Apps, who finished second in scoring behind Sweeney Schriner of the Americans. Apps became the first winner of the Calder Trophy, a brand-new award given to the top NHL rookie.

Late in the season, Chicago owner Fred McLaughlin came up with a novel idea. He iced a team of mostly American-born players. He signed U.S. amateur stars Ernie Klingbeil, Paul Schaefer, Milt Brink, Al Suomi, and Bun Laprairie, adding them to the three American-born players already on his roster, one of whom was goalie Mike Karakas. The newcomers, all virtually unknown, flunked their big-league test and soon disappeared from the scene. Other club owners called McLaughlin's experiment a farce.

The Montreal Canadiens won the Canadian Division by one point over the Maroons, and Detroit repeated as champions of the American Division, finishing six points ahead of Boston.

The Red Wings had little difficulty with the Canadiens in the first two games of the opening round of the playoffs, winning 4–0 and 5–1. However, Red Wing goalie Norm Smith suffered a badly bruised elbow in game three at Montreal and couldn't continue. The Habs won 3–1 and followed up with a victory in game four by the same score. The deciding match at the Montreal Forum was tremendously exciting. The drama ended after almost an hour of overtime when Hec Kilrea scored to give Detroit a 2–1 victory, making a second straight Cup win a distinct possibility.

When the Maroons met the Bruins in Series B, Boston's Dit Clapper lost his temper in game one and struck Dave Trottier across the head with his stick. Referee Clarence Campbell intervened, and Clapper, still incensed, punched the unsuspecting official. Clapper was given a five-minute penalty. Montreal won the game 4–1 and the fans thought they'd seen the last of Clapper, who they were certain would be given a long suspension. But the

Bruin star was lucky. He was fined $100 after Campbell reported that Clapper's blow was probably unintentional. Clapper was the best player on the ice in game two, won by Boston 4–0. But the Maroons won game three 4–1 and the Bruins' season was finished.

Series C between Toronto and the Rangers opened at Maple Leaf Gardens. A free-for-all broke out in game one with only a few seconds to play and with New York leading 3–0. Conn Smythe jumped on the ice to argue with referee Ag Smith, and Leaf defenseman Red Horner threw a wild punch at the official. There were many penalties but no suspensions. Back in New York, Babe Pratt scored the winning goal in overtime, giving the Rangers a 2–1 decision and eliminating the Leafs.

When Detroit faced the Rangers in the final series for the Cup, Red Wing goalie Norm Smith was still nursing a tender elbow and was replaced by rookie Earl Robertson, who played the entire series. After the teams split the first two games, Ranger goalie Dave Kerr registered a 1–0 shutout in game three. Neil Colville scored the only goal of the contest. Because of the annual invasion of the circus at Madison Square Garden, the remaining games were played in Detroit. In game four, Robertson turned in a 1–0 shutout performance to square the series for the Red Wings. Marty Barry scored the game's only goal. The Detroit sharpshooter added two more goals in game five, pacing the Red Wings to a 3–0 triumph and their second straight Stanley Cup.

Rookie Robertson was highly praised after his two shutouts in a row, and the Red Wings congratulated themselves for selecting him over Turk Broda when faced with the choice a few months earlier. But Robertson's moments of Stanley Cup glory were few, and Broda eventually far surpassed him in playoff heroics.

**O**NE MAN WHO THOUGHT Earl Robertson was headed for longtime stardom was Red Dutton, manager of the New York Americans. He acquired Robertson in the off season to solve the Amerks' goaltending problems.

In Chicago, Major McLaughlin made another coaching change, bringing in Bill Stewart, who doubled as a big-league baseball umpire and NHL referee. Stewart found himself umpiring in the seventh game of the World Series one day and behind the Chicago bench the next. Stewart had once made headlines as a pitcher, fanning 54 batters in three games played over two days. He knew Chicago, having pitched for the White Sox in 1919. Hockey men laughed at his appointment, talked of his inexperience, and said he'd never amount to anything in his new profession.

King Clancy was the new coach of the Montreal Maroons, but the retirement of Lionel Conacher and Alex Connell left Clancy with some weak spots that management was unable to fill. Muzz Patrick was called up from the minors and joined his brother Lynn in the Ranger lineup. Their father, manager Lester Patrick, also brought in Bryan Hextall, who turned in a fine rookie season. The Bruins introduced a slick-passing, high-scoring trio known as the Kraut Line. Bobby Bauer, Milt Schmidt, and Woody Dumart were all of German descent and hailed from Kitchener, Ontario.

Toronto won the race in the Canadian Division with 57 points, eight more than both the Americans and the Canadiens. The

*Ranger manager
Lester Patrick
(left) and his sons
Muzz and Lynn.*
(Public Archives of
Canada)

Leafs' Gordie Drillon and Syl Apps finished one-two in the scoring race with 52 and 50 points. Boston won a league record of 30 games and finished with 67 points, six ahead of the Rangers.

In the first round of the playoffs, the Leafs upset Boston by winning three straight games. Gordie Drillon scored the winning goals in both the second and third games. The battle between the second-place teams, the Americans and the Rangers, was decided in overtime in game three. The largest crowd of the season in New York, more than 16,000, saw a thriller that required one hour and 40 seconds of overtime before Lorne Carr scored for the Americans, giving them the game (2–1) and the series.

The Canadiens, on home ice, jumped in front in their series with Chicago, winning easily 6–4. But Chicago's Mike Karakas engineered a 4–0 shutout in the second game at the Chicago Stadium. Back in Montreal, Chicago's Earl Seibert scored in the dying seconds to tie the game at 2–2, and Paul Thompson won it for the Hawks in overtime.

With the Canadiens eliminated, the Hawks met the New York Americans in a semifinal series. Each team won a game, and in the deciding match, played at Madison Square Garden, all bets were on Red Dutton's Amerks. With the score tied at 1–1, the Hawks' Alex Levinsky scored a goal, but the red light didn't flash. Tempers erupted until the referee signaled a score. He'd discovered that a New York fan had grabbed the goal judge by the wrist, preventing him from switching on the light. Chicago won the game 3–1 and took the series two games to one. The Black Hawks, with only 14 wins during the 48-game regular season — one of the worst records of any Stanley Cup challenging team in history — found themselves one step away from Lord Stanley's famous basin.

When the final series opened in Toronto, the Hawks were without a goalie. Mike Karakas, suffering from a broken toe, was a last-minute scratch. The Hawks asked permission to use Dave Kerr, the New York Ranger goalie, but the request was denied. Alfie Moore, a minor-league goalie in the Leaf farm system, was recruited, although there were grave doubts he'd be much help.

Some say he was found in a tavern on the afternoon of the game, and Moore would later admit, "Sure, I had a few beers. But I had no idea I was going to play that night." Play he did, and brilliantly, leading Chicago to a 3–1 triumph. But Moore thumbed his nose at the Toronto bench when he left the ice, and that was it for him; he was ruled ineligible for game two. Rookie Paul Goodman was brought in to replace Karakas. Toronto shooters peppered Goodman and skated away with a 5–1 win.

A huge crowd jammed the Chicago Stadium when the series moved back across the border. They saluted Mike Karakas, who was back in goal, with a prolonged ovation, and Karakas treated them to some textbook goaltending. Hawk fans greeted the Leafs' Red Horner, suspected of breaking the nose of Doc Romnes in game two, with a chorus of boos and a shower of debris. A stadium usher took a gallon container of beer away from one fan in the balcony. When he asked, "What were you going to do with it?" the man replied, "Dump it all over Horner." When Doc Romnes crashed into Horner and smacked him over the head with his stick, sending the Leaf player to his knees, a Chicago sportswriter wrote: "Romnes waved his stick at Horner and the Leaf player fainted." Romnes scored the winning goal with less than five minutes to play, beating Broda with a long shot in the 2–1 victory.

"Broken Toe" Karakas was spectacular again in game four, allowing a single goal in a 4–1 Chicago victory. One wag in the press box wanted to bet that Karakas would play with all his toes broken next season.

The Chicago Stanley Cup triumph was unprecedented, an incredible achievement for a team that had won only 14 times during the regular season. Fifty per cent of the Hawk players were U.S. born and the team scored fewer goals than any in the league. But there was no denying they were champions of the world. Their stunning Cup triumph silenced those who said Bill Stewart would never be successful as a big-league coach, and those who said the Hawks would be patsies in the playoffs. However, Stewart's smashing success was quickly forgotten by Major McLaughlin, who fired him a few months later.

**B**EFORE THE 1938–39 SEASON got under way, the NHL governors had to solve a major problem — what to do with the Montreal Maroons, who wanted to bow out of hockey for a year. After much debate, the team was allowed to suspend operations. As a result, with seven teams in the league, the two-division concept was abandoned. It was decided that six teams would make the playoffs and the team that finished in first place would be awarded the Prince of Wales Trophy, symbolic of the league championship. Nobody cared much about the Prince of Wales Trophy, and they cared even less about the O'Brien Trophy, which went to the second-place club. All that mattered was winning the Stanley Cup.

The dominance of the American teams continued into 1938–39. Boston was still a powerhouse and became even stronger as a result of a surprise deal with Detroit: goaltender Tiny Thompson, the Bruins' popular veteran, was sold to the Red Wings for $15,000. Bruin fans were hopping mad, even after manager Art Ross assured them that his new goalie, a kid named Frank Brimsek, would make them forget all about Thompson. It was true. Brimsek recorded six shutouts in his first eight games. He won the Vezina Trophy with a sparkling 1.59 goals-against average and captured the rookie award. No goalie ever made a more sensational debut.

The Bruins won the league title with 74 points and engaged in a bitterly fought playoff series with the Rangers, who finished a poor second, 16 points behind the Bruins. If one player every dominated a playoff series, it was Boston's unheralded Mel Hill. Once rejected by the Rangers as being "too frail for big-time hockey," Hill scored the winning goal in game one after 59 minutes and 25 seconds of overtime. His shot after eight minutes and 24 seconds of overtime carried the Bruins to their second triumph. The Bruins won game three by a 4–1 score before the largest crowd in Boston hockey history. But the Rangers fought furiously to stay alive and won three straight games, by scores of 2–1, 2–1, and 3–1. At the Boston Garden in game seven, Hill came through again, this time scoring after eight minutes of play in the third overtime period to give Boston a 2–1 winning edge in one of the tightest series every played.

In Series B, Toronto ousted the Americans in two games, and in Series C, Detroit eliminated the Canadiens, winning two games to one. Toronto then pushed the Red Wings aside in Series D, winning two out of three. Toronto's line of Apps, Davidson, and Drillon was the best on the ice.

In the finals, Boston's Kraut Line outshone anything the Leafs had to offer when the teams split two games at the Boston Garden. Brimsek allowed the Leafs just one goal in game three and shut them out in game four as the Bruins won a pair on Maple Leaf Gardens' ice. Back on home ice, the Bruins captured the series with a 3–1 triumph. Brimsek had allowed just six goals in the five games played.

President Calder was on hand to award the Stanley Cup to the team that had waited ten years to capture it. Bruin captain Cooney Weiland accepted the trophy while his teammates stood around laughing and hugging one another and the immense crowd roared its passionate approval.

# 7 The Forties: Wartime Hockey and Postwar Growth

**N**HL HOCKEY IN THE FORTIES began in disarray because of the war raging in Europe and the Pacific. But the postwar period brought stability and prosperity. It was an era that saw the face of the game changed with the introduction of the red line at center ice. It saw the resurgence of the Montreal Canadiens and the Toronto Maple Leafs — they would share no less than seven Cup triumphs in the decade — and it brought an end to the apparent domination of the American teams.

During the decade, more and more clubs used air travel to reach their destinations. In time, air travel would help revolutionize the game, making it easy for NHL moguls to envision expansion to distant cities.

When the 1930–40 season began, the Montreal Canadiens quickly tumbled into the league basement, soon to become the only NHL team to miss the playoffs. With the Kraut Line humming along, Boston was still a powerhouse. Milt Schmidt led the league in scoring with 52 points, and linemates Bobby Bauer and Woody Dumart tied for second, each with 43 points. Boston's stellar defenseman, Eddie Shore, played home games only; he had purchased the Springfield Indians of the American League and was preparing for retirement. New coach Cooney Weiland became tired of this arrangement and in midseason Shore was traded to the Americans. He was barely missed as the Bruins raced to the NHL championship with 67 points, three more than the Rangers, who had impressed fans with a 19-game unbeaten streak during the season.

The Rangers and the Bruins met in a thrilling playoff series that began in New York with goalie Dave Kerr recording a 4–0 shutout. The Bruins squared the series with a 4–2 victory and followed up with a 4–3 win in game three. The Rangers stormed back with three straight wins — thanks largely to Dave Kerr, who collected two more shutouts — and the defending Stanley Cup champions were eliminated.

Toronto ousted Chicago in two games while the Red Wings needed three games to end the Americans' season. Game three was the last game for two great stars wearing Americans' jerseys — Eddie Shore and Nels Stewart.

The Toronto–Detroit series turned ugly when the Wings faced elimination in game two. No less than 28 players took part in a wild game-ending brawl in Detroit. Red Horner of the Leafs tried

*Goalie Turk Broda (left) and Conn Smythe.* (Public Archives of Canada)

to take on all of the Wings. Then a lady fan attacked him, pounding him with her purse and yanking on his hair. Toronto players won their share of the fights, but more important, took the series two games to none.

Toronto opened the final series for the Cup against the Rangers at Madison Square Garden. After the first two games, won by the Rangers 2–1 and 6–2, Garden workers moved in and removed the ice so that the annual circus, a big revenue producer, could begin the next day. All remaining games were played in Toronto. The Leafs' Hank Goldup scored the winner late in game three, and Turk Broda stopped the Rangers in game four with a 3–0 shutout. Before game five, Leaf manager Conn Smythe broke up a combination that had defeated New York twice, but his strategy backfired when Muzz Patrick scored in overtime to give the Rangers a 2–1 victory. Game six also required overtime, and this time Bryan Hextall scored after two minutes to bring the Stanley Cup into the Ranger camp for the first time since 1933. Conn Smythe was lavish in his praise of the victors. "I think Lester Patrick's deportment throughout the series was admirable," said Smythe. "I know if I had two of my sons on the ice I'd have been a nervous wreck."

**F**RANK BOUCHER HAD WON the Stanley Cup in his first season behind the New York Ranger bench. For the 1940–41 season, he had virtually the same lineup, although several players around the NHL were interrupting their careers and joining the Canadian and U.S. armed services. Leaf coach Dick Irvin moved on to Montreal, where he hoped to revitalize the struggling Canadiens. Conn Smythe appointed Hap Day to take over for Irvin.

The Boston Bruins lost only eight games all season and set two impressive records. They went 15 games without a road loss during one stretch and 23 games without a loss in another. The Bruins finished five points ahead of Toronto. The Americans won only eight games, and it was rumored they'd be dropped from the league if their situation didn't improve.

Boston's Bill Cowley won the scoring title with 62 points, 18 points ahead of five players who tied for second. Cowley was hampered throughout the playoffs with a wrenched knee.

The Bruins and the Leafs split the first two games of their opening-round series, played in Boston. Syl Apps, with a hat trick, paced Toronto to a 7–2 win in game three at Maple Leaf Gardens. Then came a remarkable string of 2–1 games. Boston won game four by 2–1 and Toronto took game five by the same score. The Bruins squeezed out yet another 2–1 win, and the seventh and deciding game also ended 2–1 in Boston's favor.

Fewer than 9,000 fans turned out for the deciding game in Detroit between the Rangers and the Red Wings. Detroit eliminated the  defending Cup champions with a 3–2 win in game three of the series. The Chicago Black Hawks needed three games to oust the Canadiens, and the Hawks, in turn, bowed to Detroit in two straight games in the following series.

In Boston fan support for the Bruins in their final battle against Detroit was at an all-time high. Conversely, in Detroit, the first playoff game at the Olympia drew about 10,000 fans and the second only about 8,000. In three of the four games, Detroit established a lead, only to see the Bruins come back to win. Boston captured the series in four straight games, establishing yet another record.

Andy Lytle, sports editor of the *Toronto Star*, witnessed the final series and credited Boston with superior goaltending. He wrote: "I have seen Lehman, Holmes, Hainsworth, Vezina, Worters, Chabot, and most of the great goaltenders. Of all I've seen, I rate Frank Brimsek the greatest."

**T**HE 1941–42 SEASON was only a few weeks old when Japan's sneak attack on Pearl Harbor on December 7 yanked the focus away from hockey. The following day, thousands of fans throughout the United States began lining up to join the armed forces. Over the next few weeks, dozens of NHL players turned in their sticks and skates and began wearing a different kind of uniform. Of the 14 players in the Ranger lineup on the day of that shocking blitz in the Pacific, ten were soon serving their country. By season's end, Boston entered the playoffs without the patriotic Kraut Line. But hockey carried on, with teams replacing missing stars with lesser players who wouldn't have been granted a big-league trial under peacetime conditions.

The Rangers climbed to the top of the standings and finished the season with 60 points, three more than Toronto and four ahead of the Krautless Bruins. The Rangers' Bryan Hextall was top scorer with 56 points, two more than teammate Lynn Patrick.

Toronto and New York met in the opening round of the playoffs. Toronto's big line of Apps, Metz, and Drillon outplayed the Ranger trio of Hextall, Patrick, and Watson in the first two games, won by the Leafs 3–1 and 4–2. The Rangers won game three by 3–0; Toronto took game four 2–1, with Apps and Schriner playing big roles; and the Rangers fought back for a 3–1 triumph in game five. Injuries to Lynn Patrick and Grant Warwick hurt the Rangers in game six, which was won by the Leafs 3–2 on a Nick Metz tie-breaking goal. The Leafs took the series four games to two.

In Series B, Boston edged Chicago two games to one behind Frank Brimsek's flashy netminding, and Detroit won Series C over the Canadiens, two games to one. Detroit then upset Boston in two straight games in Series D, with the largest crowd in Red Wing history on hand for game two. Red Wing fans were delighted to see a team that had finished fifth in regular-season play upset one that had finished 14 points higher in the standings.

In the final series with Toronto for the Cup, Detroit took a one-game lead with a 3–2 win in the opener at Maple Leaf Gardens. The line of Grosso, Wares, and Abel scored all three goals, Grosso getting two. Grosso stayed hot and scored two more goals in the second game, won by the Wings 4–2. Back in Detroit, Eddie Bush of the Red Wings was a one-man show, scoring once and assisting on three more goals in a 5–2 rout of the Leafs. Cocky Billy Taylor of the Leafs wasn't impressed or concerned. "Don't worry," he told reporters. "We'll come back and beat 'em four straight." The reporters tried not to laugh.

Despite Taylor's bold boast, the Red Wings appeared to be a shoo-in. No team down 3–0 in games had ever come back to win a playoff series. And it looked like curtains for the Leafs and a slap in the mouth to Taylor when the Wings rolled to a quick 2–0 lead in game four. But Conn Smythe and Hap Day had made some roster changes, benching Gordie Drillon and Bucko McDonald and bringing in Don Metz and Bob Goldham. The Leafs suddenly showed a lot more grit than they'd displayed in previous games and tied the score on goals from Davidson and Carr. But when Liscombe scored in the third period, thoughts of champagne on ice and a postgame party must have been circulating throughout the Red Wing camp. Suddenly Syl Apps knifed his way through to draw the Leafs even at 3–3, and Nick Metz added what proved to be the winning marker. That turned the tide in this memorable series. Any chance of a Detroit comeback was snuffed out when referee Mel Harwood slapped four penalties on the Red Wings late in the game, infuriating Jack Adams. The red-faced Detroit coach stormed out on the ice and attacked Harwood. President Calder, who was at the game, promptly suspended Adams for the rest of the series.

Back at Maple Leaf Gardens, the Leafs routed the Wings 9–3 with Don Metz getting three goals and Syl Apps two. The shellacking seemed to drain all the confidence out of the Wings. On home ice they lost again, this time without a goal to show for their efforts. Turk Broda shut them out 3–0, and referee Bill Chadwick was so pleased with the players' behavior that he didn't call a single penalty.

With the series squared, the seventh game in Toronto created tremendous excitement. The Wings jumped into a 1–0 lead on Syd Howe's goal, but the Leafs conceded nothing and proved themselves a real comeback team by scoring two goals in the third period. Sweeney Schriner tied the score with 13 minutes to play. Then he and Pete Langelle added goals that assured the Leafs of victory. They won the game 3–2 and the precious Cup they had last held in 1932. The greatest comeback in Stanley Cup history was over.

**T**HE 1942–43 SEASON saw the war hit everything but attendance. Red Dutton made valiant efforts to keep his New York Americans afloat, but his only hope lay in persuading other clubs to provide him with some talent. But talent was scarce. The Americans, facing the end of their lease at Madison Square Garden, dropped out of the NHL. Dutton was given the right to try again for a franchise when times improved, but the colorful Americans never resurfaced.

Dutton would soon be back in hockey, however. President Frank Calder was stricken with a heart attack while presiding over a governors' meeting. When he died in hospital a month later, Dutton was called upon to replace him temporarily, with the understanding that a permanent president would soon be appointed.

This season saw the end of overtime play during regular-season games, so that teams could cope with wartime travel restrictions. It would be decades before overtime was reinstated. More than 90 players were in the armed forces or reserves, and the Rangers lost their Shibicky–Colville–Colville forward line, one of the hottest scoring trios in the game. The Montreal Canadiens introduced a promising rookie in Maurice Richard, a fiery winger who broke his ankle early in the season. Toronto's Syl Apps was lost for the season when he broke his leg in a goal-mouth incident. Upon his recovery, Apps joined the army.

Under a new playoff system, only four teams were eligible for the Stanley Cup playoffs, with the first-place team meeting the third-place finishers and the second-place and fourth-place clubs playing another series. Chicago and New York sank to the bottom of the standings and were eliminated. The Red Wings, picking up where they left off the previous spring, won the NHL title with 61 points, four more than Boston. Toronto finished third, and Dick Irvin's Montreal Canadiens slipped into the playoffs by a single point, edging out Chicago. Doug Bentley of the Black Hawks was the league's scoring champion with 73 points, one more than the Bruins' Bill Cowley.

When Toronto met Detroit in the first round of the playoffs, the Leafs signed a pair of 17-year-olds, Ted Kennedy and Jackie

Hamilton, as replacements "in the event of an emergency." The Red Wings repeated their performance of a year earlier by taking the first three games. The Leafs embarked on another comeback, winning two in a row, but they failed to engineer another miracle. In game six at Toronto, after nine minutes of overtime, Adam Brown scored the winning goal for Detroit.

Boston and Montreal went five games before the Bruins ousted the Habs in a high-scoring series. The teams combined for 35 goals, a record for a five-game series.

In the finals against Boston, the Red Wings showed early strength and won the first three games. Perhaps they were inspired by an offer from owner Jim Norris, who promised to add $5,000 to the Wings' playoff purse if they won, and an additional $2,500 if they won four in a row. In game three, Johnny Mowers shut out the Bruins 4–0. At this point, fans anticipated a Boston comeback, for recent history indicated the Wings often stumbled with the Cup almost in their grasp. But the Wings pooh-poohed history, and goalie Mowers came through with his second straight shutout, this time by 2–0. The Red Wings won the Cup and the Jim Norris bonus.

The series sweep was sweet revenge for the Wings, especially for their coach, Jack Adams. "Remember, this Boston club swept us aside in the finals two years ago," he said. "And Toronto came back with their miracle finish last season. Those defeats really hurt. Now I guess we're at least even with Boston."

**THE ARMED FORCES** continued to take their toll on NHL rosters in 1943–44. With more stars in military uniform than ever before, the caliber of play dropped alarmingly. But the fans didn't seem to mind. All sports were considered to be a morale booster during difficult times, and NHL hockey, with its service rejects, young kids, and over-the-hill veterans, continued to attract widespread interest. Art Ross of the Bruins suggested that all records established in this period be listed as "set under wartime conditions." How poor was the quality of play? "Why, the best forward line today couldn't make the Bruins' third line a couple of years ago," stated Ross.

In New York, the Rangers' coach, Frank Boucher, then 42 years old, made a comeback as a player and averaged almost a point a game for the 15 games he played.

Each team lost star players, and one or two clubs discovered some future stars. Montreal's Maurice Richard was beginning to blossom and scored 32 goals. With sensational rookie Bill Durnan to keep pucks out, the Canadiens zoomed to the top of the NHL standings. The Habs had lost just two games by mid-January, and when the season ended, they held a record 25-point margin over second-place Detroit. Herb Cain of Boston won the scoring crown with 82 points, five more than Chicago's Doug Bentley. Detroit's Syd Howe blasted home six goals one night in a game against New York, and Leaf rookie Gus Bodnar set a record when he scored 15 seconds into his first shift on opening night against the Rangers.

Bodnar and the Leafs had the gargantuan task of trying to upset the Canadiens in the playoffs. Late in the season, Leaf coach Hap Day said of the league leaders: "The Canadiens will win the Stanley Cup. They won't lose a single playoff game. They're simply too big, too fast for the rest of the field." Day helped prove his prophecy wrong in game one when he coached his Leafs, 3–1 underdogs, to a stunning 3–1 upset of the Canadiens.

In game two, Montreal's Maurice Richard humiliated the Leafs and goalie Paul Bibeault. Richard had been a pal of Bibeault's for years, and when they met between games, Richard told his boyhood chum, "You were too hot for us in game one, Paul. But I'll give you a lot to think about in game two, my friend." Richard kept his promise by scoring five goals against Bibeault in a 5–1 rout. Richard was awarded all three stars after the game, the first time the three-star selectors had ever recognized excellence in such a manner. The Canadiens had no trouble sweeping aside the Leafs, winning the next two games 4–1 and 11–0. It took the Habs only three minutes and 36 seconds to score a record five goals in the final game rout.

In the other playoff matchup, Chicago showed some scoring punch by eliminating Detroit in two straight games with scores of 7–1 and 5–2.

But the Hawks were completely outclassed by the Canadiens in the finals. Game two in Chicago resulted in fireworks that angered the league president. Richard scored a hat trick against Mike Karakas, and on his third goal the Hawks beefed that Elmer Lach was holding on the play and should have been penalized. When the referee disagreed, the fans littered the ice with debris, causing a 20-minute delay. President Dutton was livid and decreed that in future a similar display in any rink would result in the game being forfeited to the visiting team.

Montreal won again on home ice 3–2, with Phil Watson scoring the winning goal. The final game required a third-period splurge by Montreal after Chicago took a 4–1 lead. The fans began to chant "Fake! Fake! Fake!" at the Canadiens, indicating they thought the Habs were taking it easy and calculating the gate receipts another game or two would bring. The chants angered Richard and his mates, and they ripped into the Hawks in the third period, scoring three times to tie the score. Toe Blake whipped in a goal in overtime, and the Canadiens celebrated their first Stanley Cup victory in 14 years.

**BEFORE THE 1944–45** NHL schedule began, president Red Dutton decided to step down and asked the league to find someone to replace him. Leaf owner Conn Smythe was offered the job, even though he was in hospital overseas, recovering from war wounds. When Smythe declined the offer, Dutton said he would carry on until the NHL governors found somebody else.

Early in the season, Chicago owner Fred McLaughlin died suddenly. McLaughlin was remembered for his penchant for hiring and firing coaches. One of a dozen or so he retained was Godfrey Matheson, who impressed the owner by coaching a Winnipeg midget team to a championship. Matheson introduced some novel ideas, including a whistle system. From the bench, he'd toot his

*Hector "Toe" Blake, a key player on the fabled Punch Line with Elmer Lach and Rocket Richard. Later, he coached the Canadiens to many Stanley Cups.*

whistle and his players would respond. A single toot meant the puck carrier was to pass, a double toot and he was to shoot, while three toots meant to fall back on defense, and so on. When McLaughlin got fed up with all the whistling, he fired Matheson.

All eyes now followed the Canadiens' Maurice Richard, nicknamed the "Rocket." He produced a dazzling season, scoring a record 50 goals in 50 games. The potent Punch Line finished 1–2–3 in scoring with Elmer Lach on top with 80 points, followed by the Rocket with 73 and Blake with 67.

The Canadiens lost only eight games all season and finished with 80 points, 13 more than Detroit. Bill Durnan captured the Vezina Trophy for the second time, beating out Toronto rookie Frank McCool, who won the Calder Trophy. Chicago's Bill Mosienko turned in a penalty-free season and was rewarded with the Lady Byng Trophy.

Montreal's prosperity didn't extend into the Stanley Cup playoffs. When the Habs collided with the Leafs, who had finished third, rookie goalie Frank McCool shut them out 1–0 in the Forum. Ted Kennedy, another rookie headed for stardom, scored the only goal of the game. McCool was outstanding again in game two, which went to Toronto 3–2. Back at Maple Leaf Gardens, Bob Davidson checked Richard to a standstill, holding him scoreless for the third successive game. Even so, the Canadiens fought their way back in the series with a 4–1 victory. Gus Bodnar's overtime goal won game four for Toronto 4–3, but the Canadiens stormed back in game five, giving the Leafs a solid trouncing 10–3. Richard scored four goals against McCool. If the Habs thought beating McCool would be easy in game six, they were wrong. The youngster allowed two goals, but his teammates scored three, and the highest scoring team in hockey, the one with the best overall record, was eliminated.

Elsewhere, Boston and Detroit engaged in a bitterly contested semifinal series, which began with each team winning two games away from home. Back in Detroit for game five, Mud Bruneteau scored one of his patented overtime goals to defeat the Bruins, who then won game six at the Boston Garden, forcing the series to the limit. Detroit's Carl Liscombe cut loose for four goals in the deciding contest, won by the Red Wings 5–3.

In the final series between Detroit and Toronto, Frank McCool's goaltending brilliance in the first three games was record-shattering. He rang up three straight shutouts and wasn't beaten until eight minutes and 35 seconds of game four, which was won by the Wings 5–3. Then Harry Lumley of Detroit began a shutout streak that he stretched through the next two games and into a third. He won by scores of 2–0 and 1–0 and was instrumental in pushing the series to a seventh game in Detroit.

In game seven before a packed house at the Olympia, with the score tied 1–1 in the third period, big Babe Pratt rushed in on Lumley and beat him for the winning goal. The Leafs, who had finished 28 points back of the league leaders, were the proud winners of the Stanley Cup.

For many years after that, the Stanley Cup moved between just three cities — Montreal, Toronto, and Detroit. The Boston Bruins had won it in 1941, but three decades would go by before they won it again. Twenty years would pass before Chicago players would hold it high, and the Rangers would ice teams for the next five decades without knowing the thrill of a Cup-winning season.

**W**ITH THE END OF THE WAR, players whose careers had been interrupted returned to their old clubs, and a few stickhandlers who had been elevated to the dizzy eminence of the big league were thanked and paid off, or returned to the minors where their limited skills were more appreciated.

Honored hockey names were in the news in 1945–46. P. D. Ross announced that former referee Cooper Smeaton would succeed the late William Foran as a Stanley Cup trustee. Lester Patrick, who had been an imaginative manager and coach for many years, gave way to Frank Boucher in New York. Colorful Art Ross, volatile leader of the Bruins, stepped aside for Dit Clapper, a playing-coach who welcomed back the Kraut Line. The Leafs were strengthened when half a dozen of their former stars, notably Syl Apps, were demobilized. Frank McCool, troubled with ulcers throughout his career, went home claiming ill health, a condition one scribe diagnosed as follows: "McCool was sick all right. He was sick and tired of arguing over a $500 difference in salary." McCool's brilliant record in the 1945 playoffs had led him to believe he was worth more than the Maple Leafs were paying him. After Toronto dropped ten of their first 13 games, management pleaded with McCool to return, and he did. Obviously, he had a change of heart, since he still didn't get the extra $500.

It was McCool's last season, however. Turk Broda came back from overseas and replaced him, but even with two first-rate goalies the Leafs missed the playoffs. One bright note was Gaye Stewart's 37-goal season, although he was runner-up to Chicago's Max Bentley for the scoring title.

The Montreal Canadiens, with 61 points, won the league championship for the third successive time. Boston finished with 56, Chicago with 53, and Detroit with 50.

In Chicago, despite a productive year from the Pony Line (the Bentley brothers and Mosienko), the Black Hawks were no match for the Canadiens in the first round of the playoffs. Toe Blake was a star throughout the series and scored a hat trick in game four as the Habs swept the Hawks aside in four straight games.

In the series between second-place Boston and fourth-place Detroit, the teams split the first two games. The Kraut Line sparked Boston to wins in the next two games, and the Bruins' Don Gallinger was the star of game five, scoring the winner in overtime. Winners by four games to one, the Bruins advanced to the finals against the Canadiens.

The finals opened at the Montreal Forum with the rival goaltenders, Bill Durnan and Frank Brimsek, playing spectacular hockey. The first game went to Montreal 4–3, when Rocket Richard beat Brimsek with a goal in overtime. The Habs followed up with 3–2 and 4–2 victories and hoped to win the Cup at the Boston Garden in game four. But Brimsek edged Durnan in another great goaltending duel, and the Bruins won in overtime on Terry Reardon's goal. In game five at the Forum, the Bruins caved in to relentless Montreal pressure in the third period, Brimsek was beaten three times, and Montreal skated off with a 6–3 triumph.

The Canadiens won the Cup for the second time under Dick Irvin's coaching and Tommy Gorman's management. Gorman, a former Ottawa sportswriter, pugnacious, and hockey-wise, had managed the old Ottawa Senators as far back as 1919. He played a major role in hockey for more than 25 years. "It's time," he said, "to step aside and let somebody else run the show in Montreal." Somebody else turned out to be Frank Selke, who left Toronto to take over Gorman's desk at the Forum. Selke was available because of a dispute he'd had with Leaf owner Conn Smythe.

There were more changes. In September 1946, Red Dutton retired as league president. His successor was Clarence Campbell, former referee, Rhodes scholar, and lieutenant colonel in the Canadian army. Campbell had been groomed for the position by Frank Calder and would likely have succeeded Calder had he been available at the time.

**FOR THE 1946–47 SEASON,** the NHL initiated a 60-game schedule and boosted to $127,000 the regular-season and Stanley Cup playoff pools, providing added incentive for players and teams to do well.

After finishing out of the playoffs, the Leafs underwent a shake-up. Lorne Carr, Sweeney Schriner, and Bob Davidson retired, Babe Pratt was sold to Boston, and Billy Taylor was traded to Detroit for Harry Watson. After having been wounded by shrapnel overseas, Howie Meeker joined the Leafs and captured the rookie award. In Chicago, rookie Emile Francis shared netminding duties with Paul Bibeault, played in 19 games, and had the worst goals-against average in the NHL — 5.47. Detroit acquired Roy Conacher from the Bruins and found a place on the roster for a promising rookie from Saskatchewan named Gordie Howe. He arrived just as the great Syd Howe — no relation — was retiring. Young Howe scored seven goals in 58 games and finished 49th in league scoring. He would do better in the seasons ahead.

Unable to gain a point against Boston in the final game of the season, Rocket Richard finished one point behind Max Bentley for the scoring championship. Dick Irvin's Canadiens finished in first place with 78 points, six more than the Leafs. Boston finished third with 63 points and Detroit fourth with 55. Once again, the Rangers and the Black Hawks missed the playoffs.

Perhaps Montreal fans were beginning to take playoff wins for granted; only 10,000 turned out for the opening of the series with Boston at the Forum. Montreal got off to a flying start with a 3–1 victory. In game two, with less than a minute to play, Ken Reardon scored the tying goal and then assisted on Mosdell's overtime winner. In game three at the Boston Garden, Milt Schmidt dropped back on defense and led the Bruins to a 4–2 win. But Montreal's Billy Reay fired four goals past Brimsek in game four, the Habs won the game 5–1, and took a 3–1 lead in the series. The fifth game seesawed back and forth until Richard scored his second goal with a couple of minutes to play. That tied the score 3–3, and Montreal's Johnny Quilty popped in the winner after more than 36 minutes of overtime. The Canadiens won the series four games to two and prepared to meet the winner of the Detroit–Toronto matchup.

In game one of the playoff battle between the Red Wings and the Leafs, Toronto's Howie Meeker was the hero; his overtime marker clinched a 3–2 victory. The Leafs fell apart in game two and lost 9–1, but bounced back on Detroit ice and twice thumped the Wings 4–1. Back at Maple Leaf Gardens, the Leafs overpowered Detroit and ended the Wings' season with a 6–1 rout.

The final series opened at the Montreal Forum with big Bill Durnan registering a 6–0 shutout over Toronto. Turk Broda was in shutout form in game two, enabling the Leafs to skate off with a 4–0 decision. In this game, Rocket Richard bopped two Leafs on the head — Vic Lynn and Bill Ezinicki — drawing a match penalty, a fine, and a one-game suspension. Toronto moved ahead in the series with a 4–2 win at Maple Leaf Gardens and followed up with a 2–1 overtime victory in which Syl Apps scored the winning goal. The teams returned to Montreal where the Canadiens, fighting to survive, won by 3–1. Back in Toronto, Durnan stopped a dozen shots that appeared to be labeled, but he couldn't handle them all, and Toronto won 2–1 on goals by Ted Kennedy and Vic Lynn. Hap Day had coached the Leafs to the Stanley Cup for the second time.

CONN SMYTHE WASN'T yet finished with his rebuilding program. He had the youngest club ever to win the Cup, but he lost a great leader and playmaker when Syl Apps retired at the end of the 1946–47 season. Needing a topflight center, Smythe engineered one of the great trades in NHL history to get the man he wanted — Max Bentley of Chicago. In return, Smythe gave up Gus Bodnar, Bob Goldham, Ernie Dickens, Bud Poile, and Gaye Stewart. He even persuaded Bill Tobin to throw in Cy Thomas to sweeten the deal. Then he persuaded Apps to come back for the 1947–48 season. Smythe's big deal paid off when the Leafs won the NHL championship again.

The Canadiens, on the other hand, went into a tailspin and failed to make the playoffs in the spring of 1948. Some demented fans made an empty threat to burn down the Forum if coach Dick Irvin wasn't fired. After Toe Blake broke his ankle and decided to retire, the Habs' famous Punch Line was broken up. The Red Wings put together a threesome of Ted Lindsay, Sid Abel, and

Gordie Howe, which scored with such regularity it became known as the Production Line.

The season was also marked by scandal. Two years earlier, Babe Pratt had been suspended for betting on hockey games but had been reinstated after 16 games. The new episode ended the careers of Billy Taylor of the Rangers and Don Gallinger of the Boston Bruins, who were expelled for life by League president Clarence Campbell. Campbell ruled that while no fix of a game had been attempted, association with gamblers couldn't be tolerated under any circumstances.

Toronto finished on top of the league standings with 77 points, five more than Detroit. Boston finished third with 59 points and the Rangers slipped into the fourth playoff spot with 55. Conn Smythe wasn't unhappy when his prediction of a first-place finish for Montreal was well off the mark.

In the first round of the playoffs, on home ice, Toronto captured the first two games from Boston, with Ted Kennedy scoring four goals in the second encounter. In game three at Boston, following a 5–1 Leaf win, the Toronto players and coach Hap Day were jumped by fans as they made their way off the ice. Day might have been seriously injured if Wally Stanowski hadn't leaped to his rescue. Boston owner Weston Adams even invaded the Leaf dressing room to argue a point but was promptly thrown out. The Bruins fought back to win game four, but the Leafs ended the series in Toronto with a 3–2 victory.

The Red Wings and the Rangers each won two games on home ice in their semifinal series. With Red Kelly scoring twice, Detroit won game five 3–1. Kelly dominated again in game six, scoring a goal and adding two assists in a 4–2 Detroit win. The Red Wings earned the right to advance against the Leafs.

Toronto lost a key player in the first game of the final series when defenseman Gus Mortson suffered a broken leg, but they were able to take game one 5–1 and followed up with a 4–2 victory on home ice. In Detroit the Leafs took a commanding lead with their third straight win, a 2–0 shutout for Broda. The fourth game was no contest, the Leafs romping to a 7–2 triumph and their second straight Stanley Cup. So strong was the Leaf checking and defense that Detroit's Production Line scored only one point in the series. Conn Smythe told reporters, "This is the best Leaf team I've ever had."

**H**OCKEY WAS BOOMING AGAIN. Attendance hadn't been hard hit during the war years, but the quality of play had deteriorated. By 1948 it was better than it had ever been. The clubs were making money, players' salaries were on the rise, and the Stanley Cup players' pool was boosted. Every club had its farm teams and its scouts who traveled to the boondocks seeking talented young players. Leaf scout Squib Walker signed a prospect by placing a hundred dollars in small bills on the family's kitchen table and persuading the eager young man to sign a document called a C form, which bound the teenager to the Leaf organization for life. Then, before leaving, the scout would sell the youngster a life insurance policy, taking back the hundred dollars as a down payment. Danny Lewicki and Wally Stanowski were among the dozens of future Leafs who were acquired in this manner.

Even the premium players, like Gordie Howe, were acquired at incredibly little expense. All it took to make Howe happy as a Detroit rookie was a Red Wing jacket, plus whatever kind of contract Jack Adams felt like handing him.

Roy Conacher and Doug Bentley of the Black Hawks battled through most of the 1948–49 season for the scoring title, with Conacher winning it with 68 points, two more than Bentley. Despite the fact that he'd won the Vezina Trophy four times, Montreal fans were critical of Bill Durnan, and other teams tried to acquire him, but after Durnan put together four consecutive shutouts, the critics were silenced and the trade rumors ended.

With Gordie Howe improving after missing 20 games with a knee injury, the Red Wings took first place in the league schedule and divided up $17,000 in bonus money. Boston was second, nine points back, the Canadiens finished third, and Toronto fourth. Detroit coach Tommy Ivan was far from relaxed as the playoffs opened. "Don't kid yourselves," he told his players. "Nothing is certain in the postseason until you've got the Stanley Cup locked up in your trophy case."

In game one of the playoff series between Detroit and Montreal, the teams were approaching 45 minutes of overtime when Montreal's Ken Reardon took a penalty and Max McNab scored a power play goal to win the game 2–1. Game two also went into overtime. This time Gerry Plamondon of the Habs slapped in the winner, his third of the game. Bill Durnan backstopped Montreal to a 3–2 win in game three at the Forum, but two nights later Gordie Howe, with a pair of goals, dominated in a 3–1 Red Wing victory. On home ice, Detroit won again by 3–1. Before game six at the Forum, Durnan was presented with a new car by the fans in recognition of his accomplishments over the years. He responded by allowing Detroit only one goal while his teammates scored three, two of them by Plamondon. Detroit won game seven at the Olympia 3–1 behind Harry Lumley's solid goaltending, and advanced to the next round.

In Series B, Toronto took the first two games in Boston 3–0 and 3–2, with Harry Watson scoring a pair of goals in each game. After Boston won game three, Toronto rookie Sid Smith, a minor-league call-up, starred in game four with a pair of goals and an assist in a 3–1 win. Back in Boston, the Leafs eliminated the Bruins in a rough contest by a 3–2 score. At one point, Boston fans bombarded the ice with debris. A bottle thrown at referee King Clancy just missed him.

Although the Red Wings and the Leafs were leg-weary when they emerged from the semifinal series, goalie Turk Broda seemed as fresh as a daisy. The stubborn Wings forced the Leafs into 17 minutes of overtime before Toronto's Joe Klukay picked up a pass from Ray Timgren and scored the game winner. Rookie Sid Smith had another big playoff game in the next encounter, scoring all three goals in a 3–1 victory. Broda was the star of game three, and Ted Kennedy flipped in the winning goal for another 3–1 decision over the Wings.

The Leafs had won the final series in four straight games the previous year. Could they do it again? Up to this point the famed

Production Line had been held goalless in the series. Ted Lindsay broke the drought with a goal in game four, but Broda again came up with spectacular netminding and the Wing shooters were stymied the rest of the way. Timgren, Gardner and Bentley scored for the Leafs, and the game ended 3–1.

Not since Ottawa's fabulous Silver Seven had a team won three successive Stanley Cups. Never before had a team captured the Cup six times. Never before had a coach guided his team to three straight Cup championships. The Leafs "Happy" Day was a happy man that night.

But Detroit would come snarling back, looking for revenge, one year later.

**B**EFORE THE 72-GAME 1949–50 season got under way, the Red Wings traded ace defenseman Bill Quackenbush and Pete Horeck to Boston in return for Pete Babando, Jimmy Peters, Clare Martin, and Lloyd Durham. Other clubs made changes, too. The Bruins sold Frank Brimsek to Chicago and replaced him with Jack Gelineau. The Rangers brought up Gus Kyle and teamed him up with Allan Stanley on the blue line.

Chicago coach Charlie Conacher found himself in hot water during the season, faced with court action after he slugged sportswriter Lou Walter of Detroit. The NHL fined Conacher $200 and the suit was withdrawn after he apologized to Walter.

Leaf goalie Turk Broda made headlines in what became known as the Battle of the Bulge. Ordered to lose seven of his 197 pounds, Broda made Conn Smythe's deadline with half a pound to spare. Another goalie, Bill Durnan of Montreal, talked of retiring at the end of the season. Late in the schedule he was replaced for six games by Gerry McNeil, and the rookie's goals-against average was an impressive 1.50.

The Red Wings, with plenty of scoring and depth, soared to the NHL championship with 88 points, one more than Montreal. Toronto finished third with 74 points, followed by the Rangers with 67. Ted Lindsay won the scoring championship with 78

One of the many battles over the Cup between the Red Wings and the Leafs in the 1940s.

(Turofsky)

points, nine more than Sid Abel and ten more than Gordie Howe. Rocket Richard led the goal scorers with 43.

The Detroit Red Wings squared off with Toronto in one semifinal series. Well aware that the Leafs had beaten them in 11 straight playoff games, the Wings were shocked when the domination continued in a 5–0 opening-night Leaf victory. A further blow was the injury to Detroit's brilliant winger Gordie Howe in a collision with Ted Kennedy along the boards. Howe was carried off the ice on a stretcher, suffering from a fractured nose, a broken cheekbone, and a severe concussion. A team of surgeons relieved pressure on the brain from a broken blood vessel and was credited with saving Howe's life.

The Wings squared the series with a 3–1 win in a rugged second game. Kennedy, blamed by Detroit fans and some Red Wing players for the Howe injury, was the principal target for a number of body slams. Clarence Campbell warned the teams of fines and suspensions if the feuding continued. The teams split the next two games and Toronto edged in front when Turk Broda fashioned a 2–0 shutout in game five. The Red Wings bounced right back with a 4–0 shutout, forcing a seventh game, in which big Leo Reise became a hero. After three periods of scoreless hockey, Reise scored at 8:39 of overtime, and Red Wing fans howled with pleasure and delight.

In Series B, the Montreal Canadiens were hard hit by injuries when they met the Rangers. Five penalties to the Habs' Ken Reardon and the outstanding goaltending of Charlie Rayner were the key factors in New York's opening-night victory by a 3–1 score. Reardon was added to the Montreal injury list with a dislocated shoulder in game two, which the Rangers won 3–2. In game three, Rayner came up with another big effort and Pentti Lund scored three times in New York's third straight win. The score was 4–1. In game four, ailing Bill Durnan was replaced in the Montreal goal by Gerry McNeil. McNeil's work was solid and Elmer Lach's overtime goal gave the Habs their first win by 3–2.

The Rangers were forced to play game five at the Montreal Forum when the circus once again usurped Madison Square Garden. Charlie Rayner turned aside every Montreal attack and emerged as the game's hero with a 3–0 shutout. New York won the series four games to one.

For the finals against Detroit, the Rangers chose Maple Leaf Gardens as their "home rink." The Rangers were underdogs, mainly because of having to play all their games on the road, but they pushed the final series to the limit. With the series tied 2–2, New York's Don Raleigh scored in overtime for the second straight time, giving the Rangers a 2–1 victory and the series lead. New York was looking for its first Stanley Cup since 1940 in game six, but Detroit outscored them 5–4 and forced a seventh game. The Red Wings captured the Stanley Cup in overtime on April 23. With the game tied 3–3, Pete Babando scored the series-winning goal from George Gee.

# The Fabulous Fifties

**B**EFORE THE 1950–51 SEASON, Jack Adams of Detroit engineered the biggest deal in NHL history, an eight-player swap with Chicago. Sent to the Black Hawks were goalie Harry Lumley, Al Dewsbury, Don Morrison, and Pete Babando, hero of the final game of the 1950 Stanley Cup series. In return, Adams got defenseman Bob Goldham and forwards Metro Prystai, Gaye Stewart, and goalie Jim Henry. The big deal gave sensational young goalie Terry Sawchuk a chance to take over from Lumley in Detroit. Sawchuk racked up 11 shutouts and a stunning 1.98 goals-against average in his rookie season and won the Calder Trophy.

In Toronto, Al Rollins was brought in to share goaltending duties with Turk Broda, and Joe Primeau replaced Hap Day as coach. Charlie Conacher resigned as coach in Chicago and gave way to Ebbie Goodfellow. Lynn Patrick moved from the Rangers to Boston, where he replaced George Boucher behind the Bruin bench.

Bernie "Boom Boom" Geoffrion was one of two exciting rookies in the future of the Montreal Canadiens. Geoffrion played in only 18 games in 1950–51, so was eligible for Calder Trophy honors the following season. Hab fans were shocked and disappointed when Jean Beliveau, the most heralded junior player in history, turned down a huge contract from Montreal and decided to play another year to two with the Quebec Aces of the Quebec Senior Hockey League. Rocket Richard, still steaming over a game misconduct penalty that referee Hugh McLean had given him the night before, attacked McLean in the lobby of a New York hotel. He drew the heaviest fine of the season — $500.

With Gordie Howe almost back to full health and wearing a helmet, the Detroit Red Wings became the first NHL team to surpass 100 points in a season. The Wings won 44 games and collected 101 points. Toronto finished a close second with 95 points. The Canadiens were third with 65, and Boston won the final playoff position with 62.

After finishing 36 points in front of third-place Montreal, the Red Wings may have been overconfident when they faced the Habs in the first round of the playoffs. Rocket Richard put Detroit in a deep hole by scoring overtime goals in each of the first two games to give Montreal a two-game lead in the series. Back at the Forum, Sawchuk came through with a 2–0 shutout, and Howe and Abel starred in game four, won by Detroit 4–1. On Detroit ice, Boom Boom Geoffrion scored what proved to be the winning goal in a 5–2 Montreal victory, and the upset was complete two days later when the Habs edged the Wings 3–2 in a rare penalty-free game. What caused the mighty Red Wings to lose their steam in this series? Montreal coach Dick Irvin thought he knew the answer. "The Rocket threw one punch that flattened Ted Lindsay," he chortled. "After that the Red Wings just up and quit."

If the Boston Bruins planned to knock the stuffing out of the Leafs in Series B, they meant it as a metaphor. But in the game won 2–0 by the underdog Bruins, a flying skate knocked the stuffing out of Al Rollins's goal pad. The pad went for repairs and so did Rollins, out with torn knee ligaments. The second game in Toronto went into overtime tied 1–1, and the midnight curfew forced cancellation of further play. The match was ruled "no contest." Turk Broda, at 36, proved to be a capable replacement for Rollins, and when the series returned to Boston, he sparkled in a 3–1 Leaf victory. Broda came right back with a 3–0 shutout and then starred in yet another Toronto win, 4–1. The Leafs completed their comeback with a 6–0 rout of the battered and bruised Bruins.

In the finals against the Canadiens, the Leafs were heavy favorites. During the regular season, Montreal had won only two of the 14 games played between the clubs. In the opener, Sid Smith, one of four 30-goal scorers in the league, poked in the winning goal in a 3–2 overtime victory for Toronto. "If that's the best they can do in their own backyard, they're not so much," said Montreal coach Dick Irvin after the loss. Rocket Richard was the overtime hero in game two when Montreal edged the Leafs 3–2. Then Leaf captain Ted Kennedy got into the overtime act, firing a bull's-eye past Gerry McNeil and winning the game by a 2–1 count. Game four also went into overtime before Harry Watson of the Leafs scored at 5:15. Game five, played at Maple Leaf Gardens on April 21, was the most dramatic of them all. The Leafs had fought from behind to tie the score at 2–2 with only 32 seconds on the clock. They pulled their goalie, and Sid Smith shot through a maze of players. He saw the puck hit the post. "Oh damn," he said in frustration. Then he saw the red light flash. The puck had bounced out onto the stick of Tod Sloan, who whipped it into the net. "God, it was a great feeling," Smith recalled.

The goal that dropped the final curtain on a memorable playoff series — some call it the most thrilling series ever played — was smashed high into the net behind Gerry McNeil by an onrushing Bill Barilko, of whom Frank Selke once said, "I dislike the guy so much I'd do anything to get him for the Habs." Pandemonium broke loose when Barilko scored. Coach Joe Primeau hurdled the boards and hurried out to embrace the big defenseman. The players rushed over and threw Primeau up on their broad shoulders. Conn Smythe led Turk Broda onto the ice as the fans cheered for their favorite fat man. It was a great night for Barilko, who had been gathering slivers on the bench earlier in the season. For Joe Primeau, it completed a grand slam. He had coached Memorial, Allan, and Stanley Cup winners, the first coach to earn such honors. It also meant that Primeau had filled the largest coaching shoes in hockey, the ones vacated by Hap Day, rated by many as the greatest coach of all time. There was no Cup presentation after the game, much to the disappointment of the Leaf fans. The superstitious Conn Smythe wouldn't permit the Cup in his building for fear it would jinx his team.

Following the celebration on the ice, hockey writer Red Burnett visited the tomb that was the Montreal dressing room, where little Gerry McNeil, who had turned in one of the greatest netminding displays in Cup history, pulled off his jersey. "He sat in his steaming underwear," observed Burnett. "Tears trickled down his cheeks as he fumbled with the straps on his goal pads. In 20 minutes he didn't manage to undo a single buckle."

**T**HE **1951–52 SEASON** wound up in a flurry of headlines for Bill Mosienko of the Chicago Black Hawks. Mosienko, a high-flying right winger, shattered a long-standing record on March 23 when he scored three goals in a mere 21 seconds against goalie Lorne Anderson of the New York Rangers. Chicago won 7–6 and Anderson was dismissed, never to play another big-league game.

On the same night, Gordie Howe of Detroit scored three times against Montreal in a 7–2 rout. Howe's hat trick gave him 47 goals for the season, tops in the NHL, and his 86 points earned him

*Dauntless goalie Terry Sawchuk in action.*

$1,000 as the NHL scoring champion. Detroit finished on top of the league standings with an even 100 points. Montreal was second with 78, 22 points behind. Then came Toronto with 74 and Boston with 66.

The Leafs were very much the underdogs in Series A with the Red Wings. In the first two games, Detroit goalie Terry Sawchuk turned in a pair of superb performances to record 3–0 and 1–0 shutouts. Turk Broda, overweight and balding, a netminder who had seen no real action since the preceding spring's Stanley Cup finals, started the third game for Toronto because Conn Smythe had promised him at least one playoff start. The old warrior was peppered with shots, and the Red Wings won their third straight, 6–2. Al Rollins replaced Broda in game four, and the Leafs fought hard to avoid the stigma of four successive playoff defeats, but the Detroit machine was overpowering. The Leafs succumbed 3–1. Their loss marked the end of a Toronto dynasty that had won the Stanley Cup in four of the five preceding seasons. One general manager was prompted to say, "It's the best thing that could have happened for the league. The Leafs have won too many Stanley Cups the past few seasons."

Meanwhile, the Bruins and the Canadiens were clawing at each other in Series B. With Rocket Richard leading the way with a pair of goals, the Habs sped to a 5–1 rout in game one. They won the second game 4–0, thanks largely to Boom Boom Geoffrion, who scored three times. But the game proved to be a costly one for Montreal when Ken Mosdell was carried off the ice with a broken leg. The Bruins fought back with a 4–1 win in Boston, then tied the series with a 3–2 victory. When the Bruins made it three straight wins, taking game five 1–0, Lynn Patrick joyfully announced, "The Habs are dead." He should have known better. In game seven, one of the "dead" Habs engineered the most dramatic play of the series, and one of the most dramatic plays ever. With the score tied 1–1 in the second period, Rocket Richard crashed to the ice after a collision with Leo Labine. Six stitches were required to close Richard's head wound, but he returned to the game. Late in the third period, he took a pass from Butch

Bouchard, sailed past four Bruins, warded off Bill Quackenbush's check with sheer strength and determination, and hooked a one-handed shot past Sugar Jim Henry. It was a brilliant solo effort. A four-minute ovation hailed the Rocket's effort and a dozen sweepers hustled around the ice cleaning up the programs, galoshes, popcorn boxes, and other debris that had been hurled into the air and onto the ice following the glorious goal. Later Lynn Patrick said, "It was the most sensational goal in NHL history. A truck wouldn't have stopped Richard on that play."

But in the final series, without a truck, the Red Wings not only stopped the Rocket but the entire Canadiens team. Tony Leswick's two goals led the Wings to a 3–1 win in the opener. In game two, Ted Lindsay's second-period goal, with the puck dribbling into the net off the chest of Butch Bouchard, gave the Wings a 3–1 win. Terry Sawchuk fashioned a 3–0 shutout in game three, in which Gordie Howe, held scoreless in six previous playoff games, finally clicked for a pair of goals. Ted Lindsay was credited with the other, a 65-footer. The Red Wings became the first team in playoff history to sweep eight straight games without a loss in Cup competition when they shut out Montreal 3–0 in the fourth game. It was Sawchuk's second consecutive shutout and his fourth in eight games.

IN 1952–53, VETERAN Detroit star Sid Abel wasn't around to help the Wings seek a record five-straight NHL championships. He was traded to Chicago where he took over as playing-coach and led the Black Hawks to a playoff spot.

On December 18, Jean Beliveau made a sensational debut with Montreal, scoring five goals in his first three games. Fans hungered to see more of the big centerman, but he decided to return to Quebec and finish the season in the Quebec league.

At the close of the season, Gordie Howe was again the NHL scoring champion. He came within an ace of tying Rocket Richard's mark of 50 goals in a single season, finishing with 49 goals and 95 points. An official's ruling cost Howe a 50-goal season after he claimed he tipped in a shot by Red Kelly against the

Bruins. Kelly and several other Red Wings supported Howe, but the official scorer stubbornly insisted the goal was Kelly's.

Detroit finished first overall with 90 points. Second-place Montreal earned 75, and Boston and Chicago tied for third with 69 points. Because the Hawks had fewer wins, 27 to the Bruins' 28, they were relegated to the fourth playoff spot. The Black Hawks had gone on a late-season tear, losing only three of their last 12 games. It brought them their first participation in postseason activity in seven years. For the first time since Maple Leaf Gardens opened its doors in 1931, the Leafs faced a nonprofit spring. So did the Rangers.

Because Detroit had needed only eight games to capture the Stanley Cup the previous spring, they were favored to dispose of Boston in Series A of the Stanley Cup semifinals. Terry Sawchuk picked up where he left off in the 1952 playoffs, with a 7–0 shutout over Boston in game one. It was his fifth shutout in nine playoff games. Over that span, he had allowed just five goals.

"The second game won't be so easy," warned Jack Adams. It wasn't. Boston goalie Jim Henry was sensational, making 43 saves in a 5–3 Bruin triumph. Jack McIntyre of the Bruins broke up game three with an overtime goal, giving Boston two wins in a row. They came right back with a 6–2 victory in game four at the Boston Garden. Back in Detroit, the Bruins gave up two goals in 55 seconds and lost 6–4. But on home ice again, they ended the Red Wings' season with a 4–2 win. Lynn Patrick praised Porky Dumart for holding Gordie Howe in check throughout the series.

In Series B, the Chicago Black Hawks dropped a 3–1 decision to Montreal in game one and lost again in game two after they blew a two-goal lead. Jim Norris wasn't a happy owner and warned his players, "You know I don't like losers." On home ice, Chicago bounced back and won games three and four to square the series. Vic Lynn, who hadn't scored a single goal in 29 games, whipped in the winner in game four. Montreal coach Dick Irvin claimed one of the Hawk goals was ten feet offside. "He's full of baloney," snorted Sid Abel.

The Black Hawks made it three in a row with a 4–2 win in game five at the Forum. The trio of playoff victories matched the number of wins they'd recorded against the Canadiens during the regular season. Before the sixth game, the Habs' regular goaltender, Gerry McNeil, asked to be relieved from duty "for the good of the team." Rookie netminder Jacques Plante, who had seen action in only three NHL games, sparkled in a 3–0 whitewashing of the Hawks. It was the first of many great playoff games Plante would play for Montreal.

The fired-up Habs rolled over Chicago 4–1 in the deciding game, with rookie Eddie Mazur scoring twice, while Richard and Geoffrion completed the scoring. When asked to comment on the forthcoming final series with Boston, Dick Irvin said, "You know they've just beaten Detroit, so they'll probably claw us to pieces. I don't see how we can win even a single game."

Irvin was a lousy prognosticator. The final series opened in Montreal and the Canadiens emerged with a 4–2 decision in game one. Bruin goalie Sugar Jim Henry twisted an ankle in game two and was replaced by another Henry, Gordon "Red" Henry, up from the Hershey Bears. Both Henrys stymied the Habs, and Boston tied the series with a 4–1 victory.

Dick Irvin, too, was busy shuffling goalies. Gerry McNeil was back for the third game and shut out the Bruins 3–0, and was his bouncy self in the fourth game, while Red Henry was shelled for seven goals, three by Richard, in a 7–3 romp. The sixth game went into overtime in Montreal. Elmer Lach, a spry 35-year-old veteran, sent a harmless-looking shot toward the Bruin net at 1:22 of sudden-death play. Sugar Jim Henry, back in the Boston goal, didn't notice it slide into his net. "Neither did I," admitted Lach after the game. "Man, was I surprised when that red light went on." Canadiens won the game, the series, and the Stanley Cup.

**B**EFORE THE 1953–54 SEASON, Montreal finally persuaded Jean Beliveau to leave Quebec City and sign a Canadiens' contract. Photos of the historic occasion were flashed from coast to coast. But early in the season Beliveau was slashed across the ankle and missed several games.

*The Red Wings' iron man — Gordie Howe, a true hockey titan.*
(Norman James)

The Chicago Black Hawks dropped into the league basement, losing 51 of the 70 games they played, and concern was expressed over the future of the franchise. Despite the gloomy situation, however, Al Rollins stood tall in the Chicago net and won the Hart Trophy as most valuable player in the league.

Detroit's Red Kelly won his third Lady Byng Trophy in four years. He also captured a new award, the James Norris Trophy, as top defenseman.

The Red Wings were league leaders for a record sixth successive season, finishing with 81 points. The Canadiens were second with 81, followed by the Leafs with 78 and the Bruins with 74. For the fourth time in a row, Gordie Howe won the Art Ross Trophy as scoring champion with 81 points, 14 points ahead of Rocket Richard.

With Howe, Lindsay, and Sawchuk leading the way, it took Detroit just five games to eliminate Toronto in the opening round of the playoffs, while Montreal was busy ousting Boston four straight. In game two against the Bruins, Dickie Moore scored two goals and assisted on four others in an 8–1 shellacking of the Beantowners. Moore's six points were a playoff record, as was his opening goal, coming after just ten seconds of play.

The final series for the Cup between Detroit and Montreal was a thriller that lasted seven games. Detroit won the opener 3–1, and goalie Jacques Plante was accused of "ducking his head" on a shot by rookie Dutch Reibel. Before the series, Plante had complained of stomach cramps and there had been some doubt he'd be able to play. Rocket Richard burst out of a scoring slump with a pair of goals in game two, won by the Canadiens 3–1. With Doug Harvey and Jean Beliveau sidelined with injuries, Montreal was no match for Detroit in the third game, which the Red Wings won 5–2. When coach Dick Irvin was told that both his injured stars would be back for the next outing, a reporter commented: "Irvin will probably make playoff history tonight when he smiles." But Irvin had nothing to smile about when Terry Sawchuk shut out his Habs 2–0.

Goalie Gerry McNeil turned in a sensational performance in game five. After two months' absence from competitive action, he blanked the Red Wings through three periods. At the other end of the rink, Sawchuk was also working on a shutout. Finally, in overtime, Ken Mosdell broke up the scoreless deadlock with a backhand drive that streaked by Sawchuk. Canadiens won 1–0 and cut the Red Wing margin to three games to two.

McNeil was brilliant again in game six when two goals by Floyd Curry and singles by Richard and Geoffrion were enough to beat the Wings 4–1. For the second time in NHL history, the seventh game of a final series went into overtime before a winner could be declared. The hero turned out to be Detroit's little Tony Leswick, who ended the thrilling series at 4:26, scoring on a freak shot when the puck was deflected in off Doug Harvey's glove.

**W**HEN THE 1954–55 REGULAR SEASON rolled to a close, Detroit had finished on top of the NHL standings for the seventh straight time. But hockey fans weren't buzzing so much about the forthcoming Stanley Cup playoffs as they were about the stunning announcement from league head-quarters that Rocket Richard has been suspended. On March 13, during a game in Boston, Richard had gone wild after being cut on the head in a melee with Boston's Hal Laycoe. When linesman Cliff Thompson tried to intervene, Richard smacked him with a punch under the eye. League president Clarence Campbell called Richard on the carpet, and on March 17 he announced his decision to suspend the superstar for the rest of the season and the playoffs.

Campbell's decision touched off an angry outburst from thousands of fans, including death threats against the league president. That evening the Detroit Red Wings began to play the Canadiens at the Forum, but the game was never finished. Campbell was pelted with garbage and at least one fan took a wild punch at him. A tear gas bomb was thrown, and police ordered an immediate evacuation of the arena. Detroit, leading 4–1 at the time, was awarded the game.

Outside the building, an angry mob indulged in a frenzy of looting and burning along St. Catherine Street. More than 100 arrests were made and damage was estimated at more than one million dollars. It was the blackest hour in Montreal hockey history and it came on the eve of the Stanley Cup playoffs. The Rocket's suspension cost him his only chance at the individual scoring title. On the final weekend he was passed by teammate

*Rocket Richard attempts to flip the puck past the Leafs' Al Rollins.*
(Bill Galloway)

Boom Boom Geoffrion. At the Forum, Richard fans greeted Geoffrion's achievement with a chorus of boos.

When the opening rounds of the playoffs got under way a few days later, Dick Irvin promised Montreal fans "something you have never seen before." He kept his word by alternating his goalies — Jacques Plante and rookie Charlie Hodge — every few minutes to face the shots of the Boston Bruins. The novel strategy worked as the two netminders shared a 2–0 shutout in game one. Montreal won game two by a 3–1 score.

Back in Boston the teams played a pair of sizzlers. With Sugar Jim Henry replacing rookie John Henderson in goal, the Bruins played aggressive hockey and whipped the Habs 4–2. But Donnie Marshall's overtime goal in game five gave Montreal a 4–3 win and put the Bruins on the edge of elimination. Montreal ended the Bruins' season with a 4–1 victory in game six.

The Toronto Maple Leafs faced the Detroit Red Wings in their semifinal series without the services of defenseman Tim Horton. He was out for the season with a broken leg and a broken jaw, suffered in a late-season collision with the Rangers' Bill Gadsby. Detroit outscored the Leafs 7–4 in a wide-open first game, and Ted Lindsay set up both goals in a 2–1 Red Wing victory in game two. Detroit won the next game by the same score and completed a sweep of the series with a 3–0 shutout on Toronto ice. Lindsay inquired of a reporter after the victory: "Was that really Ted Kennedy's last game? If so, he went out without much grace. For the second year in a row he was the only guy who refused to shake hands with us." For a player who had been goaded beyond description by Lindsay's verbal taunts and finally whacked over the head by Lindsay's stick, it was hardly surprising that Kennedy refused to wish Lindsay well. He did, however, go out of his way to congratulate Red Wing defenseman Bob Goldham.

The Red Wings were listed as 13–5 favorites for the final series with Montreal. In the opening match, unsung hero Marty Pavelich broke up a tie game with a breakaway goal at 17:07 of the third period. Ted Lindsay then fired an insurance goal into the empty net and Detroit skated off with a 4–2 victory. The Wings stretched a winning streak to 15 games with a 7–1 rout in game two. Lindsay was the star with four goals. During the game, he and Howe targeted Dickie Moore. Howe speared him and Lindsay added a butt end. Moore was so enraged that he flew at Lindsay and received a minor, a misconduct, and a game misconduct for his trouble.

The Canadiens won their first home game when Boom Boom Geoffrion scored a hat trick in a 4–2 win over the Wings. They followed up with a 5–3 triumph to square the series at two games apiece. Back at the Olympia, Gordie Howe produced a dazzling three-goal performance to pace Detroit to a 5–1 drubbing of Montreal. Howe's goals brought his points total to 19, a playoff record. The Canadiens bounced back on home ice with a 6–3 victory, with Geoffrion scoring two goals. The series was tied with all victories coming on home ice.

In the deciding game, home ice again paid off when Detroit won 3–1. Jimmy Skinner became the second rookie coach — Joe Primeau was the first — to win a Stanley Cup championship. By winning at the Olympia, the Red Wings stretched their unbeaten record on home ice to 24 games. League president Campbell presented the Cup to Marguerite Norris, who had taken over the presidency of the Red Wings. The name Marguerite Norris soon became the only woman's name to grace the Stanley Cup.

**B**EFORE THE 1955–56 NHL SEASON, players and coaches were on the move. Dick Irvin left the Canadiens and moved on to face the challenge of rebuilding the Chicago Black Hawks. The Hawks played 28 games that season in which they either scored only one goal or were shut out. Irvin was replaced behind the Montreal bench by Toe Blake. In New York, Phil Watson was signed to coach the Rangers, replacing Muzz Patrick, who moved into the general manager's office. In a blockbuster trade, Detroit sent Terry Sawchuk to Boston in return for five Bruins. Jack Adams already had a solid replacement for Sawchuk in young Glenn Hall. New players on the Ranger roster included Andy Bathgate, Ron Murphy, Dean Prentice, Harry

Howell, and a colorful character named Leapin' Lou Fontinato. And Montreal opponents now had another Richard to worry about — the Rocket's quiet but flashy kid brother, Henri.

By winning the NHL championship and the Prince of Wales Trophy in the spring of 1956, the Montreal Canadiens broke the record of seven straight league titles strung together by Detroit. The Canadiens won 45 games, eclipsing the league record of 44 set by Detroit in 1950–51. Detroit finished in second place with 76 points, New York was third with 74, and Toronto was fourth with 61. NHL scoring champion Jean Beliveau finished the season with 47 goals and 88 points, both records for a centerman. Bert Olmstead set an assist record with 56, and Jacques Plante won the Vezina Trophy. Doug Harvey was named top defenseman and, as Jack Adams predicted, Glenn Hall won the Calder Trophy.

The Canadiens won all seven games against the Rangers during the regular schedule and were overwhelming favorites to sweep the New Yorkers aside in the opening round of the playoffs. Rocket Richard scored three goals in the first game, a 7–1 rout. But the Rangers stormed back with a 4–2 victory on Forum ice. Gordie Bell, a journeyman goalie, replaced Gump Worsley in the Ranger net and played a starring role in the surprise victory. "We're going to take it all now," boasted Ranger coach Phil Watson to anyone who would listen. But Watson was silenced by the results of back-to-back weekend games, both won by Montreal, 3–1 and 5–3. And he was stunned after his team took a 7–0 shellacking in game five, with Rocket Richard assisting on five of the goals to tie a playoff record. After the one-sided series, Watson shook his head and said, "It's hard to believe my club was dominated so completely."

The Toronto Maple Leafs weren't given much chance in their semifinal matchup with Detroit. The Toronto path to the playoffs had been paved by Tod Sloan, who turned in a 37-goal season. But Sloan was recovering from a mild concussion when postseason play began. Calder Trophy winner Glenn Hall was sensational in the first game, won by the Wings 3–2. Sloan, still nursing a headache, ran into more hard luck in game two, won by the

Wings 3–2. He went down with a fractured shoulder after taking a check into the boards from Gordie Howe.

When the series returned to Toronto, there was some off-ice excitement. An anonymous caller phoned the Toronto newspapers and threatened, "You don't have to worry about Howe and Lindsay tonight. I'm going to shoot them." Lindsay had the last laugh at his would-be assassin when the tough little winger scored the tying and winning goals as Detroit won in overtime 5–4. After the win, Lindsay inverted his stick and pointed it at the Gardens crowd as if seeking the "shooter" who'd threatened him.

Before the fourth game, it was said that Leaf goalie Harry Lumley was angry with overcritical sportswriters. Lumley took his ire out on the Red Wings, swatting pucks as if they were annoying scribes in a 2–0 shutout. It marked the first time Toronto had beaten Detroit in a Cup match in three years.

In the final seconds of the fifth game, with the Leafs trailing 2–1, Lumley was benched in favor of an extra attacker. But the strategy backfired when Lindsay scored in the empty net and the Leafs were eliminated.

Detroit, seeking its third straight Stanley Cup, was below par for the opener against Montreal, and the Habs came up with a four-goal third period to win it 6–4. In a lackluster game, the Canadiens made it two in a row with a convincing 5–1 victory. Jack Adams said the next game would prove "whether my boys have any pride left." Ted Lindsay and Gordie Howe responded to Adam's barbs by scoring third-period goals to give the Wings a 3–1 comeback victory on home ice.

Jean Beliveau, hailed by Toe Blake as "the greatest living hockey player," triggered Montreal to within a single victory of the Stanley Cup in game four when he scored twice in a 3–0 Montreal win. Two nights later at the Forum, the Habitants were crowned Stanley Cup champions after they eliminated Detroit by a 3–1 count. The turning point came when Jean Beliveau and Rocket Richard scored power-play goals within 52 seconds of each other in the second period with Marcel Pronovost in the penalty box.

**D**URING THE 1956–57 SEASON, hockey fans in the United States were able to watch NHL hockey on their television screens for the first time. CBS carried the NHL Game of the Week with Bud Palmer and Fred Cusick doing the commentary.

This was the season Ted Kennedy attempted a comeback with the Leafs, a team that introduced a rookie left-winger named Frank Mahovlich. Terry Sawchuk quit the Boston Bruins under mysterious circumstances and was replaced by Don Simmons. When Boston reporters wrote derogatory things about him, Sawchuk threatened to sue them. Elsewhere, word leaked out that certain NHL players were trying to form a players' association with Ted Lindsay as president.

The league was forced to change a rule regarding penalties. Because the Montreal Canadiens had such a potent power play, they often scored two or three times when an opposing player was penalized. Before this season, the player was required to spend the full two minutes of a minor penalty in the box. Under the new rule, a penalized player was allowed to come out of the box whenever a power-play goal was scored against his team.

The Detroit Red Wings won the NHL championship with 88 points. On the strength of four Stanley Cups in the past seven years, they were overwhelming favorites to dump the third-place Boston Bruins. The Montreal Canadiens, defending Stanley Cup champions and second-place finishers with 82 points, were similarly favored to defeat New York, who managed only 66 points during the season.

Boston's eager Bruins, picked by most experts in the fall as the team least likely to succeed, not only made the playoffs with a third-place finish and 80 points, but engineered some surprises once they got there. They stunned Detroit with a 3–1 victory in game one at the Detroit Olympia before suffering a 7–2 thrashing in game two. Aroused by stinging criticism from club officials and fans, the Wings played aggressively and 22 penalties were called, an NHL record in the playoffs. Bruin veteran Cal Gardner scored at 13:28 of the third period to give the Bruins a 4–3 win in game three. It was Gardner's first goal of the season against Detroit. One play was the turning point of the fourth game: rookie goalie Simmons stopped Gordie Howe on a breakaway. Boston won the game 2–0 and took a 3–1 lead in games back to Detroit.

In the fifth and series-winning game, the Bruins scored three goals in the third period. One was Cal Gardner's shot at 15:16, giving the Bruins a 4–3 lead that they held to the end. It was a major upset. The odds against the Bruins before the series had been 12–5.

Similar odds favored the Canadiens in their series with the Rangers, since the Canadiens had scored a league-high 210 goals and the Rangers had allowed a league-high 227. Game one fit the pattern, with third-period goals by Geoffrion, Beliveau, and Richard powering the Habs to a 4–1 decision. But game two required overtime, the first at Madison Square Garden since 1940, and Andy Hebenton's shot ended it at 13:38, giving the Rangers a 4–3 victory.

The Rangers were now faced with the task of winning three playoff games in ten days at the Forum, where they had managed only three wins in the past three seasons. Coach Phil Watson figured his goalie, Gump Worsley, was the key. "Gump has been outstanding," he said. "But keep it quiet. Gump weakens when he's exposed to too much praise." Worsley weakened in game three, won by Montreal 8–3. Geoffrion fired three goals and Beliveau, enjoyed a five-point outing. The Rangers tightened their defenses in game four but still lost by 3–1. Following game five, won by Montreal 4–3, Rocket Richard happily posed for pictures after his overtime goal had put Montreal into the Stanley Cup finals against Boston. A shot from his brother, Henri, had hit him in the midsection and dropped to the ice. The Rocket had reached it before Worsley could and flipped it into the net.

In game one of the finals against the Bruins, the Rocket played like an inspired rookie and drilled four goals past Don Simmons in a 5–1 win. Simmons grumbled: "My back's sunburned from all those red lights. The Rocket humiliated me. He beat me four different ways."

In game two, Simmons was the victim of Jean Beliveau's second-period goal, which stood up for a 1–0 Hab triumph and a shutout for Jacques Plante. In game three it was Geoffrion's turn to shine. He scored a pair of goals in a 4–2 victory. Rookie Phil Goyette was a dominant player in the game, prompting Boston coach Milt Schmidt to moan: "I almost drafted the guy last year but I figured he was too small for the NHL."

The Bruins regrouped on home ice, and Don Simmons played brilliantly in a 2–0 shutout of the Habs. Montreal mayor Jean Drapeau had traveled all the way to Boston to have his photo taken with the Canadiens grouped around the Stanley Cup. Simmons's shutout spoiled the politician's ego trip.

The roughest game of the series was the final one, a 5–1 Cup-winning victory for Montreal at the Forum. A rash of high-sticking, slashing, and solid bodychecking almost turned the game into a donnybrook.

**THE 1957–58 NHL SEASON** opened with Terry Sawchuk shunted back to Detroit in return for a blue-chip prospect, Johnny Bucyk, who would enjoy a 23-year career in the league and score 556 goals, placing him eighth on the list of all-time goal-scoring leaders.

The colorful Canadiens suffered an awesome number of injuries during the season but still finished at the top of the NHL standings with 96 points. The Rangers moved up to second place with 77 points. The Red Wings finished third with 70 points, one point ahead of the fourth-place Bruins. Chicago missed the play-offs for the eleventh time in 12 years. In Toronto after the Leafs' fifth-place finish, Stafford Smythe declared: "Every Leaf is expendable except Mahovlich."

In the playoffs, Maurice Richard, still the most exciting player in hockey at the advanced age of 36, fought off the effects of a partially severed Achilles tendon to delight the Forum crowd in the opening game against Detroit. He belted a pair of goals past Terry Sawchuk in the first four minutes of an 8–1 rout. The Rocket exploded again in game two, a 5–1 win for Montreal. He scored twice in the third period and had another goal washed out because he was camped in Sawchuk's crease. In the second period of game three, Jacques Plante was smashed to the ice by Detroit's Bob Bailey and was unconscious for three minutes, but he returned to thwart every Red Wing shot after that and was able to hang on until Andre Pronovost scored in overtime to give Montreal a 2–1 victory.

Richard almost single-handedly beat the Wings in game four. The ageless wonder, playing in his 1,000th game, scored three goals, leading the Habs to a 4–3 win and a berth in the finals.

Boston and New York met in Series B, which opened at Madison Square Garden. Dave Creighton of the Rangers scored twice in a 5–3 victory in game one. Jerry Toppazzini's overtime goal in game two resulted in a 4–3 Boston win. Following the game, the circus clowns and elephants moved in, forcing the Rangers to play all remaining games in Boston.

Boston's Don Simmons was a hot goalie in game three and backstopped the Bruins to a 5–0 shutout. Two days later, Gump Worsley was almost as sharp for New York, and the Rangers knotted the series with a 5–2 win. Boston's Fern Flaman, who'd played in 85 games without scoring a goal, connected for two in Boston's 5–1 fifth-game victory. Ranger coach Phil Watson was so upset after the game that he barred reporters from the dressing room. His team was humiliated 8–2 in the next encounter, and the Bruins found themselves in the Stanley Cup finals.

In game one of the 1958 finals, Dickie Moore, recovering from a broken wrist, scored the winning goal in a 2–1 victory. The Bruins fought back with a 5–3 upset two days later. Rocket Richard, stymied in the first two games, scored twice in game three, and the Canadiens won 3–0, with Plante registering the shutout. The Bruins' Fleming Mackell, a hungry hockey player with seven mouths to feed at home, played a starring role in game four as Boston slapped down Montreal 3–1 to tie the series.

But the Bruins still hadn't found a way to control Richard. He fired a sudden-death overtime goal to give the Habs a 3–2 win on home ice. On national television, before the overtime, Montreal general manager Frank Selke predicted that Richard would score the winner. "There's no thrill like scoring a winning goal in over-time," said Richard. "It makes you feel so young, you think you can play forever." Richard should know — he'd scored a total of 18 playoff-winning goals since joining the Canadiens 16 years earlier.

It was Boom Boom Geoffrion, returning to the hockey wars two months after major bowel surgery, who fired two goals in a 5–3 Cup-winning triumph over the Bruins in game six. It was Montreal's ninth Stanley Cup victory. Nobody had ordered champagne to help the winners celebrate, so they sipped orange juice from Lord Stanley's famous silver trophy as the flashbulbs popped.

A SUDDEN LATE-SEASON SURGE by the Toronto Maple Leafs, the equally sudden collapse of the New York Rangers, the scoring of Dickie Moore and Jean Beliveau, the battered nose of the Rangers' Lou Fontinato — these were the events for which the 1958–59 NHL season would be remembered. During a game in New York, when Ranger tough guy Lou Fontinato saw Detroit's Gordie Howe swing his stick at Eddie Shack, he challenged the big right-winger to drop the gloves. Howe obliged and ended the bout with a punch that splattered Fontinato's nose all over his face. Photos of Leapin' Lou's fractured beak and bloody cheeks were in every paper the following day.

The 1958–59 season produced one of the most exciting finishes in hockey history as the Leafs, under newcomer Punch Imlach, came from nowhere in the final days of the schedule to win five straight games and squeeze into the playoffs in the final period of the final game. The Rangers stumbled through their last couple of weeks, losing six out of seven and finishing one point behind Toronto.

Montreal captured the league title with 91 points, followed by Boston with 73, Chicago with 69, and Toronto with 65. Dickie Moore won his second consecutive scoring crown with a record

*Adoring fans ask for autographs from a young Jean Beliveau.* (David Bier)

96 points, while teammate Jean Beliveau scored twice in the final game to finish second with 91 points, the highest point-total ever obtained by a center.

Throughout the season the Chicago Black Hawks had trouble with the defending champion Canadiens. The best the Hawks could do against the Habs was one victory and five ties in 14 meetings. That was why the third-place finishers had all the odds stacked against them when they faced Montreal in the first round of the playoffs.

Montreal won the opener 4–2 when muscular Marcel Bonin, who had played in 25 Stanley Cup games without scoring a goal, hammered in a pair. Bonin credited some old hockey gloves he'd borrowed from Rocket Richard for his change of luck. The gloves came through again in game two as Bonin scored two more goals and Montreal won easily 5–1. At that point in the series, Chicago owner Jim Norris issued unsigned checks to his players for $3,350. They came with instructions: "Bring them back to me after you've won the Cup and I'll sign them."

The Black Hawks rebounded with a 4–2 victory. The game was delayed when Beliveau was taken to hospital suffering from a spinal injury after he absorbed a crunching check from Glen Skov. The big centerman was lost for "an indefinite period."

After Marcel Bonin's lucky gloves produced another goal in game four, Bobby Hull scored his first Stanley Cup goal to tie the score. Two more Chicago goals, one by Glen Skov into an empty net, gave the Hawks a 3–1 triumph. In game five Bonin scored his seventh goal in five games, and the Habs were victorious 4–2. The sixth and series-winning game in Chicago was a spectacular see-saw struggle, which finally went to Montreal by a score of 5–4. The game was marred by a near riot when referee Red Storey failed to call a tripping penalty on Junior Langlois of Montreal, who had dumped hometown hero Bobby Hull. Bottles, cans, coins, a deck of cards, and even a chair were tossed onto the ice. Two fans tried to attack Storey. One interloper was clobbered by the stick of Montreal defenseman Doug Harvey and cut for 15 stitches. A few days later, when referee Storey heard that league president Clarence Campbell had criticized his handling of the incident, telling a reporter that "Storey froze," the veteran official turned in his stripes and resigned.

If the Toronto Maple Leafs, winners of five straight games entering the playoffs, were on a hot streak, so were the Boston Bruins. The Bruins had finished the season in spectacular style, winning six of their final seven games. Both clubs entered the semifinal series with confidence. Veteran goalie Harry Lumley, who took over when Don Simmons was felled by an attack of appendicitis, was sensational in the Bruins' opening 5–1 victory. Toronto bounced back to win game two 4–2.

Gerry Ehman was the Toronto hero in game three at Maple Leaf Gardens. He scored the tying goal and the winning marker in overtime as the Leafs shaded the Bruins 3–2. The fourth game was another overtime thriller, decided when Frank Mahovlich scored to give the Leafs a 3–2 verdict. It was Johnny Bower, described as a miracle man, who was instrumental in the Leafs' third straight win, a 4–1 victory on Boston ice. "You know, I almost benched the guy in favor of Ed Chadwick," Punch Imlach told reporters after the game.

The Bruins upset the Leafs 5–4 in Toronto, and two nights later in game seven, Ehman again played the hero, scoring the winning goal in a 3–2 squeaker. The Leafs captured the series, four games to three.

Imlach sent his Leafs into the Stanley Cup finals against Montreal, hoping that "balance would beat brilliance." Bonin was back in the news in game one, scoring the winner in a lackluster 5–3 Montreal win. Doug Harvey masterfully set up Claude Provost for a pair of goals in game two, a 3–1 Hab victory.

Back in Toronto, the Leafs played aggressively in a 3–2 over-time win, with Dick Duff firing the winner after 10:06 of extra play. Boom Boom Geoffrion played a big role in Montreal's 3–2 decision over the Leafs in game four, setting up the first two goals and blasting in the third one himself. Despite Imlach's prediction that "we'll come back," the Canadiens rolled to a 5–3 victory in the fifth and deciding game. In front of more than 14,000 roaring fans at the Forum, the Habs set an NHL record of four consecutive Stanley Cup triumphs.

**E**ARLY IN THE 1959–60 SEASON the goalie face mask became a permanent part of the game. On November 1, 1959, Jacques Plante was struck in the face by Andy Bathgate's slap shot. Several stitches were required to close the wound, and Plante refused to return to the ice until coach Toe Blake allowed him to wear the face mask he'd been using in Montreal practices. Blake, no fan of the mask, reluctantly agreed. Plante won the game, and when he emerged a winner in the ten games that followed, the mask became part of his regular equipment.

*The wiry Jacques Plante without his trademark mask.*
(Toronto Star)

New faces in the NHL included those of J. C. Tremblay in Montreal and Bill Hay and Murray Balfour in Chicago. Hay and Balfour would be teamed up with Bobby Hull to form Chicago's Million-Dollar Line.

Early in February, Red Kelly and Billy McNeill of Detroit were traded to New York for Bill Gadsby and Eddie Shack. When Kelly refused to report to the Rangers, Clarence Campbell phoned him to say, "If you don't report, you will never play for or coach an NHL team as long as you live." Kelly stayed put. A few days later a deal was made with the Leafs — Kelly for journeyman defenseman Marc Reaume. It would turn out to be one of the best deals Toronto ever made.

Montreal won its third successive regular-season title with 92 points. Toronto finished second with 79, Chicago third with 69, and Detroit fourth with 67. Bobby Hull of the Black Hawks won a thrilling duel with Boston's Bronco Horvath for the scoring title, 81 points to 80. Hull's linemate, Bill Hay, was named rookie of the year.

In the Stanley Cup semifinals, Montreal faced Chicago. With Bobby Hull sidelined with abscessed tonsils and Stan Mikita out with a swollen eye, the Hawks were at a disadvantage in game one and lost 4–3. The second game went to Montreal by the same score, but it was accomplished the hard way — in overtime. Veteran Doug Harvey scored at 8:38 of extra play to put Montreal two games up. A one-sided 4–0 victory for Montreal then placed the Hawks on the verge of elimination. During the game, Chicago fans bombarded the ice with debris, and the disorganized home team failed to get a shot on Plante in the final ten minutes. A 2–0 shutout for Plante in game four swept the Hawks aside.

Toronto met Detroit in Series B. After the Red Wings won the opener 2–1, Leaf coach Punch Imlach reached into his bag of psychological tricks. He placed $1,250 in the middle of the dressing room floor during the pregame warm-up. "That's the difference between winning and losing this series," he told his players. Inspired, the Leafs went out and skated to a 4–2 win. Desire for the playoff loot may have held over to the next game in Detroit, which went into three overtime periods before Frank Mahovlich scored his second goal in a 5–4 Leaf victory. The Wings were sharper than the Leafs in game four and won in overtime when Jerry Melnyk beat Bower.

Before game five, veteran Leaf defenseman Allan Stanley told reporters: "Forget those guys who say I'm too old and too tired to be effective. I might just beat those Red Wings all by myself." Then he cut loose for a pair of goals and assisted on two more in a 5–4 Toronto win. Stanley had scored only three goals in 40 previous Cup matches. In game six, Toronto trailed 2–1 with just one period to play. Then Bob Pulford scored twice to spark a strong comeback and Mahovlich potted the winner, his third in six games. Now only their arch-rivals, the Montreal Canadiens, stood between the Leafs and the Stanley Cup.

The high Imlach forehead was creased in a frown before the final series with the Canadiens. "My players aren't sharp and they're tired. I was afraid of a letdown after the Detroit series and it's happened." Indeed, the Leafs appeared to be sluggish in game one at the Forum, where they were beaten 4–2. Henri Richard buzzed around the Leaf defenders all night and picked up a goal and three assists.

Playing a strong defensive game, the Canadiens squeezed out a 2–1 victory in the second meeting, and in the third game they came up with a 5–2 victory. Phil Goyette collected two goals, while Henri and Rocket Richard and Donnie Marshall got the others. The Rocket retrieved the puck after his goal, the 82nd playoff goal of his career, and rinksiders figured he was telegraphing his imminent retirement.

Montreal ousted the Leafs 4–0 in the fourth game to win their fifth consecutive Stanley Cup. The eight-game sweep equaled the mark set by the Red Wings of 1951–52. The Canadiens took their victory in stride, even coach Blake, whose winning playoff record soared to 27–2. As Doug Harvey put it: "When you win the final series in four games, there's just not much to get excited about."

# 9 The Swinging Sixties

**W**HEN THE 1960–61 NHL SEASON opened, two of hockey's all-time great scorers had packed away their skates. Rocket Richard, holder of 17 NHL records, including a career mark of 544 goals, announced his retirement from the Canadiens, and Terrible Ted Lindsay, after 14 seasons, 999 games, and 1,623 penalty minutes bowed out in Detroit.

The season produced a thrilling duel for the scoring crown between two Canadiens, Boom Boom Geoffrion and Jean Beliveau. Geoffrion came on with an impressive late-season rush, scoring 18 goals in 11 games to tie Rocket Richard's record of 50 goals in a season. He won the scoring title with 95 points, five more than runner-up Beliveau.

Toronto and Montreal battled for the league championship, which Montreal won by two points, 92 to 90. Chicago finished third with 75 points and Detroit fourth with 66. Johnny Bower of the Leafs ended Jacques Plante's five-year hold on the Vezina Trophy, and Leaf teammate Dave Keon captured the Calder.

After Montreal's first-place finish, it was widely predicted that they would soon reign as Stanley Cup champions for the sixth year in a row. But three key Hab stars — Jean Beliveau, Billy Hicke, and Donnie Marshall — were injured in the opening game of Montreal's playoff series with Chicago, a game won by the

Canadiens 6–3. Coach Blake was furious with the "dirty tricks" of the Black Hawks and accused them of using their sticks like tomahawks. Ed Litzenberger, a former Canadien, helped win game two for Chicago, scoring the winning goal with less than three minutes to play. A marathon third game went into three overtime periods before the Hawks' Murray Balfour scored to give the home team a 2–1 win. Again, Blake erupted in anger over the refereeing. At the end of the game, he dashed across the ice and threw a wild punch at referee Dalt McArthur. President Clarence Campbell fined Blake $2,000, the largest individual fine in league history. In game four, Dickie Moore and Billy Hicke each scored twice in a 5–2 Canadiens' win, but Chicago stormed back in game five at the Forum with Glenn Hall recording a 3–0 shutout. Hall was brilliant again in game six and earned his second consecutive shutout by 3–0, dashing Montreal hopes for a sixth straight Stanley Cup. Rocket Richard called the series "the dirtiest I have ever seen." Boom Boom Geoffrion, sidelined with a leg injury during the playoffs, was so anxious to help his team that he removed his cast and tried, rather unsuccessfully, to play in the final game.

Series B between Toronto and Detroit went five games before Toronto was ousted. It was a stunning upset because the Leafs had finished 24 points ahead of Detroit after regular-season play. Gordie Howe played a prominent role in game five, his 100th Stanley Cup playoff game. Jack Adams needled Punch Imlach at the finish. "Thanks, Punch," he said gleefully. "You did it for us. You insulted us with your 'Leafs in four' newspaper talk. Our boys can read, and I think this stung them."

The all-American final series opened in Chicago with Bobby Hull scoring twice in Chicago's 3–2 win over Detroit, a game in which Red Wing goaltender Terry Sawchuk was injured. With backup goalie Hank Bassen in goal for game two, the Red Wings played tighter defensively, Alex Delvecchio scored two goals, and rookie Howie Young added another for a 3–1 Red Wing victory. Back in Chicago for game three, the Hawks checked Detroit's big line of Howe, Delvecchio, and Stasiuk to a standstill and won 3–1. Detroit fought back with a 2–1 squeaker to even the series. Bruce

McGregor's first NHL goal was the game winner. Two goals each from Mikita and Balfour helped Chicago forge ahead in the series with a 6–3 win in game five. A strong third period in game six produced three Chicago goals, and the Black Hawks skated away with a 5–1 triumph and the Stanley Cup — their first Cup victory since 1938.

**B**EFORE THE 1961–62 SEASON opened, 36-year-old Doug Harvey joined the Rangers as player-coach. In return for Harvey's release, the Canadiens received defenseman Lou Fontinato. Former Ranger coach Phil Watson was signed by Boston to replace Milt Schmidt, and the Leafs' Punch Imlach had his contract as manager-coach extended another three years.

Bobby Hull, now 23 and in his fifth NHL season, went on a goal-scoring spree that netted him 50 goals in 66 games. His 50th — and record-tying goal — came in the final game of the season and tied him with New York's Andy Bathgate for the scoring title. The Art Ross Trophy went to Hull because he'd scored more goals than Bathgate.

*A youthful Golden Jet — the incomparable Bobby Hull jousting with the Maple Leafs' Marcel Pronovost and Johnny Bower. Note the wickedly curved stick.*

The Canadiens captured their fifth straight regular-season title behind the remarkable goaltending of Jacques Plante, who won the Vezina and Hart trophies. Rookie Bobby Rousseau captured the Calder Trophy.

The Habs finished with 98 points, 13 in front of second-place Toronto, Chicago finished third with 75 points, and the Rangers wound up fourth with 64. The Boston Bruins, under Phil Watson, won only 15 games and finished in last place with a meager 38 points.

The oddsmakers, ignoring or forgetting Chicago's upset of the Habs in the 1961 playoffs, favored the Canadiens in the semifinal playoff matchup with the Black Hawks. But the Habs were missing Henri Richard, their top playmaker, out with a broken arm. Montreal jumped into a 2–0 lead in the series on home ice by winning 2–1 and 4–3, but back in Chicago the Black Hawks rebounded with a pair of wins, 4–1 and 5–3. Game four was the roughest game of the season, according to Toe Blake. At one point, when the Habs ran into a number of penalties, Blake lost his temper and tried to assault referee Eddie Powers.

Chicago goalie Glenn Hall shaded Jacques Plante 4–3 in a goaltending battle in game five at the Montreal Forum, and Hall came right back in game six with a 2–0 shutout on home ice to eliminate the Canadiens. For the second year in a row, Chicago had upset Montreal in a playoff series and by the same margin, four games to two.

When the Rangers faced the Leafs in Series B, it marked the first time in 20 years the two clubs had met in playoff competition. Toronto took the first two games at Maple Leaf Gardens 4–2 and 2–1. The Rangers squared the series back in New York, winning 5–4 and 4–2. In the fourth game Rod Gilbert, a handsome rookie playing in only his fourth game, starred with two goals and an assist on the winning tally. A feature of game five was a marvelous goaltending duel between Gump Worsley and Johnny Bower. Red Kelly scored the winner in a 3–2 thriller that needed a second period of overtime.

When game six got under way, perhaps the Rangers were bothered by the "Toronto jinx" — they hadn't won on Toronto ice in 16 games. The Leafs scored three goals in the first ten minutes of play and rolled to an easy 7–1 victory and a berth in the finals. Dave Keon and Dick Duff each scored a pair of goals.

The Leafs' momentum carried on into the finals against Chicago. Foolish penalties hurt Chicago in game one, and the Leafs skated off with a 4–1 triumph. Both teams seethed over the officiating of Frank Udvari in game two, won by Toronto 3–2. Back on the familiar ice of the Chicago Stadium, the Hawks' fierce checking and hard shooting paid off in a 3–0 shutout. The Hawks followed up with a 4–1 victory in game four in which Sawchuk was injured, and there was a long delay while backup Don Simmons put on the pads and replaced him. The match ended with a stick-swinging clash between Frank Mahovlich and Stan Mikita.

The Leafs' Bob Pulford emerged as the star of game five, scoring three times in an 8–4 Leaf victory in Toronto. Don Simmons was the winning goaltender, having taken over for the injured Johnny Bower. Stan Mikita was the best of the Hawks, and his two assists gave him 21 playoff points, a new record.

Toronto won the Stanley Cup on the road, defeating the Black Hawks 2–1 in Chicago on April 22. There was no scoring until Bobby Hull banged the puck past Simmons midway through the third period. The Chicago Stadium crowd celebrated Hull's goal with a shower of debris, and there was a long delay while scrapers cleared the ice. When play resumed, Bob Nevin quickly tied the score, and then Tim Horton rushed down the ice and passed to Duff, who beat Hall for the game winner.

**BEFORE THE 1962–63 SEASON,** Doug Harvey gave up the dual role as player-coach with the Rangers and signed a one-year contract as a player only. Muzz Patrick decided to take on the duties of manager-coach and later he assigned the coaching role to former Ranger Red Sullivan. Sid Abel succeeded Jack Adams as manager of the Red Wings when Adams, after 35 years with Detroit, moved on to become president of the Central Pro Hockey League.

After Boston managed only one win in 14 games, Phil Watson was fired and Milt Schmidt went back behind the Bruin bench. Chicago goalie Glenn Hall's amazing consecutive-game streak finally came to an end after 502 starts. Back problems forced the durable puckstopper to take a night off in early November; he hadn't missed a game since joining the NHL in 1954. He recovered in time to win the Vezina Trophy at the end of the season.

At a late-night party in Toronto following the annual all-star game, a deal was allegedly made whereby the Leafs would sell Frank Mahovlich to Chicago for one million dollars. The next day members of the media gave the story front-page coverage. By then Leaf officials had sobered up and announced that Mahovlich wasn't for sale and the Chicago offer had been turned down.

In late January, Montreal coach Toe Blake was once again beefing about referees. His target was Eddie Powers, whom he accused of officiating as if he had a bet on the outcome. Clarence Campbell slapped a $200 fine on Blake for his remarks. "That's totally inadequate," said referee Powers as he turned in his resignation.

On March 9, Lou Fontinato of the Canadiens fell headlong into the boards and suffered a crushed vertebra. After surgery, he made a slow recovery, but he never played hockey again.

Four teams engaged in a race to the wire for first place in the league standings, and Toronto won for the first time in 15 years, finishing with 82 points, one more than Chicago. Montreal was third with 79 points, two more than Detroit.

Gordie Howe, with 86 points, won the Art Ross Trophy as scoring champion for the sixth time. Pierre Pilote of Chicago won the Norris Trophy and Dave Keon took the Lady Byng for the second successive year. Leaf defenseman Kent Douglas won the Calder Trophy.

The Leafs were 2–1 favorites when they met the Canadiens in Series A of the playoffs, and they made the oddsmakers look good by winning the first three games by scores of 3–1, 3–2, and 2–0. The shutout in game three was Johnny Bower's first in 38 playoff games. Gilles Tremblay scored two power-play goals in pacing Montreal to a 3–1 victory at the Forum in game four, but the Leafs stormed back on home ice for a 5–0 shutout in game five, winning the series four games to one.

In Series B, after Chicago won the first two games on home ice, Gordie Howe celebrated his 35th birthday by collecting a goal and two assists in Detroit's 4–2 win in game three. Bobby Hull, bothered by an injured shoulder, suffered a badly broken nose in this match when he was struck in the face by Bruce McGregor's stick. Detroit evened the series with a 4–1 victory in game four. Hull scored the Black Hawks' lone goal despite breathing problems from his nose injury. In game five at Chicago, Norm Ullman starred with two goals and an assist in Detroit's 4–2 win. Ullman had another productive night in game five — two goals and three assists — as Detroit won 7–4 and took the series four games to two.

The Toronto Maple Leafs were obviously hungry for an early lead when they faced Detroit in the final series for the Cup. Dick Duff dominated in game one, scoring two goals in the first 68 seconds of play; Toronto went on to win 4–2. The Leafs came right back with another 4–2 win on home ice. The Big M was out of action with a knee injury and his place was taken by Ed Litzenberger. Alex Faulkner, Newfoundland's gift to the NHL, scored a pair of goals in the Red Wings' first win in the series, a 3–2 victory at the Olympia. After Faulkner's second goal, former NHLer Howie Meeker predicted: "When he gets back to Newfoundland, his hometown of Bishop Falls will stage the biggest celebration since the end of the war. There'll be a motorcade of 1,000 cars, and it'll be the biggest welcome any individual athlete ever received in Canada."

Toronto took the series lead, three games to one, when Dave Keon scored the winning goal in a 3–2 Leaf win. Another 3–1 victory at Maple Leaf Gardens in game five won the Cup for Toronto. Keon scored two goals — one into an empty net with five seconds on the clock — and Eddie Shack added another. Captain George Armstrong accepted the Cup on behalf of his teammates from league president Clarence Campbell.

**T**HREE INTERESTING ROOKIES joined the NHL for the 1963–64 season, and all three would play a major role years later in Team Canada's unforgettable 1972 victory over the Soviet Union. John Ferguson joined Montreal, replacing Dickie Moore, Paul Henderson surfaced as a Red Wing, and Phil Esposito became a freshman with the Chicago Black Hawks. Esposito's coach was another newcomer; in the off season, Billy Reay had replaced Rudy Pilous as the Hawks' mentor.

In his 19th NHL season, Gordie Howe broke Rocket Richard's record for career goals when he scored his 545th in November. And two major trades occurred in 1963–64. The Canadiens sent Jacques Plante, Donnie Marshall, and Phil Goyette to New York in return for Gump Worsley, Dave Balon, Leon Rochefort, and Len Ronson. Plante said Frank Selke had called him "a cancerous growth in the Montreal organization." Late in the season, Toronto traded Dick Duff, Bob Nevin, Arnie Brown, Rod Seiling, and Bill Collins to the Rangers in return for Andy Bathgate, who was in the worst slump of his career, and Don McKenney. The two ex-Rangers would figure prominently in the 1964 playoffs.

Montreal finished the season in first place with 84 points, one point ahead of Chicago. Toronto wound up in third place with 78 points and Detroit in fourth place with 71.

Tempers were short when the Leafs and Canadiens hooked up in one semifinal series. The teams set a playoff record for penalties in game one, and little Charlie Hodge, the Vezina Trophy winner, shut out the Leafs 2–0. Frank Mahovlich played his best game in years in game two, a 2–1 Toronto victory. The Leafs outplayed the Habs in game three and were leading 2–1 with three minutes to play. Then two goals 25 seconds apart, by Gilles Tremblay and Henri Richard, gave Montreal a stunning 3–2 victory on Toronto ice. Mahovlich was again in top form in game four and led the Leafs to a 5–3 win with two goals and three assists. The teams went back to Montreal where the Canadiens moved ahead in the series with a 4–2 win. They might have wrapped up the series back in Toronto if it hadn't been for Johnny Bower. He sparkled in a 3–0 shutout, forcing game seven. The ageless netminder was just as sensational in the final game at the Forum, and inspired by his play, the Leafs skated to a 3–1 victory. Even though Dave Keon scored all three Toronto goals, he was overlooked by the game's three-star selectors.

In Series B, Chicago opened with a 4–1 win over Detroit. Early in game two, won by Detroit 5–4, Terry Sawchuk pinched a nerve in his shoulder and was replaced in goal by rookie Bob Champoux. Norm Ullman scored three of the Red Wing goals. Sawchuk came out of hospital to record a 3–0 shutout in game three, but the Hawks fought back to tie the series with a 3–2 victory in overtime. When Sawchuk's shoulder problem forced him back to the hospital, Roger Crozier took over in the Detroit goal for game five at the noisy Chicago Stadium. The Hawks beat Crozier and the Wings 3–2 to take the series lead. But it was deadlocked again when the Wings walloped Chicago 7–2 two nights later. Norm Ullman was the Detroit hero with three goals and two assists. In game seven at Chicago, the Wings silenced the huge crowd by jumping to a 2–0 lead. Sawchuk lasted in goal for two periods, then Crozier took over. Chicago tied the score, but goals by Delvecchio and MacDonald put the game out of reach. Detroit advanced to the finals, winning the series four games to three.

The final series for the Cup opened in Toronto. The first game wound up in dramatic fashion, with Bob Pulford scoring the winning goal with just two seconds left on the clock. The second game needed almost eight minutes of overtime before Larry Jeffrey scored the winner in a 4–3 Detroit victory. Game three at the Olympia was decided in the final few seconds. After Detroit took a 3–0 lead, the Leafs fought back to tie the score with just over a minute to play. Alex Delvecchio surprised Johnny Bower with a shot that ended the game with just 17 seconds left in regulation time. Toronto came back with a 4–2 win on Detroit ice to tie the series. Andy Bathgate's blast from 45 feet eluded Sawchuk for the game-winning goal, and later Frank Mahovlich added an insurance marker. Back at Maple Leaf Gardens, Sawchuk won a goaltending battle with Bower and the Red Wings took the series lead with a 2–1 victory.

*Bobby "Boomer" Baun, one of the toughest Maple Leafs ever to lace on skates.*

The sixth game in Detroit will forever be remembered as the "Bobby Baun" game. In the third period, Baun lay on the ice in pain from an injured ankle. When the Toronto training staff carried the rugged defenseman off the ice, they appeared to be carting away Toronto's chances for a third straight Stanley Cup, for the Leafs were skating on rubber legs against the youthful Red Wings, who were hungry for the Cup after a nine-year wait. But the Leafs hung on, and suddenly it was early in overtime and there was "Boomer" Baun, standing at the Red Wing blue line on one leg frozen with local anesthetic. The puck came to him, he whacked at it, and his shot deflected off Bill Gadsby's stick and bulged the net behind Sawchuk. Baun forgot his injured leg and leaped into the air, yelling "Ya-hoo!" His amazing shot forced a final game in the series.

The Toronto Maple Leafs won their third consecutive Stanley Cup on the night of April 23, 1964, when they blanked the confident Red Wings 4–0. The Leaf injury list included George Armstrong with a damaged shoulder, Red Kelly with damaged knee ligaments, Bobby Baun with a suspected fractured fibula, and Carl Brewer with separated ribs. Kelly had spent the day in bed dictating letters in his role as Leonard Kelly, Member of Parliament. His wife Andra was amazed when he hobbled to his feet and said he was going to the game. At the Gardens, he and Baun had painkilling injections, and Kelly scored the goal that put the Stanley Cup on ice. It was Kelly's 142nd playoff game, a record number. After a swig of champagne, Bobby Baun finally agreed to have his injured leg X-rayed. Sure enough — it was a fractured fibula.

**F**OR THE 1964–65 NHL SEASON, there was a new man in the Canadiens' front office. Sam Pollock succeeded aging Frank Selke as Montreal's general manager. In New York, Emile Francis, a successful junior operator in Guelph, Ontario, took over as general manager of the Rangers.

When Detroit left veteran goaltender Terry Sawchuk unprotected, the Leafs snapped him up. In Bower and Sawchuk, the Leafs had the oldest goalie duo in NHL history. Sawchuk was 34, while Bower, whose age was unknown, was at least 40. The two old-timers gave Toronto outstanding goaltending and allowed the fewest goals against. When the NHL awards were handed out, Bower and Sawchuk refused to accept the Vezina Trophy unless they could share it, and unless they each got the $1,000 bonus that went with it.

Roger Crozier, who succeeded Sawchuk in the Detroit nets, posted an impressive 2.42 goals-against average and won the Calder Trophy as top rookie. Ted Lindsay made a successful comeback with the Red Wings and scored 14 goals, silencing critics, including Clarence Campbell, who said his comeback attempt was "a big mistake."

The Red Wings captured their first NHL championship since 1957 and finished with 87 points, four more than the Canadiens. Chicago won third place with 76 points, only two points ahead of Toronto.

Chicago's Stan Mikita battled Norm Ullman all season for the individual scoring title and won the Art Ross Trophy with 87 points, four more than Ullman. Ullman scored the most goals — 42.

Series A between Chicago and Detroit saw the Red Wings win the first two games at the Olympia by scores of 4–3 and 6–3. Chicago bounced back with a pair of wins to tie the series. In game four Glenn Hall was brilliant in goal and Bobby Hull's game winner at 9:04 of the third period helped produce a 2–1 victory. Norm Ullman's three goals — two of them in a span of five seconds — paced Detroit to a 4–2 victory in game five, but the Hawks came right back to win game six 4–0 behind Hall's stellar netminding. Chicago eliminated Detroit at the Olympia, winning game seven 4–2. Mikita broke a 2–2 tie in the third period with the game-winning goal and Nesterenko added an insurance marker.

Series B between Toronto and Montreal became open warfare. In game one at the Montreal Forum, referee Vern Buffey called 37 penalties before the Canadiens completed their 3–2 win. The Leafs' Kent Douglas drew a match penalty for trying to decapitate Dave Balon with his stick. Bobby Rousseau, Jean Beliveau, and Henri Richard were the stars of game two, which also went to Montreal 3–1. Back on home ice, the Leafs' Dave Keon scored the overtime winner in game three, and Johnny Bower was sensational in game four, a 4–2 Leaf triumph. Red Kelly contributed a pair of goals in the win. Bower made one mistake in game five at Montreal; he allowed a 50-foot slapshot off Bobby Rousseau's stick to find his net, the winning goal in a 3–1 Montreal win. The biggest goal in game six came in overtime, when Claude Provost scored at 16:33 to beat Bower and the Leafs 4–3.

The final series between Montreal and Chicago opened at the Montreal Forum. The Canadiens had Gump Worsley in goal, playing in his first Cup final series in a dozen years. But they were missing Jacques Laperriere, who had suffered a broken ankle in the series with Toronto. The Black Hawks were forced to get along without two key injured players, Pierre Pilote and Ken Wharram.

Rookie Yvan Cournoyer scored the winning goal in game one, which went to Montreal 3–2, and Gump Worsley shut out the Hawks 2–0 in game two, a game in which neither team was in top form. Back in Chicago, the Hawks' Ken Wharram was back in uniform and his electrifying goal was the game winner in a 3–1 victory. Chicago came right back to win game four 5–1 to even the series. In that game, Charlie Hodge replaced Gump Worsley in the Montreal goal and gave up a 70-footer to Bobby Hull, a turning point in the contest. To no one's surprise, Toe Blake was livid over the officiating of Vern Buffey, who handed out 15 penalties to the Habs and only eight to the Hawks.

Charlie Hodge made up for a mediocre performance in game four by shutting out Chicago in game five at the Forum 6–0. John Ferguson pummeled Eric Nesterenko in a one-sided fight, and Jean Beliveau collected two goals. When the teams returned to the Chicago Stadium, the Black Hawks tightened up defensively and squeezed out a 2–1 victory to tie the series. Doug Mohns clicked for the winning goal midway through the third period.

Gump Worsley was back in goal for the critical seventh game at the Montreal Forum. Worsley blanked the Hawks 4–0, and the Habs scored all their goals in the first period. Beliveau scored after 14 seconds of play. Other goals came off the sticks of Duff, Richard, and Cournoyer. A new hockey award, the Conn Smythe Trophy, was awarded to the most valuable player of the playoffs, and the winner was Jean Beliveau, who scored eight goals in 13 games.

**I**N OCTOBER 1965, the NHL made a monumental decision — to double in size by expanding the league into six new cities. Joining the NHL in time for the 1967–68 season were franchise holders in Los Angeles, Oakland, Minnesota, Pittsburgh, Philadelphia, and St. Louis. The franchise fees were two million dollars per team. Canadian fans were irate when Vancouver's bid for a franchise was rejected, and there was talk of organizing a boycott of Molson beer, the major sponsor of hockey telecasts. Punch Imlach claimed Vancouver's bid was turned down because Montreal and Toronto would have had to share television revenues with a third Canadian team if it had become a league member.

The Leafs were pleased when Red Kelly gave up politics to concentrate on hockey. Ted Lindsay retired (for the second time), and so did Jacques Plante and Carl Brewer. Detroit defenseman Doug Barkley was forced to give up the game when he suffered a detached retina.

The season's big scorer was Bobby Hull of Chicago, who rammed in 44 goals in 45 games, then slumped a bit and connected for goal number 50 in his 57th game. On March 12 at the Chicago Stadium, Hull blasted a slapshot past Cesare Maniago to break the 50-goal record he shared with Rocket Richard and Boom Boom Geoffrion. The Golden Jet wound up with 54 goals and 97 points to win the scoring title, 19 points ahead of Stan Mikita and Bobby Rousseau, who tied for second.

With Hull to lead them, the Hawks battled with Montreal for the NHL championship but fell short by eight points. Toronto finished third, and Detroit, pennant winners in 1965, slipped to fourth.

Flying fists and body slams were featured in the opening-round playoff series between Toronto and Montreal, won by the Canadiens in four straight games. In game two, referee Bill Friday doled out 22 penalties, and in game four a 12-minute brawl resulted in 125 penalty minutes served.

Detroit had it almost as easy as the Habs in their semifinal matchup with Chicago, winning four games to two. Bobby Hull managed only two  goals in the series, mainly because of the pesky checking of Bryan Watson.

In the finals, Detroit stunned the Canadiens by winning the first two games in Montreal by scores of 3–2 and 5–2. Goalie Roger Crozier was outstanding in both games. Back in Detroit, Montreal winger Gilles Tremblay broke open a tie game with a pair of third-period goals and paced the Habs to a 4–2 win. Crozier was injured in game four and was replaced by Hank Bassen, who gave up the winning goal to Ralph Backstrom in a 2–1 Montreal win. In game five, the Red Wings couldn't keep up with the fast pace set by Montreal and bowed 5–1. Game six was tied 2–2 at the end of regulation time, and early in overtime Henri Richard scored a controversial goal that brought Montreal the

Stanley Cup. In attempting to score, Richard slid into the Detroit goal with the puck under his body. While the Wings howled in frustration, referee John Ashley ruled the goal was legal, and another Stanley Cup battle was over. The Conn Smythe Trophy was awarded to a member of the losing team, goalie Roger Crozier, who had played courageously despite considerable pain.

**T**HE BOSTON BRUINS took on a youthful look for the 1966–67 NHL season. Harry Sinden, 33, replaced Milt Schmidt as coach, and 18-year-old Bobby Orr signed a two-year contract for a reported $70,000 at a time when the average big-league salary was $15,000. Orr would enjoy a spectacular rookie season, winning the Calder Trophy and finishing third in scoring on the Bruins. But even with Orr on defense, the Bruins quickly fell into the league basement.

Boom Boom Geoffrion came out of retirement, joined the Rangers, and scored 17 goals. With Geoffrion, Rod Gilbert (fully recovered from spinal surgery), Phil Goyette, Don Marshall, Harry Howell, and Ed Giacomin, the Rangers had enough quality players to win fourth spot in the final standings. Going into the final weekend, they could have finished as high as second.

The Chicago Blacks, paced by Bobby Hull and Stan Mikita, finally won their first NHL championship with 94 points, a whopping 17 points ahead of Montreal. Toronto finished third with 75 points, three more than New York. Hull scored 52 goals, but it was Stan Mikita, with a record 62 assists, who captured the Art Ross Trophy. He also captured the Lady Byng and the Hart trophies, the first player to win three major awards in one season.

In Montreal a rookie goalie, Rogatien Vachon, filled in capably for Gump Worsley when Worsley was struck in the eye by an egg thrown during a game in New York.

Bobby Hull knew all about hockey injuries, especially at playoff time. In the past, he'd performed in postseason play despite bad knees, a broken nose, a bruised back, and an aching shoulder. On the eve of Chicago's opener in the semifinals against Toronto, he was nursing a badly bruised ankle and a damaged knee.

The Black Hawks were overwhelming favorites to eliminate Toronto from the playoff picture. The Hawks had been unbeatable on home ice all season against the Leafs. The pattern continued in the playoff opener at the Chicago Stadium, when goalie Denis Dejordy performed superbly in a 5–2 Hawk win. Hull was able to play but bowed out in the third period, complaining, "I ache all over. I feel 80 years old tonight." In game two, Leaf goalie Terry Sawchuk was the individual hero and turned aside all but one shot in a 3–1 Toronto win. The Leafs came right back to capture game three by 3–1, with Sawchuk again playing a starring role. In the pregame warm-up, one of Hull's slapshots sailed over the protective glass and smashed into the nose of Leaf owner Harold Ballard, breaking it in four places.

Chicago won game four at Maple Leaf Gardens by a 4–3 score to even the series. Ken Wharram got the Hawks off to a quick start by scoring nine seconds after the opening whistle, and Bobby Hull connected for the winning goal. Late in the game, Glenn Hall stopped a shot off Jim Pappin's stick, lost two teeth, and needed 25 stitches to close a deep cut on his chin. A Toronto reporter called the game "a spectacular show of drama, blood, and guts." Terry Sawchuk was the story in game five, a 4–2 Leaf win. "I saw him make those saves and I still can't believe it," said Bobby Hull. "We had enough chances to win six games." The Leafs ousted the Hawks by winning 3–1 two nights later, and once again Sawchuk played brilliantly.

Game one between the Canadiens and the Rangers in Series B produced a believe-it-or-not ending. With the Rangers leading 4–1 and eleven minutes left to play, the Habs suddenly caught fire. They scored three goals in just under two minutes to tie the score. Then Backstrom and Beliveau scored to win the game 6–4 and send the Rangers to their dressing room in stunned disbelief. The Rangers never recovered from their inexplicable first-game letdown and dropped the next three games. Suddenly their season was over. During the series, Ranger president Bill Jennings blasted referee John Ashley, calling him "incompetent" and "bush league." Two years earlier, Jennings had been fined $500 for breaking down the door to the referees' room and hurling abuse at Vern Buffey.

The Canadiens entered the Stanley Cup finals for the 16th time since the NHL became a six-team league in the 1942–43 season. They were undefeated in 15 games. Just before the opener, Punch Imlach told reporters: "You can tell that junior B goaltender Vachon he won't be playing against a bunch of peashooters when he plays against the Leafs." When Vachon allowed only two goals in a 6–2 victory, he said with a grin, "It was kind of Punch to mention me." Henri Richard scored three goals in the game and Yvan Cournoyer added a pair. Imlach gambled on Johnny Bower in game two and Bower stopped the Habs cold, shutting them out 3–0. Imlach was hoping for six goals in the game so that he "could shove it down their throats." Bower was superb, stopping three attacks on his body by John Ferguson. The first time Ferguson's stick sliced his eyebrow, the second time it cut across his nose, and the third time it left an ugly bruise on his collarbone. Ferguson said later, "They were accidents, just part of the game."

Bower was just as good in game three. In the second longest game ever staged at Maple Leaf Gardens, he stopped 60 shots and the Leafs nudged the Habs 3–2. Bob Pulford's goal after 28:26 of

*"Ageless" Johnny Bower juggles the puck and foils Boston Bruin Johnny Bucyk.*
(Turofsky)

overtime ended one of the most thrilling encounters seen in years.

In the warm-up before game four one of Bower's overworked leg muscles gave out and he was replaced in goal by Terry Sawchuk, who had an off night and lost 6–2. But the team that lobbed pucks past Sawchuk with nonchalant ease in the fourth game found him unbeatable in the fifth. Sawchuk, maligned and taunted two days earlier, was a masterful puckstopper at the Forum and spurred the Leafs to a 4–1 win.

Coach Toe Blake put Gump Worsley in the Montreal starting lineup for game six, even though he'd played only one complete game and parts of two others in the past three months. The gamble fizzled when Worsley gave up three goals to Sawchuk's one. Imlach's "Old Folks Athletic Club" had won the Stanley Cup. "This was the sweetest of my four Cups," commented Imlach.

**E**XPANSION BECAME A REALITY in the 1967–68 season, doubling the number of franchises from six to twelve. The six older clubs became members of the East Division, and the newcomers banded together in the West Division. After playoffs within the divisions, the surviving East Division team would meet the best from the West for the Stanley Cup.

When the West Division clubs drafted players from the existing teams to stock their rosters, some big names changed uniforms. Goalie Glenn Hall went to St. Louis and Terry Sawchuk was drafted by Los Angeles. The Philadelphia Flyers plucked two excellent young netminders from the Boston roster in Bernie Parent and Doug Favell.

Milt Schmidt, now Boston's general manager, pulled off a blockbuster deal with Chicago, acquiring Phil Esposito, Ken Hodge, and Fred Stanfield in return for Gilles Marotte, Pit Martin, and goalie Jack Norris. Esposito, Hodge, and Stanfield soon blossomed into prolific scorers in Boston.

Scotty Bowman began his coaching career with the St. Louis Blues, and Red Kelly, rookie coach of the Los Angeles Kings, guided his club to a 10–12–2 mark against Eastern opposition, the best record for a West Division club against the established teams.

New arenas sprang up. The $18-million Forum in Los Angeles opened in December, the $6-million Metropolitan Sports Center in Bloomington, Minnesota, became the home of the North Stars, and the $12-million Spectrum was home base for the Philadelphia Flyers. There was consternation when the roof blew off the Spectrum late in the season and the Flyers were forced to play "home" games in Quebec City and Toronto. The opening of the new $25-million Madison Square Garden in New York soon followed.

There were exciting races in both divisions. The Boston Bruins, hit hard by the expansion draft, became a surprise powerhouse in the East, but their drive for a championship was hampered by injuries to Bobby Orr and Ted Green. The Montreal Canadiens, in last place at Christmas, suddenly turned themselves around, rattled off 16 games without a loss, and grabbed first place, ahead of New York, Boston, and Chicago. The Philadelphia Flyers (32–33–1) failed to finish above .500 but still grabbed first place in the West, one point ahead of Los Angeles. St. Louis finished third and Minnesota fourth.

When Boston met Montreal in an East Division quarterfinal, fans anticipated a rough-and-tumble series. Boston had accumulated 1,000 penalty minutes during the 74-game schedule and Montreal 700. But the Bruins wilted in four straight games. New York grabbed a 2–0 lead over Chicago in the other playoff matchup, but the Black Hawks stormed back to win four in a row. "Jets against propellers." That was how Black Hawk coach Billy Reay described his team's 9–2 loss to Montreal in game one of the East Division championship round. Reay took a pair of foolish penalties in game two, one for calling referee John Ashley a "homer" and one for delaying the game. The penalties were a turning point and Montreal won 4–1. The Habs went on to eliminate Chicago in five games.

In the West Division, Philadelphia and St. Louis battled through seven games before the Blues won out. In game five, a third-period fight resulted in 49 minutes in penalties and $3,800 in fines. One of the stars in game seven was 43-year-old Doug Harvey of the Blues, who assisted on the winning goal.

Fans witnessed another thrilling seven-game series when Wren Blair's Minnesota North Stars met Red Kelly's L.A. Kings. In game seven, the Kings relied heavily on Terry Sawchuk, who was playing in his 100th playoff game. But Sawchuk was bombed in a 9–4 rout, and Minnesota advanced to the West Division finals.

Four overtime games highlighted the seven-game series between the North Stars and the Blues. Glenn Hall sparkled in goal for St. Louis, but Minnesota's Ron Schock was the series hero when he scored in the second overtime period of game seven to send the Blues into a history-making final series against Montreal.

The Canadiens had enjoyed a week's rest before they faced the leg-weary Blues in the final battle for the Stanley Cup. But despite losing four straight to the powerful Habs, the Blues made it a close, interesting series. Each game was decided by a single goal and two games needed overtime. The first of those was won by Bobby Rousseau, the second by Jacques Lemaire.

In winning the Stanley Cup on May 11, 1968, the Canadiens helped culminate the longest Cup hunt in history. It took 40 games to decide the winner. Immediately after the Canadiens' final 3–2 victory, coach Toe Blake announced his retirement. "I can't stand the pressure anymore," he said. At 55, the man who had spent 26 years in the Montreal organization, who had guided teams to nine league titles and eight Stanley Cups said, "I'd like to coach for another 100 years, but I can't do it."

When St. Louis goalie Glenn Hall was named winner of the Conn Smythe Trophy as MVP of the playoffs, Stafford Smythe was upset. "I don't think my father intended his trophy to go to a player from a team that failed to win a single game in the finals," he said. Many hockey officials were furious with vacationing Stan Mikita of Chicago for failing to appear at the trophy presentation luncheon. "Disgraceful" and "inexcusable" were verdicts delivered by one of the governors in discussing the center, who won three major awards for the second time.

**D**URING THE 1968–69 SEASON, scoring records tumbled around the league. Bobby Hull crashed through the 50-goal plateau for the fourth time and finished the season with 58. Even so, he was overshadowed by his former teammate Phil Esposito, who surged to the top of the scoring race and finished with an all-time high of 127 points. Hull finished second with 107 points, and Gordie Howe, an ancient 40 years old and in his 23rd season, astonished everyone by collecting a career-high 103 points for third place in the race.

There was an impressive individual record–tying performance in the East Division. Red Berenson of St. Louis scored six goals in a game against Philadelphia — his victim was goalie Doug Favell — to match a mark set 25 years earlier by Detroit's Syd Howe.

The Boston Bruins had become hockey's version of the Gashouse Gang. Their success was built around an explosive scoring machine coupled with muscle that intimidated many rivals. The Bruins won 42 games and collected an even 100 points, but they still finished three points back of the more consistent Montreal Canadiens. New York finished a strong third and Toronto was fourth. St. Louis again dominated the West Division, finishing on top with a 19–point bulge over runner-up Oakland. Philadelphia was third, Los Angeles fourth.

In Series A, the Rangers were primed to give plenty of trouble to the Canadiens, who were guided by rookie coach Claude Ruel. But it didn't turn out that way. New York proved to be an easy conquest for the Canadiens and folded in four straight games. In game three, Montreal trounced the Rangers 4–1. The defeat was the first for the Rangers on home ice in more than three months. Game four produced the first penalty-free playoff game in 18 years.

In Series B, the Boston Bruins humiliated Toronto 10–0 in game one. The Leafs' Pat Quinn dished out the game's hardest check when he smashed into Bobby Orr, whose head was down, and the Boston superstar fell unconscious to the ice. Several spectators tried to maul Quinn along the boards. Late in the game, Toronto's Forbes Kennedy ignited a brawl, half shoved, half punched linesman George Ashley, and was banished from the game. Kennedy was subsequently suspended and fined $1,000. He never played another game in the NHL. Toronto was eliminated in four games, and after the final match at Maple Leaf Gardens, Stafford Smythe fired general manager and coach Punch Imlach.

In the West Division, the Blues won the title. The Oakland Seals surprised many by grabbing second place while the Philadelphia Flyers, losers of only two of their final 15 games, were third. Los Angeles nosed out Minnesota and Pittsburgh for the fourth playoff spot.

In Series C, the Blues proved to be far too talented for the Flyers and captured the series in four straight games. Jacques Plante registered back-to-back shutouts in games two and three and almost clicked for a third in a 4–1 win in game four. With a perfect playoff record, the Blues sat back to await the winners of the Los Angeles–Oakland series.

Only 5,449 fans turned out to watch the opening game, won by the Kings 5–4 on Ted Irvine's overtime goal. Oakland won the next two games, then Los Angeles won a pair. The Seals took game five, but the Kings fought back with two straight wins to advance against the Blues. The long, difficult series had obviously sapped the strength of the Kings, for they bowed out of the contest against St. Louis in four straight games.

Meanwhile, the Boston Bruins and the Montreal Canadiens were producing scintillating hockey in the East Division playoffs. The Bruins outplayed the Canadiens in the first two games on Forum ice but still wound up with two overtime defeats, 3–2 and 4–3. Phil Esposito scored two goals and assisted on three more in game three as the Bruins trampled the Habs 5–0. In game four, Derek Sanderson paced the Bruins to a 3–2 victory but retired when John Ferguson nailed him with his knee. "He got me, too," complained Ron Murphy, "with a two-hander over the head. It's too bad the referee wasn't paying attention 'cause he missed a real good game." Rogie Vachon was sensational in game five, robbing Esposito half a dozen times, and Montreal moved into the series lead three games to two. The greenest rookie couldn't have been happier than Jean Beliveau was when he scored the winner in overtime in game six to eliminate the Bruins. Beliveau's marker at 11:28 of the second overtime gave the Habs a 2–1 squeaker and sent Montreal into the Stanley Cup finals for the 20th time. "If we skate like that in the next series with St. Louis, there is no way they can stay with us," said Beliveau.

It was true. The Canadiens overpowered and outlegged the Blues in four straight games to capture the Stanley Cup, which was getting to be known as "the Habs' family heirloom."

**T**HE FIFTY-THIRD SEASON of the NHL, 1969–70, was the longest in history and was packed with changes in team personnel. Red Kelly moved from Los Angeles to take over as coach in Pittsburgh. Hal Laycoe replaced Kelly in L.A., but after 24 games he was gone and Johnny Wilson moved behind the Kings' bench. Keith Allen, who had coached Philadelphia for two seasons, moved into the front office as assistant to manager Bud Poile, making way for Vic Stasiuk to coach the Flyers. Bill Gadsby, rookie coach of the Red Wings, saw his team win its first two games, then he was fired and Sid Abel took over.

The loss of Ted Green, seriously injured in a preseason stick-swinging scrap with Wayne Maki of the Blues, failed to slow down the Boston Bruins. Led by Bobby Orr, they smashed numerous records. Orr himself scored a record number of goals by a defenseman, 33, and collected 87 assists and 120 points, two more records. He became the first defenseman to win the scoring title and skated off with the Ross, the Hart, the Norris, and the Smythe trophies.

Chicago, a preseason bet to finish in the league basement, soared to the top of the East Division standing largely because of the splendid goaltending of rookie Tony Esposito, who had been drafted from Montreal. Both the Black Hawks and the Bruins finished with 99 points, but Chicago was awarded first place on the basis of more wins. Detroit finished third. New York, with a nine-goal outburst in the final game, beat out Montreal for the fourth playoff berth on the basis of more goals scored. Montreal's failure ended a 22-year string of appearances in postseason play and marked the first time no Canadian team was in the playoffs.

Scotty Bowman's St. Louis Blues clinched their second consecutive West Division crown. Red Kelly's coaching helped move Pittsburgh into second place, while Minnesota finished third. Philadelphia and Oakland tied in points for fourth place with 58, and the Seals won a playoff berth because of five more wins than the Flyers.

In the East Division playoffs, Chicago met Detroit in Series A and eliminated them in four straight games. Series B between Boston and New York was a lively affair, won by the Bruins in six games. Bobby Orr scored a pair of goals to lead Boston to a 4–1 victory in game six. Boston then met Chicago in what was expected to be a thrilling series, but the Hawks fell flat, showing little of the class they'd displayed against Detroit. The Bruins pushed them aside in four straight games.

The Blues and the North Stars fought through six games before the Stars succumbed. Meanwhile, the Pittsburgh Penguins were coasting to a four-game sweep of the Oakland Seals. When the Blues and the Penguins met for the West Division championship, St. Louis goalie Jacques Plante set a career playoff record for shutouts with 14. With Plante at his stingiest best, the Blues defeated the Penguins, four games to two.

But the Blues were in over their heads against Boston in the Stanley Cup finals. The opening contest, played in St. Louis, saw Jacques Plante knocked cold by a slapshot off the stick of Fred Stanfield. Some spectators thought Plante had been killed by the shot. Plante suffered a severe concussion and credited his face mask with saving his life.

The Blues, losers of all final-series games in two previous playoff engagements with Montreal, were just as frustrated against Boston. They were swept aside in four games, and on May 10 at the Boston Garden, the Bruins won the Stanley Cup for the first time since 1941. It seemed fitting that in the final game Bobby Orr took a short pass from Derek Sanderson and scored the winning goal after 40 seconds of overtime. The Bruins set a team record by winning ten consecutive playoff games.

Orr's series-winning goal, his ninth of the playoffs and 20th point — both Cup records for a defenseman — earned him the Conn Smythe Trophy as playoff MVP. "This is the happiest day of my life," he said with a grin. "We have a hell of a team, and let's hope we can do it all over again next year." Two days after a noisy Stanley Cup parade through the streets of Boston, Harry Sinden turned in his resignation and announced he was entering the business world.

# 10 The Savage Seventies

**F**OR THE 1970–71 SEASON, two new clubs joined the scramble for the Stanley Cup when Buffalo and Vancouver dutifully paid their $2–million entrance fees. All but three of the 14 NHL clubs were based in the United States. Punch Imlach was chosen to mold the Sabres into a contender, while Bud Poile, manager, and Hal Laycoe, coach, were in charge of the Canucks.

Boston defenseman Ted Green returned to action on the Bruin blueline after his near-fatal altercation with Wayne Maki during a preseason game in September 1969.

The Chicago Black Hawks were shifted to the West Division in 1971 after winning the league title in the East. They proved too powerful for the other clubs in their division, which consisted of expansion teams, and finished 20 points ahead of runner-up St. Louis. The Philadelphia Flyers grabbed third place, one point ahead of the Minnesota North Stars.

The Boston Bruins went on a season-long rampage, setting 37 team records and collecting a record 121 points, 11 more than the second-place Rangers. Montreal, under new coach Al MacNeil, settled for third place, and Toronto finished fourth.

Boston's Phil Esposito shattered previous marks with an amazing 76 goals and 152 points. "Never in my wildest dreams did I imagine a season like this," said Esposito. "Why, I said last

September there'd be less scoring this year because of the new rule limiting the curvature of the stick."

A new twist was added to the playoffs — a crossover series between East and West division teams in the semifinals.

When the postseason action got under way in the West, the Chicago Black Hawks — sparked by Bobby Hull's six goals — disposed of the Flyers in four games, while the Minnesota North Stars upset the St. Louis Blues in six.

In the East, the Bruins and Canadiens played one of the most dramatic series ever. The Bruins won the opener, despite a penalty call against Bobby Orr, who lost his poise and tried to attack referee John Ashley. Boston was winning game two 5–1 but incredibly blew the lead and lost the game 7–5. The Bruins came back to win the third game but lost the fourth. They won the fifth but lost the sixth. In the deciding game Montreal emerged with a 4–2 victory. It was one of the greatest upsets in Stanley Cup history, and much of the credit went to the goaltending of a tall, 23-year-old rookie, Ken Dryden.

The Rangers eliminated the Leafs four games to two in Series B. During a fight at Madison Square Garden in this series, Toronto goaltender Bernie Parent had his goal mask ripped off by Vic Hadfield. Hadfield threw the mask into the crowd and a fan ran off with it. Unable to play without the mask, Parent gave way to backup goalie Jacques Plante.

In one of two crossover series, the Black Hawks won a berth in the finals by dumping the Rangers in six games. In the other, Montreal took a tough, hard-won victory over Minnesota, four games to two.

The Canadiens climaxed one of their most dramatic Stanley Cup victories ever by winning the final series on the road. The combination of Henri Richard's scoring exploits and Ken Dryden's sensational goaltending led to a 3–2 Montreal triumph in game seven at the Chicago Stadium. The Habs won the deciding game after roaring back from a 3–2 series deficit and after trailing 2–0 in the final game.

The Canadiens' ascent from the previous season, when they finished out of the playoffs, to their 15th modern-day Stanley Cup a year later was an amazing feat. Dryden's phenomenal goaltending earned him the Conn Smythe Trophy, Frank Mahovlich set two playoff records with his 14 goals and 27 points, and Henri Richard said his game-winning goal in game seven was "the biggest goal of my life."

**W**HEN THE NHL opened its doors on the 1971–72 season, many of its most famous personalities had retired. Gordie Howe, 43, moved into the Detroit front office, and Jean Beliveau, 40, joined the Montreal Canadiens' management. Glenn Hall, 40, bowed out after 16 years' service, as did George Armstrong after 20 years in the league. John Ferguson, hockey's heavyweight champ, also called it a career.

Al MacNeil didn't survive in Montreal. Although Henri Richard had had his differences with MacNeil, he did say before the coach's firing: "I should have kept my mouth shut. I'll be very disappointed if Al MacNeil is not my coach when we gather next fall ... I mean that. If he's through, that's a crime ... a damn crime." Scotty Bowman took over as coach of the Canadiens and talked in glowing terms of a rookie draft choice named Guy Lafleur.

The NHL announced yet another change in the format for the Stanley Cup playoffs. Teams finishing first in each division would meet the fourth-place finishers. The old system had been first versus third and second versus fourth. The new arrangement was designed to provide further incentive for clubs to finish as high in the standings as they could.

At season's end the Philadelphia Flyers were the most disappointed team in hockey. They had been only seconds away from a playoff spot in the West Division. Buffalo's Gerry Meehan scored on them at 19:56 of the final period to give the Sabres a 3–2 win. Meehan's goal left the Flyers in a fourth-place tie with Pittsburgh but because the Penguins had the better won-and-lost record against the Flyers during the season, they walked off with the playoff berth.

Chicago won the West with 105 points, 19 points ahead of second-place Minnesota. St. Louis finished third with 67 points and

Pittsburgh was fourth with 66. In the East, the Boston Bruins were hot down the stretch and coasted to the division title with 119 points. The Rangers were close behind with 109 points, one more than Montreal. Toronto lagged behind in fourth place with 80 points.

Phil Esposito captured the scoring crown for the third time in four years with 133 points, including 66 goals. Both marks were the second highest ever recorded.

When the East Division playoffs got under way, the Rangers were hobbled by injuries to key players. Jean Ratelle was recovering from a broken ankle, Brad Park had fluid on his knee, and Rod Gilbert was a doubtful starter due to assorted aches and pains. Against the Habs, Ranger lesser lights blossomed. Pete Stemkowski, Bobby Rousseau, and Bill Fairbairn were the heroes as New York won the series four games to two. Walt Tkaczuk triggered the game- and series-winning goal in the Rangers windup 3–2 victory over the Habs.

The Leafs lacked scoring punch in their series with Boston and bowed to the Bruins in five games.

In the West, the Chicago Black Hawks, losers of only one of their last 17 regular-season games, swept Pittsburgh aside in four games, while the St. Louis Blues ousted the Minnesota North Stars four games to three.

The Black Hawks went on to meet the Rangers, and after a seemingly endless string of playoff disappointments, the Broadway club rewarded their supporters with a four-game sweep of the West Division champions. When the Rangers wrapped up the series with a 6–2 win on April 23, it marked the first time in 23 years that New York had clinched a playoff series on home ice.

The Blues' Cup hopes vanished in a crossover series with Boston. Veteran Bruin Johnny Bucyk led the way with six goals and six assists as the Blues were ousted in four straight games.

Bobby Orr, skating on a gimpy knee, dominated the Stanley Cup final series between Boston and New York. Boston captured the first two games on home ice; New York came back with a 5–2 win in game three, but Orr scored twice and assisted on the third

*Bobby Orr, the offensive Bruin defenseman who revolutionized the way hockey is played.*
(Robert Shaver)

Bruin goal in a 3–1 win in game four. The Rangers fought back — with Bobby Rousseau scoring twice — to win game five. In game six at Madison Square Garden, Orr scored one goal and assisted on another while Gerry Cheevers was busy recording a 3–0 shutout. At the final whistle the Bruins danced around the ice while the Rangers and their fans stared glumly at the jubilant Cup holders.

A huge crowd, estimated at more than 10,000 fans, pushed their way into every cranny of Boston's Logan Airport to greet the Bruins on their return home. When someone asked Phil Esposito what the difference was between the two Stanley Cup finalists, Espo laughed and said, "We had Orr, didn't we? Isn't that enough?" Orr collected over $22,000 in playoff earnings as well as a new sports car as the Conn Smythe Trophy winner. When all the partying was over, Orr announced plans to have off-season surgery on his knee, a setback that would keep him out of the much discussed September series with the Soviet Union.

**F**OR THE 1972–73 HOCKEY SEASON, the NHL welcomed two more franchises: the Atlanta Flames, with Cliff Fletcher as general manager and Boom Boom Geoffrion as coach, and the New York Islanders, with Bill Torrey in the front office and Phil Goyette behind the bench. The league had added ten new teams in a five-year span.

In September, hockey fever was at a peak when Team Canada faced the Soviet Union in a historic eight-game series that was decided in Moscow on Paul Henderson's dramatic winning goal with only seconds to play.

A new professional league — the World Hockey Association — grabbed several top NHL stars, including Bobby Hull, Gerry Cheevers, and Derek Sanderson, and there was the usual number of coaching and management changes. In Los Angeles Bob Pulford took over, in St. Louis Al Arbour was fired and replaced by Jean-Guy Talbot, and in Pittsburgh Red Kelly got the ax, with player Ken Schinkel taking over. Meanwhile, Bep Guidolin was called upon to replace Tom Johnson behind the Boston Bruin bench.

The NBC television network — with Tim Ryan, Hall-of-Famer Ted Lindsay, and your happy-to-be-there author — carried NHL games. During intermissions, Peter Puck, a popular cartoon character, explained hockey fundamentals and related some fascinating Stanley Cup stories.

When the 80-game schedule was over, the Buffalo Sabres became the first of the new expansion teams to knock an established club out of the playoff picture. The Sabres grabbed the fourth and final playoff berth in the East Division, squeezing in ahead of the Red Wings. The top team in the East was Montreal, losers of only ten games all season. The Canadiens met the Sabres in one East Division quarterfinal series, while the second-place Boston Bruins squared off with their old rivals, the Rangers, in another. When Montreal coach Scotty Bowman was told that his team was a heavy favorite to win the Cup, he said, "You know how the playoffs go. The team that gets the best goaltending often wins it all."

Montreal had trouble handling Buffalo in the first round, and Hab fans breathed a sigh of relief when the Canadiens won in six games. Buffalo coach Joe Crozier had feuded with Bowman throughout the series, but when it was over he walked off the ice with his arm around Bowman's shoulder. "Any man who coaches a team that loses only ten games all year has to be a hell of a guy," said Crozier.

In the Rangers–Bruins series, a crushing body check delivered in game two by New York heavyweight Ron Harris on Phil Esposito was the turning point in the series. Esposito limped off with torn knee ligaments and Boston hopes limped off with him. Chicago dumped St. Louis and Philadelphia took care of Minnesota in other opening-round play.

Montreal then eliminated Philadelphia in five games in a semi-final crossover matchup, while Chicago did the same to New York. After failing once more to advance, the Rangers' Rod Gilbert was almost inconsolable. "How could this happen to us again?" he asked. "It's been so long for us ... since 1940."

The world series of hockey between the Montreal Canadiens and the Chicago Black Hawks opened at the Montreal Forum on May 2. "Surprise, everyone, the Hawks are here," forward Chico Maki told Montreal reporters. "Were you guys among all those who wrote us off this season?"

Montreal scoring strength overpowered Chicago in game one. Chuck Lefley connected twice against Tony Esposito in an 8–3 rout. Yvan Cournoyer followed up in game two with a pair of goals in a 4–1 victory. On home ice, the Black Hawks scored two empty net goals in a 7–4 victory, but the shutout goaltending of Ken Dryden (3–0) in game four gave Montreal a stranglehold on the series.

Before game five back in Montreal, those of us involved in the NBC telecasts predicted a thrilling goaltending battle between two of the finest, Ken Dryden and Tony Esposito. In a bistro on the eve of the game, Lindsay, Ryan, and I stayed late at the bar. So did the two Chicago goaltenders, Esposito and Gary Smith. Midnight came and went, and more rounds were served. Finally, in the wee small hours, Tim Ryan could stand it no longer. He approached the Chicago netminders with words of advice. "You guys had better get to bed," he said bluntly. "Especially you, Tony. We expect a hell of a game from you tomorrow." The two puckstoppers laughed and signaled the bartender. "One for the road," they ordered.

What happened on national television the next day was one for the book — this book. Neither Esposito nor Dryden appeared capable of stopping beach balls as pucks flew past them like hailstones. Chicago won the game 8–7 as two floundering goalies helped set a new record for goals by two teams in a playoff game. Mistake followed mistake and it almost seemed as if the players were scoring on every shot. "We know where Esposito was last night," said Tim Ryan after the game. "Now I can't help wondering where the hell Dryden was."

The Canadiens won a 6–4 shootout on Chicago ice in game six. After falling behind 2–0, Henri Richard, the gritty little Hab captain, scored with 12 seconds to play in the first period. His marker gave the Canadiens a lift and they roared back to win the game and the Cup on Yvan Cournoyer's record-setting 15th goal. Cournoyer, one of the most dangerous shooters and scorers in the league, finally won his first major individual award — the Conn Smythe Trophy.

**I**F THE MONTREAL CANADIENS were going to make a serious bid for the Stanley Cup following the 1973–74 season, they would have to do it without Ken Dryden. The goalie stunned the hockey world by announcing his decision to retire, at least for one season, in order to article with a Toronto law firm. Equally stunning was news that Gordie Howe and his sons Mark and Marty had signed contracts with the Houston Aeros of the WHA.

Early in the season, Alex Delvecchio ended a 23-year playing career and replaced Ted Garvin as coach of the Red Wings. Bobby Clarke of the Flyers, at age 24, became the youngest team captain in NHL history. By February, Ned Harkness was all through as Detroit's general manager, replaced by assistant general manager Jimmy Skinner. In the same month, popular Tim Horton of the Buffalo Sabres was killed instantly when his Italian-made sports car left the highway and crashed.

Four Boston Bruins finished on top of the individual scoring race. Phil Esposito captured his fifth title with 145 points. He was followed by Bobby Orr with 122, Ken Hodge with 105, and Wayne Cashman with 89. With that kind of point production, it was no wonder the Boston Bruins captured the East Division title. They finished with a 14-point bulge over second-place Montreal. The Rangers were third and the Leafs fourth.

What a demonstration Philadelphia Flyer fans put on when the Flyers clinched first place in the West, ahead of heavily favored Chicago. Orange and black balloons floated down from the Spectrum rafters and fans roared their approval of the team that had accumulated 112 points. Los Angeles took third place, four points ahead of Atlanta.

In the playoffs, Boston had little difficulty pushing Toronto aside in their quarterfinal series. Goalie Gilles Gilbert, acquired from Minnesota a few months earlier, chalked up his first playoff shutout in game one. The Bruins tripped the Leafs 6–3 in game two and infuriated coach Red Kelly. "They're the worst trippers, hookers, fakers," fumed Kelly. "There isn't a team around that gets away with more than those guys." Kelly's rantings didn't upset the Bruins. They swept the Leafs aside by winning four straight.

The confident New York Rangers skated all over Montreal in game one of their matchup, winning 4–1. But Yvan Cournoyer scored a hat trick in game two to even the series. Two more goals by Cournoyer paced the Habs to a 4–2 victory in game three. The fourth game was a seesaw affair, decided on Bruce McGregor's goal followed by an empty-netter by Pete Stemkowski. The Rangers won 6–4. In game five a gamble paid off for the Rangers. Trailing 2–1 with a minute to play, Eddie Giacomin left his net, Brad Park's desperation shot was juggled by goalie Bunny Larocque, the puck squirted out to Bruce McGregor, who scored with 16 seconds left to play. New York's Ron Harris scored in overtime for a 3–2 triumph. The Rangers' Pete Stemkowski scored two empty net goals in game six to eliminate the Canadiens.

In the West, the Philadelphia Flyers handled Atlanta with ease in the first two games at the Spectrum. In Atlanta, a bench-clearing brawl erupted in game three and a hotly disputed Flyer goal so infuriated goalie Dan Bouchard that he shoved referee Dave Newell and swung his goal stick at linesman Neil Armstrong.

Bouchard got off with a misconduct penalty. The Flyers won the game 4–1.

A Bitter Bloodbath with the Broad Street Bullies was the alliterative headline of one newspaper describing the bristling crossover series between the Flyers and the Rangers. After Bernie Parent coasted to a 4–0 shutout in game one and three fluky goals led to a Flyer win in game two, the Rangers roared back with a resounding 5–3 victory. Ranger coach Emile Francis was furious with Dave Schultz for beating on Ranger favorite Rod Gilbert during the game.

In game four, the Rangers evened the series with a 2–1 victory in overtime on Rod Gilbert's goal. In this game, the Flyers' Barry Ashbee was struck in the eye by a Dale Rolfe slapshot. Your author, standing at rinkside with an NBC microphone, impulsively stepped onto the ice and was given a firsthand account of the injury by linesman Matt Pavelich. It marked the first — and last — time a broadcaster mingled with the players on the ice during a game. Your intrepid reporter was subsequently warned by president Clarence Campbell not to try it again. Ashbee, unfortunately, lost the sight in his eye and his NHL career was finished. Several months later he died of leukemia. The Flyers won on home ice two days later by 4–1, but the Rangers evened the series back in New York, also by 4–1. Bernie Parent's goaltending brilliance held the Rangers at bay in game seven and the Flyers won a close 4–3 decision.

Few shots, few goals, few problems was a succinct way to describe Chicago's advance to the Stanley Cup quarterfinals at the expense of the Los Angeles Kings. Chicago won in five games and outscored L.A. in the series by a mere 10–7. In game three, the Black Hawks were outshot 32–10 and still won by 1–0. The Hawks scored on their first shot on goal and managed only nine shots after that. "We never did get to see the Kings' goalie," said Dennis Hull with a chuckle. "Who was he, anyway?"

In the crossover series with Boston, the Hawks' airtight defense went missing. They were stung for 27 goals in the series, won by Boston in six games.

The final series for the Stanley Cup between the Flyers and the Bruins opened at the Boston Garden on May 7. The Bruins struck quickly and held a 2–0 lead after one period. The Flyers scored one goal in the second, and Bobby Clarke's goal tied the score in the third. At 19:38, just as overtime seemed inevitable, Bobby Orr blasted a shot past Bernie Parent, and Boston grabbed the opener 3–2. The second game started out like a carbon copy — Boston opened a 2–0 lead and the Flyers fought back to tie. But here the ending changed. After the Flyers' Andre Dupont scored to force overtime, Bobby Clarke was primed. He banged a rebound past Gilles Gilbert early in the first extra period and the Flyers celebrated a 3–2 win.

Back on Spectrum ice, the Flyers won two in a row to take the series lead, three games to one. But the Bruins weren't finished. They stormed back at home to win game five 5–1. But it turned out to be their final fling.

*Bobby Clarke, the Baron of the Broad Street Bullies.* (Robert Shaver)

When the teams met back in Philadelphia for game six, the pregame spotlight was on former singing star Kate Smith. Kate's rendition of "God Bless America" had been a good-luck omen for the Flyers dozens of times, and on this afternoon, before a nation-wide TV audience, Kate appeared in person. The arena lights dimmed, the spotlight picked her up on the ice, and she belted out her famous song. A tremendous roar from the crowd drowned out her final notes and the game was under way.

Unlike the other games in the series, game six wasn't marred by fighting and rough play. The fans were treated to fast, exciting hockey and outstanding goaltending. The Flyers scored a first-period goal, Rick MacLeish deflecting Dupont's hard shot behind Gilbert. In the third period, with the minutes slipping away, the goal by MacLeish became enormous. The Bruins put everything into a late charge, but Parent was unbeatable. The game ended unofficially when Bobby Orr took a controversial penalty for holding Bobby Clarke with less than two minutes to play. At the final buzzer, the Spectrum rocked with noise. The Flyers, with not one player in the lineup who had ever experienced a Cup victory, became the first expansion team to capture the famous trophy. No longer would Philadelphia be known as a city of losers.

"I've been around a long time," said winning coach Fred Shero as the champagne flowed. "I dreamed of this moment for 25 years, ever since I played for the Rangers and we lost the Cup to Detroit. This Flyer team may never be duplicated. They gave everything a man could ask for. And if you wanted more than that, then they simply came up with it."

Bernie Parent was named winner of the Conn Smythe Trophy. He collected $24,500 in bonus money and earned a three-word tribute from Phil Esposito. "Bernie was super," said the Boston sharpshooter.

**T**HERE WAS A NEW PLAYOFF look in the NHL for the 1974–75 hockey season. With two new clubs in the fold, Washington and Kansas City, the league had ballooned to 18 teams. Four divisions were formed, and the format looked like this:

### Prince of Wales Conference

| Adams Division | Norris Division |
|---|---|
| Boston Bruins | Montreal Canadiens |
| Buffalo Sabres | Detroit Red Wings |
| Toronto Maple Leafs | Los Angeles Kings |
| California Seals | Pittsburgh Penguins |
| | Washington Capitals |

### Clarence Campbell Conference

| Patrick Division | Smythe Division |
|---|---|
| Philadelphia Flyers | Chicago Black Hawks |
| New York Rangers | Minnesota North Stars |
| Atlanta Flames | St. Louis Blues |
| New York Islanders | Vancouver Canucks |
| | Kansas City Scouts |

It was announced that the final division standings, not points, would count for playoff positions at the conclusion of the 80-game schedule. The first three teams in each division would earn a playoff spot while the four division champions would get a bye into the quarterfinals.

A best-of-three preliminary round pitted the team with the most points against the team with the fewest points, the team with the second-highest point total against the team with the second-lowest point total, third highest against third-lowest, fourth-highest against fourth-lowest. Only the division winners would avoid the possibility of an upset in the preliminary round.

In the quarterfinals, the four survivors of the preliminary rounds would play the four division winners, again with the team with the highest point-total meeting the team with the lowest point-total, second-highest meeting second-lowest, and so on. The quarterfinals, the semis, and the finals would all be best-of-seven affairs.

The defending Stanley Cup champion Philadelphia Flyers finished the regular schedule with a tremendous rush, winning 12 and tying two of their final 14 games to wind up tied atop the overall standings with both Buffalo and Montreal. All three teams finished with 113 points, but the Flyers were awarded the championship on the strength of most wins — 51 to the Bruins' 49 and the Canadiens' 47. All three earned a playoff bye, as did Vancouver.

The eight teams in the preliminary round were Los Angeles (105 points) meeting Toronto (78 points), Boston (94) hosting Chicago (82), Pittsburgh (89) opposing St. Louis (84), and the Rangers (88) playing the Islanders (also 88 points but with fewer wins than the Rangers).

Individually in 1974–75, Boston's Bobby Orr won his second NHL scoring title with 135 points, breaking teammate Phil Esposito's four-year hold on the Art Ross Trophy. Montreal's Guy Lafleur became the first player in the 58-year history of the Montreal Canadiens to score more than 50 goals. Lafleur, with 53, was pleased when Rocket Richard phoned to congratulate him.

Three of the playoff favorites — Boston, the New York Rangers, and Los Angeles — ran into disaster in the preliminary round. The Black Hawks, thought to have only an outside chance against the powerful Bruins, bounced back from an opening 8–2 walloping to eliminate Boston with 4–3 and 6–4 victories. Tony Esposito made 52 saves in game three.

After the Islanders and the Rangers each won a game, the Isles' Jean-Paul Parise became the third-game hero, scoring the winning goal after just 11 seconds of overtime. Pittsburgh advanced to the quarterfinals with two straight wins over St. Louis while the Leafs upset the Kings 2–1 in games.

In the quarterfinals, the Leafs met the Flyers, the Penguins faced the Islanders, the Sabres opposed the Black Hawks and the Canadiens played the Canucks. The Flyers swept the Leafs aside in four games, the Buffalo Sabres ousted Chicago, four games to one, and Montreal eliminated the Canucks on Guy Lafleur's overtime goal in game five at the Forum. The New York Islanders amazed everyone by falling behind 3–0 in games to Pittsburgh, then storming back with four straight wins. Not since the Leafs stunned Detroit with a four-game comeback in 1942 had a team performed such a "miracle."

Home ice was a big advantage to both teams when Buffalo moved into the semifinals against Montreal. The Sabres won two games at home, then lost two at Montreal. Game five in Buffalo went into overtime before René Robert's shot ended it. The Sabres broke the home-ice jinx in game six by winning 4–3 at the Montreal Forum. Buffalo fans rejoiced. Their young Sabres had made it all the way to the Stanley Cup finals.

In the other semifinal, the Islanders appeared to have used up all their energy in their thrilling come-from-behind battle with Pittsburgh, because the Philadelphia Flyers defeated them three games in a row. Then the Isles began working on a second "miracle." They won game four, then game five, and then game six. The hockey world was spinning. Could the Islanders come up with one more big win?

The dramatic seventh game was held at the Spectrum. The Flyers trotted out Kate Smith to sing "God Bless America" and the game was only 19 seconds old when Gary Dornhoefer scored to put the Flyers in front 1–0. Then Rick MacLeish took charge and scored the hat trick to oust the storybook Islanders 4–1.

The "expansion" final between Philadelphia and Buffalo was expected to be a battle between Bernie Parent, the Flyers' last line of defense, and the Sabres' high-scoring French Connection Line of Gilbert Perreault, Richard Martin, and René Robert.

Parent was the victor as he stymied the Sabre attack repeatedly in games one and two at the Spectrum. Richard Martin was the only Sabre to beat him in game one as the Flyers scored a 4–1 victory. Bobby Clarke scored the winning goal in a 2–1 Flyer win in game two. On Buffalo ice, the Sabres came from behind to tie the score in the third period at 3–3 and force overtime. Near the end of the first overtime period, René Robert slapped the puck through the pads of the startled Parent, giving Buffalo a 4–3 win. The Sabres were in top form in game four and whipped the Flyers

4–2. When the series returned to Philadelphia, the Sabres were concerned about a Spectrum jinx: they hadn't won there since entering the league five years earlier. They were right to be worried. The Flyers jumped into an early 3–0 lead and never looked back, coasting to a 5–1 triumph.

Buffalo goalie Gerry Desjardins had looked a little shaky in game five so coach Floyd Smith switched to veteran Roger Crozier for the sixth game in Buffalo. Both goalies — Parent and Crozier — were spectacular through two periods, neither allowing a goal. Early in the third, the Flyers' Bob Kelly came from behind the Sabres' net and squeezed the puck into the far corner for the game's first goal. It was all the Flyers needed. They protected the lead well, and when Bill Clement whipped in an insurance marker late in the game, it was all over. The Flyers beat the harried Sabres with pure, clean, fundamental hockey. There were only two fights in the six games.

The Flyers, the first expansion team to win the Cup, had proved their 1973 win was no fluke. They sipped bubbly from the Stanley Cup once again and, two days later, were paraded through the streets of Philadelphia, this time with 2.3 million fans cheering them on. "Nobody likes us," said coach Shero. "Nobody outside of Philadelphia, that is."

Bernie Parent became the 11th winner of the Conn Smythe Trophy as playoff MVP. He was also the first player in Stanley Cup history to capture it two years running.

**A**T THE BEGINNING of the 1975–76 NHL season, Montreal coach Scotty Bowman said, "This season I want my players to think about winning the Vezina Trophy. In the past three seasons, the team winning the Vezina also won the Stanley Cup." Obviously Bowman's players got the message and were stingier than ever, helping Ken Dryden win the Vezina with a 2.03 goals against average.

But it was Montreal's offense that pleased Hab fans. The Canadiens won a record 58 games and chalked up a record 127 points. Star winger Guy Lafleur ended the 12-year monopoly of

Boston and Chicago sharpshooters in the individual scoring race and pulled away from runner-up Bobby Clarke to finish with 125 points and 56 goals, both records for a right-winger.

For the third straight season, the Philadelphia Flyers captured the Clarence Campbell Conference title and their own Patrick Division with 118 points. Boston won the Adams Division, and Chicago, on the final night of the season, skated off with the Smythe Division laurels.

When the clubs squared off in the best-of-three preliminary round, they were matched as follows: Buffalo, with the most points, met St. Louis, with the least; the New York Islanders, with the second-highest point total, opposed Vancouver, with second-lowest. The Los Angeles Kings, third-highest, met the Atlanta Flames, third-lowest, and the Toronto Maple Leafs, with the fourth-highest total hosted the Pittsburgh Penguins with the fourth-lowest total.

Both the Atlanta Flames and the Vancouver Canucks were swept out of the prelims in quick order. Between them they could manage only five goals in four games.

The Toronto Maple Leafs, backed by the extraordinary goaltending of Wayne Thomas, allowed the Penguins only two goals and an empty-net tally while winning their series two games to one. Buffalo had problems with lowly St. Louis when goalie Ed Staniowski led the Blues to a 5–2 upset in game one. The Sabres took the next two games, but both required overtime goals. Danny Gare scored the winner in game two and a Don Luce goal won game three.

After sitting around for several days while the prelims were being settled, the Montreal Canadiens launched an all-out attack against Chicago in the quarterfinals. The Habs overwhelmed the Black Hawks 13–3 in goals, swept the series 4–0, looked around, and said, "Who's next?"

The Sabres and the Islanders split the first four games of their series, both clubs winning at home. In Buffalo in game five, the Sabres watched with dismay as Bert Marshall — who hadn't scored a goal all season — knocked in the winner with just 19 seconds to play. Back on the Island, despite Punch Imlach's inspirational pep talk, the Sabres lost 3–2 and their season was over.

The quarterfinal series between the Leafs and the Flyers was one of the most controversial of all time. Flyers Joe Watson, Mel Bridgman, and Don Saleski were charged with criminal offenses following game three in Toronto. The trouble began when Don Saleski, seated in the penalty box at Maple Leaf Gardens, was mistaken for a spittoon by some irate fans. When Saleski rose and waved his stick, a policeman grabbed it and tried to yank it away from him. Saleski's teammates rushed to the area and Joe Watson did some stick-swinging of his own as fans scattered in all directions. Before the night was over, the teams had amassed 45 penalties, with the Flyers collecting 30 for a playoff record.

Watson was charged with common assault, assaulting a policeman, and possession of a dangerous weapon. Bridgman was charged with one count of assault causing bodily harm for battering Borje Salming in a one-sided fight, and Saleski faced two charges of common assault and one of possession of a dangerous weapon.

In game four, Borje Salming drew a three-minute standing ovation when he scored a dazzling goal to help sink the Flyers 4–3 and square the series. Don Saleski scored three times to pace the Flyers to a win in game five, and tempers erupted again in game six in Toronto. A total of 185 penalty minutes was called. Leaf captain Darryl Sittler ignored the rough play and scored a record-tying five goals against Bernie Parent. The Series was knotted 3–3. Leaf coach Red Kelly attributed the win to "pyramid power" and pointed to the special pyramids he'd placed under the Leaf bench. But Kelly's pyramids were toppled in game seven when the Flyers scored five third-period goals to sink the Leafs 7–3.

The Boston Bruins fought a grueling seven-game series with the Los Angeles Kings. Game six, played in Los Angeles, was described as the most exciting game ever played there. When the Kings won it 4–3 in overtime, their fans' applause went on and on, long after the players had left the ice. But the Bruins captured the deciding game; Brad Park and Jean Ratelle, acquired in a trade with New York earlier in the season, played key roles in the Boston victory.

In game one of the semifinals, the Bruins shocked the Flyers by winning 4–2 at the Spectrum. The win snapped a Flyer unbeaten streak of 24 games on home ice. But the Flyers dominated the Bruins in the next four games and won them all. Reg Leach was the triggerman on five of six goals in game six, a 6–3 Flyer win. Leach matched the five goals scored by Toronto's Darryl Sittler against Philadelphia a few nights earlier. Both players tied a play-off mark held by two Canadiens — Rocket Richard in 1944 and Newsy Lalonde in 1919.

Scotty Bowman's Canadiens, well rested after a long layoff, won the first three games of the semifinal series with the Islanders. The Islanders fought back with a 5–2 victory in game four but fell by the same score two nights later. After the traditional postseries handshakes, Islander coach Al Arbour said he was proud of his team. His four-year-old club had topped the century mark with 101 points. No team so young had ever reached that pinnacle before.

Montreal's attempt to wrest the Stanley Cup away from the Philadelphia Flyers began at the Montreal Forum on May 9. Guy

*A familiar sight in the 1970s — the Flyers brawling with the Canadiens.*

Lapointe's goal with less than a minute and a half to play gave the Habs a 4–3 victory in the opener. Ken Dryden lost his shutout bid in game two when Dave Schultz scored late in the third period. Still, Montreal won 2–1 and went two up in the series. When the series switched to Philadelphia, Steve Shutt scored a pair, and defenseman Pierre Bouchard notched the winning goal in the third period to move the Habs into a commanding 3–0 lead in the Cup finals.

Before the fourth game the Flyers threw everything at the Canadiens — pregame standing ovations, flashing floodlights, and the Flyers' perennial good-luck charm, Kate Smith; when Smith warbled before games in Philadelphia, the home team almost always won. Her record was 47–4–1. But all to no avail. Guy Lafleur scored the winner and Pete Mahovlich collected an insurance goal in a 5–3 triumph.

The Canadiens' run to the Cup was impressive. They had played a total of 93 league and playoff games, winning 70, tying 11, and losing only 12.

Reg Leach, a scoring phenomenon in the playoffs with 19 goals and 24 points, was awarded the Conn Smythe Trophy as the play-off MVP. He said, "The Canadiens have one hell of a hockey team. They've got guys who skate 400 miles an hour and there was no way we could keep up with them."

**B**EFORE THE 1976–77 SEASON opened, the NHL approved two franchise shifts for the first time in 40 years, permitting the California Seals to move east to Cleveland where they became the Barons, and the Kansas City Scouts to move west to Denver where they became the Colorado Rockies.

Several teams were in financial trouble. The Cleveland Barons were saved from bankruptcy by the players themselves, through the infusion of a $1.3-million loan courtesy of the NHL Players' Association. Speaking of money matters, Players' Association director Alan Eagleson informed his clients that the NHL teams would lose between $15 and $18 million over the course of the season.

A surprising off-season development was the decision of free agent Bobby Orr to sign a $3-million multiyear contract with the Chicago Black Hawks. Orr's departure from a city that adored him was reported to have cost the Bruins 5,000 fans per game.

The Montreal Canadiens put together a fabulous season, breaking ten records and tying another as overall champions of the NHL and winners of the Prince of Wales Trophy. They were the first team to win 60 games in a season and lost fewer games (eight) than any team in history. Both records still stand.

In winning the NHL scoring title, Guy Lafleur finished 14 points ahead of the Kings' Marcel Dionne. Ken Dryden and Bunny Larocque combined to win the Vezina Trophy.

The Philadelphia Flyers won their division and conference titles for the fourth straight season. Boston edged Buffalo by two points to win the Adams crown, and St. Louis captured the Smythe Division title. Ranger manager John Ferguson found it hard to accept that St. Louis finished with 73 points and earned a bye, while his Rangers, with just one point less, missed the playoffs in the tough Patrick Division.

Twelve teams made the playoffs, with the four division winners earning a bye through the best-of-three preliminary round. The closest thing to an upset in the prelims occurred when Toronto lost its only game at home but took both games on Pittsburgh ice to advance to the quarterfinals. Darryl Sittler figured in nine of the 13 Leaf goals against the Penguins. Before game three, Tiger Williams told a national TV audience: "Them Penguins is done like dinner."

The Islanders swept aside the Black Hawks in two games, Buffalo ousted Minnesota, also in two, and the Kings needed three games to get past Atlanta. The St. Louis Blues, champions of the Smythe Division, ran into Montreal in a quarterfinal matchup. It was a one-sided affair. Guy Lafleur sparkled offensively with five goals and seven assists as the Habs demolished the Blues in four straight games.

Goaltending was the story in the Islanders–Sabres series. Billy Smith was brilliant in goal for the Isles, while rookie Don

Edwards of the Sabres appeared to have playoff jitters. The Sabres went out in four games.

Experts predicted a low-scoring series between the Bruins and the Kings, largely due to the presence of Canada Cup-winning goalie Rogie Vachon in the L.A. goal. But just the opposite happened. The Bruins blitzed Vachon for 25 goals in the first four games. The Kings fought back with wins in games four and five, but in game six the Bruins whacked in three goals in the first eight minutes, then hung on for a 4–3 victory.

The Toronto Maple Leafs were underdogs in their quarterfinal series with the Flyers. After all, they hadn't won a game at the Spectrum since December 1971. The Leafs silenced the noisy Flyer fans by winning the first two games at the Spectrum and were leading 3–2 in game three on home ice with 38 seconds to play. Then Rick MacLeish dealt them a crushing blow, scoring a goal to tie the game and another in overtime to win it. The Leafs were shattered by what happened two nights later. They were leading 5–2 at 12:44 of the third when Bridgman scored. Then Bladon scored and Clarke tied it up with 16 seconds on the clock. Reg Leach came through with the overtime winner. Leaf owner Harold Ballard was steaming. "No team should blow leads like that," he fumed. The Flyers took the next two games to advance to the semifinals.

The Flyers ran into a snarling band of Bruins in the semifinals and bowed with barely a whimper. After posting two overtime wins at the Spectrum, the Bruins held the Flyers to just one goal in the next two games at the Boston Garden and dumped the once-proud Flyers out of the playoff picture.

Meanwhile, the Canadiens had to work extremely hard to eliminate the Islanders in six games. The Habs won the first two games, then were outmuscled by the Isles who won game three by a 5–3 count. His pride stung, the Canadiens' Ken Dryden shut out the Islanders 4–0 in game four. In game five, the Islanders again outbumped Montreal for a 4–3 win. Bob Gainey did all the scoring in game six, scoring one goal after just seven seconds of play to miss by a second the record for the fastest goal from the start of a playoff game. He scored again in the third period, and the Habs hung on for a 2–1 victory. The Islanders' season was over, but there were signs that they would make quite a hockey statement in seasons to come.

Montreal general manager Sam Pollock was concerned that the Islander series had taken its toll on his players and asked for a one-day postponement of the final series. His request was denied. But if his Habs were leg-weary, they didn't show it in game one when they thrashed the Bruins 7–3 at the Forum. "We had too long a layoff," explained Don Cherry, the colorful Bruin coach. Earlier he had said he welcomed the rest for his injured stars.

In game two, Ken Dryden earned a shutout, blanking the Bruins 3–0. After this game, Boston's John Wensink threatened to "cut off Guy Lafleur's ears" in a future meeting. In game three, the Bruins were too busy trying to keep pace with the Habs to worry about roughhouse play, much less Lafleur's hearing apparatus. The Canadiens struck for a 3–0 lead and skated off with a 4–2 victory to take a stranglehold on the series.

What turned out to be the final game provided the best hockey of the series, a fast-moving, hard-hitting affair that might have gone either way. The Bruins struck first when Bobby Schmautz beat Dryden with a clean shot after Dryden emerged from a pileup minus his face mask. Jacques Lemaire tied the score early in the second period and it remained deadlocked through the next forty minutes. At 4:32 of overtime, Lafleur chased the puck into the corner at the Boston end. Gary Doak left Lemaire unchecked in front of the net and moved on Lafleur. Lafleur hit Lemaire with a perfect pass and Lemaire's shot beat Cheevers, who had played brilliantly.

For the 20th time, the names of Montreal players would be inscribed on the Stanley Cup. After being awarded the Conn Smythe Trophy, Guy Lafleur, who led all playoff scorers with 26 points, said, "This is the biggest achievement of my career. But the trophy could have gone to any other player on our team."

Looking back on the season, Ken Dryden, 29-year-old goaltender of the Cup champions, expressed his concern for the lack

*Poetry on ice —
Montreal's Guy
Lafleur building
up steam for
one of his
patented end-
to-end rushes.*

of challenges facing the Canadiens. "I'm not complaining," said Dryden. "We had a great team and a fine record, but there were an inordinate number of games that we won without even a reasonable amount of difficulty."

New York Ranger general manager John Ferguson, who had beefed about the playoff system all season long, was delighted when incoming president John Ziegler announced that the NHL would borrow a page from the National Football League playoff book and adopt a "wild card" format for the coming season.

**I**N 1977–78 IT APPEARED for a while that six new teams would be joining the NHL. At a meeting in Chicago, the league agreed to bury the hatchet with the rival WHA and bring Cincinnati, Quebec, New England (Hartford), Edmonton, Winnipeg, and Houston into the fold. The merger would cost each WHA club $2.9 million. But at a later meeting in New York, a group of NHL owners led by Toronto's Harold Ballard squashed the merger plans. Furious at the snub, the WHA franchise owners vowed the war between the leagues would continue.

The NHL owners did agree on a new playoff format. Under the new procedure, the two top NHL clubs in each of the league's four divisions would qualify for postseason play. Four other teams would be admitted to the playoffs as "wild card" entries, based on their respective point totals.

It was inconceivable that the Montreal Canadiens could match their record of the previous season — 60 wins, just eight defeats, and a whopping 132 points. Still, they came close. When the 80-game schedule was complete, they had 59 wins and only ten losses for 129 points. The Habs had been beaten only three times in the past 50 games, and over the season they had established a record for consecutive games without a defeat — 28. The Canadiens finished on top of the overall standings for a record 19th time, holding a 16-point bulge over second-place Boston.

To emphasize the strength of the defending champions, midway through the season they traded Peter Mahovlich and Peter Lee to Pittsburgh for Pierre Larouche, a 50-goal scorer, and then couldn't find a regular spot for him in the lineup.

Guy Lafleur became the first Canadien to win the scoring title three times when he registered 60 goals and 132 points. He was only the second player to score at least 50 goals for four straight seasons. Phil Esposito had five 50-goal seasons with Boston.

A new name appeared on the Clarence Campbell Bowl. The New York Islanders ended the four-year reign of the Philadelphia Flyers as the best team in the Campbell Conference. The Isles soared to 111 points, six more than the Flyers. Center Bryan Trottier finished second to Lafleur in the scoring race with 123 points, and Mike Bossy set a scoring mark for rookies with 53 goals.

Two surprise teams made the playoffs under the new wild-card format — Detroit and Colorado. The Red Wings finished second to Montreal in the Norris Division with 78 points, one more than Los Angeles. Colorado found a nugget in rookie defenseman Barry Beck and finished second to Chicago in the Smythe Division.

In the best-of-three prelims, Philadelphia met Colorado, Buffalo played the Rangers, Toronto squared off with Los Angeles, and Detroit was matched with Atlanta. The Red Wings disposed of the Flames, Philadelphia pushed Colorado aside, and Toronto ousted

Los Angeles. All three series were over in two games. After the final Kings' game, owner Jack Kent Cooke fired coach Ron Stewart.

In the quarterfinals, the Boston Bruins bombed Tony Esposito for half a dozen goals in a 6–1 first-game victory. Boston coach Don Cherry warned his players about complacency. "Remember we shelled Chicago 8–2 in the playoffs of 1975," said Cherry. "And Esposito came back and murdered us in the next two games. It's a setup, I tell you." It was no setup. Boston won the next three games and Chicago's season was over.

Montreal disposed of Detroit in five games, and it took the same number for Philadelphia to eliminate Buffalo. For the third year in a row the Sabres had failed to go past the quarterfinals, and they looked back on only one win in 17 quarterfinal starts. "The Sabres will have a new look next season," vowed their general manager Punch Imlach. "If we're going to lose, there's no sense losing with the same faces every year."

The Flyers advanced into the semifinals against the Boston Bruins, hoping to relive the glory days of their Cup championships in 1974 and 1975. The Bruins jumped into the series lead, winning the first two games at the Boston Garden. Before game three in Philadelphia, the Flyers pulled a surprise by playing Kate Smith's "God Bless America." Earlier in the season, Kate sang before a Penguin game and the match ended in a tie. "If all she can do is tie Pittsburgh," said a Flyer spokesman, "maybe it's time for the old girl to step aside." But this time the Smith magic worked; the Flyers beat Boston and Kate was credited with her 50th win.

The Bruins came through with a 4–2 triumph in game five and, with Gerry Cheevers playing a sensational game, ended the Flyers' season with a 6–3 victory in game six. When reminded that the Bruins had beaten the Flyers in eight of their past nine playoff meetings, Don Cherry said, "That's right. And Cheevers has personally won four of those games for us."

Meanwhile, the Toronto Maple Leafs and the New York Islanders were thrilling their fans in a quarterfinal series that wasn't decided until overtime of the seventh game. "Them Islanders is worse than done dinner," predicted Toronto's Tiger Williams before game one. "They're burnt toast." Tied 1–1 after 60 minutes, the Islanders got a big break early in the overtime when Billy Harris raced in alone, only to be foiled by goalie Mike Palmateer. Seconds later, Lanny McDonald got a similar opportunity at the other end. He didn't miss, beating Chico Resch for the series-winning goal.

The Leafs moved on to meet Montreal in the semifinals, but the series turned out to be a one-sided affair. The Canadiens had too much firepower and the Leafs, weakened by injuries and exhausted after the grueling series with the Islanders, went down in four straight games.

Don Cherry's "lunch bucket" Bruins were eager to take on the Canadiens in the Stanley Cup finals. At the Montreal Forum, Boston's Brad Park scored early in the first period of the opener, but the Habs stormed back with four straight goals and won 4–1. In game two, the Bruin checkers hounded Guy Lafleur through 60 minutes of a 2–2 tie and on into overtime. But suddenly the scoring champ found a bit of skating room and drilled a shot past Cheevers for a 3–2 Montreal win. Boston fought back on home ice with Cheevers registering a 4–0 shutout.

The Bruins' Bobby Schmautz was the hero in game four. His goal after 6:22 of overtime gave Boston a 4–3 win and tied the series at 2–2. The Bruins appeared to have the game won in regulation time but Lafleur golfed the puck behind Cheevers with 33 seconds left in the third period.

Back at the Forum for game five, Montreal's Larry Robinson scored an early goal after a spectacular rush, and the Habs never looked back. They won 4–1. A standing ovation greeted the Bruins before game six in Boston, and another ovation followed Brad Park's opening goal on the power play. After that, Bruin fans were silenced. Steve Shutt tied the score, Mario Tremblay scored two goals and Rejean Houle added another as Montreal triumphed 4–1, capturing the series four games to two. Once again, the Canadiens lifted the Cup high — this time at the Boston Garden.

"It was Larry Robinson who killed us," stated Don Marcotte, who had neutralized Guy Lafleur throughout most of the series. Robinson collected 21 playoff points and won the Conn Smythe Trophy.

After fledgling NHL president John Ziegler presented the Canadiens with the Cup, he wandered into the Bruins' dressing room to congratulate the losers. As he shook hands with several of the players, Rick Middleton nudged a teammate and asked, "Who the hell is that guy?"

**B**EFORE THE NEW SEASON, 1978–79, began, the owners of the Cleveland Barons, George and Gordon Gund, cast about for a new home. They discussed a merger with both Vancouver and Washington and were rebuffed, but made a deal with Minnesota. The Barons merged with the North Stars and the Cleveland franchise folded. At the entry draft, the North Stars added even more strength by selecting center Bobby Smith number one overall.

Molson Breweries of Canada purchased the Montreal Canadiens for $20 million from Carena-Bancorp, Inc., after which general manager Sam Pollock retired. He was replaced by Irving Grundman. The troubled Colorado Rockies had a new owner, Arthur Imperatore of New Jersey, and the Washington Capitals had attendance problems with average crowds under 7,000, down an average of 3,800 from the season before.

The Rangers introduced a new coach in Fred Shero, and two new Swedish stars, Anders Hedberg and Ulf Nilsson, formerly of the WHA Winnipeg Jets. Scouts from Toronto and Chicago went to see Wayne Gretzky play in the WHA and were unimpressed. "Too small," they concluded. "Not likely ever to make it in the NHL."

On November 8, Bobby Orr retired after a 12-year pro career that saw him shatter numerous records. He had won the Norris Trophy as the NHL's top defenseman eight times.

The 1978–79 season featured a sizzling three-way race for first place overall between the Montreal Canadiens, the Boston Bruins, and the New York Islanders. The Islanders won the honors, ending the three-year domination of the Canadiens. The Isles were led throughout the season by Bryan Trottier (134 points), Mike Bossy (69 goals), Denis Potvin, and goaltenders Billy Smith and Chico Resch.

In the preliminary round of the 1979 playoffs, Philadelphia eliminated Vancouver two games to one, Toronto pushed Atlanta aside 2–0, Pittsburgh defeated Buffalo 2–1, and New York held L.A.'s Triple Crown Line of Dionne, Taylor, and Simmer to a single goal and swept the Kings in two games.

In quarterfinal play, three of the four series ended after the minimum four games. Montreal swept past Toronto, Boston ousted Pittsburgh, and the Islanders ended Chicago's season. In the fourth series, the Rangers outscored Philadelphia 28–8 and won the round 4–1.

The Rangers, seeking their first Stanley Cup in 39 years, overcame a major obstacle in the semifinals, upsetting the Islanders in a tense six-game series. Outstanding goaltending by John Davidson was a key factor in the Ranger triumph. Through six games in the other semifinal series between Montreal and Boston, home ice meant wins for both teams. Game seven in Montreal appeared to be in the Bruins' grasp when, with just 3:59 to play, Rick Middleton scored on a power play, sending Boston into a 4–3 lead. But incredibly, Don Cherry's club was caught with too many men on the ice. The Bruins were just 74 seconds away from victory when Guy Lafleur's power-play goal sent the match into overtime. During the first extra period, Yvon Lambert drilled a shot off the pads of goalie Gilles Gilbert for a 5–4 Montreal victory.

"I can't describe to you how I felt," said the thunderstruck Cherry after the astonishing faux pas that led to the Bruins' defeat. "I couldn't believe it. I wanted to sit down and cry." Harry Sinden, his boss, wanted to cry, too. Instead he fired Cherry, despite the coach's five-year record of 231–105–64.

When the New York Rangers faced the Montreal Canadiens in the final series for the Stanley Cup, their goalie, John Davidson, was nursing a gimpy left knee. Davidson and the Rangers kept the injury a secret, and the gritty goaltender dragged his aching leg through five tough games. In game one, New York capitalized on Montreal mistakes and skated off with a 4–1 win. Ulf Nilsson was a Ranger star in the game, back in the lineup after breaking an ankle only ten weeks earlier. The Rangers opened up a 2–0 lead in game two and then watched in dismay as the Canadiens fought back for a 6–2 victory. Montreal came right back with a 4–1 decision in game three. In game four, Bob Gainey and Ranger captain Dave Maloney collided violently in the 46th minute of play. Maloney went down, while Gainey skated away with the puck and slipped it behind Davidson to tie the score 3–3. Larry Robinson's shot in overtime zipped in and out of the Ranger net so fast that it escaped the notice of the goal judge and referee Andy Van Hellemond. The Habs howled but to no avail, and another blast, this time from Serge Savard, ended the game 4–3.

More than 18,000 fans jammed the Montreal Forum for game five, hoping to see the Canadiens win their first Stanley Cup at home since 1968. They weren't disappointed. After Montreal's Rick Chartraw and New York's Carol Vadnais traded goals, Jacques Lemaire drilled a long shot past Davidson in the opening seconds of the second period. Then Rejean Houle set up two goals, one by the tireless Bob Gainey and the other by Lemaire, and the Habs captured their eighth Cup in 12 years.

# 11 The High-flying Eighties

**T**HE STANLEY CUP BELONGED to two teams in the eighties. In the first half of the decade, the New York Islanders captured hockey's highest award with four consecutive wins. Then Wayne Gretzky led the Edmonton Oilers to triumph in five of the next seven seasons.

A number of remarkable players excelled during the decade. The "boy wonder" of hockey, Wayne Gretzky, joined the league for the 1979–80 season and began smashing every record in sight. In 1984, arriving with a lot of hoopla and an amazing amount of talent, Mario Lemieux began turning the Pittsburgh franchise around. Messier, Coffey, Trottier, Bossy, Lafleur, Dionne, Hawerchuk, and Czech defector Peter Stastny were some of the other superstars of the decade.

Three other brilliant performers faded from the scene in the eighties. After 32 years as a pro, Gordie Howe ended his incredible career, one that encompassed five decades, 801 goals, and 1,767 regular-season games. Before finally bowing out, Gordie lined up on March 20, 1980, with his sons Mark and Marty in a memorable game between the Whalers and the Red Wings — an NHL "first." Bobby Hull also called it quits after 16 NHL seasons and 610 career goals.

For the 1978–79 NHL season, the NHL expanded to 21 teams, adding four clubs from the defunct World Hockey

Association. The league rearranged its divisions to make room for Hartford, Quebec, Winnipeg, and Edmonton. Washington moved from the Norris to the Patrick Division to accommodate Hartford in the Norris. Quebec was added to the Adams Division as a fifth team, and the Smythe Division welcomed Winnipeg and Edmonton.

There was plenty of reshuffling within the teams, as well. Scotty Bowman was hired as the Buffalo Sabres' general manager with the hope that the success he'd achieved in Montreal — five Stanley Cup wins — would rub off on the Sabres. The Toronto Maple Leafs brought back Punch Imlach as general manager after attempting to sign Don Cherry as coach. Cherry was already committed to a multiyear contract with the Colorado Rockies.

The season was marked by one of the biggest Leaf trades in over a decade. Punch Imlach swapped popular right-winger Lanny McDonald and defenseman Joel Quenneville for left-winger Pat Hickey and right-winger Wilf Paiement from the Rockies. Leaf leader Darryl Sittler was so distressed at losing McDonald, his best friend and linemate, that he resigned as Leaf captain.

By midseason the Philadelphia Flyers' record of 25 wins and ten ties was the longest undefeated streak in North American professional sports history. The streak was punctured on January 7 when the Minnesota North Stars bounced the Flyers 7–1. The Flyers captured first place overall with 116 points and finished with a 48–12–20 record.

The Edmonton Oilers ended their rookie NHL season by clinching the 16th and final playoff position. They won eight of their last 11 games and were paced by 19-year-old newcomer Wayne Gretzky, who scored 51 goals and tied Marcel Dionne for scoring honors with 137 points. However, Dionne was awarded the Art Ross Trophy on the basis of more goals (53). Gretzky was further disappointed when he was ruled ineligible for the rookie award because of his brief career in the WHA. The Calder was won by Quebec's Peter Stastny, who was eligible despite having been a world-class player for years in his native Czechoslovakia.

The best-of-five preliminary rounds in the playoffs matched the first-place club with the 16th-place finishers, second-place versus 15th, and so on. The outcome was predictable when the first-place Flyers swept past the Oilers in three games. The Canadiens pushed the Whalers aside, Chicago ousted St. Louis, the North Stars whipped the Leafs, the Islanders knocked off the Kings, the Rangers had no trouble with Atlanta, the Bruins eliminated the Penguins, and the Sabres overpowered the Canucks. In game three of the Vancouver-Buffalo series, Sabres' coach Scotty Bowman was knocked unconscious by the stick of Dave "Tiger" Williams. Williams claimed the blow was "unintentional," but he was still slapped with a one-game suspension.

Bowman became the winningest coach in Stanley Cup history when the Buffalo Sabres won the first two games of their quarter-final series with the Chicago Black Hawks. The Sabres swept the series in four straight games. The underdog Minnesota North Stars needed seven games to overthrow the mighty Montreal Canadiens. It was the first time the Canadiens had lost the seventh game of a playoff series on home ice and marked their earliest elimination since 1974. Meanwhile the Philadelphia Flyers ousted the New York Rangers 4–1 and the Islanders disposed of the Bruins by the same margin.

In the semifinals, the Islanders' roll continued as they took the first three games from Buffalo. But Buffalo battled back to capture the next two. With the teams evenly matched, the presence of Butch Goring, acquired from Los Angeles at the trade deadline, seemed to give the Islanders the deciding edge. They knocked the Sabres out with a win in game six. In other action, the Minnesota North Stars looked as if they were primed for another upset when they beat the Philadelphia Flyers 6–5 in the first game of the series. But the Flyers caught fire and silenced Minnesota's Stanley Cup chatter by sweeping the next four games.

On May 13, the Stanley Cup finals between the Islanders and the Flyers opened at the Spectrum in Philadelphia. Denis Potvin's goal in overtime gave the Isles a 4–3 win in game one. The next three games weren't so close. The Flyers destroyed the Isles in game two with an 8–3 decision to even the series. New York prevailed in the next two games, scoring five power-play goals in game three to defeat the Flyers 6–2, and winning 5–2 in game four. But the Flyers battled back to beat the Islanders 6–2 in game five.

The sixth game was both thrilling and controversial. First, Philadelphia protested that Denis Potvin should have been called for a high-stick goal when he hit a waist-high pass from Mike Bossy past Pete Peeters to tie the game at 11:56 in the first period. The protest fell on deaf ears. The second dispute was a legitimate claim by the Flyers that rookie Duane Sutter was a foot offside when he scored the go-ahead goal for the Isles less than three minutes later. Despite the missed call by linesman Leon Stickle, the Flyers battled back to tie 2–2 on a goal by Brian Propp. No sooner had Philadelphia tied it than New York leaped ahead with goals from Mike Bossy and Bob Nystrom. The Flyers' Bob Dailey and John Paddock put the puck past Islander goalie Billy Smith and forced the game into overtime.

*One of the keys to the New York Islanders' four straight Cups was goaltender Billy Smith.*

At the 7:11 mark — a gambler's number — of sudden-death play, John Tonelli fed Bob Nystrom a perfect pass, which Nystrom promptly blew by Philadelphia's Pete Peeters. The goal gave the Islanders the game and their first Stanley Cup in the seven-year history of the club. General manager Bill Torrey summed up the Islanders' quest for the Cup when he said in postgame celebrations, "Nobody gave the Stanley Cup to us. We beat Boston and Buffalo and Philadelphia — three of the top four teams. Nobody can say we're not the best."

IN 1980–81 RETIREMENT after 18 years in the league was a sudden, midseason decision for Phil Esposito of the New York Rangers. The star sharpshooter recorded 717 goals and a point total of 1,590, second only to Gordie Howe. Also retiring was Dave Schultz. At the time, "The Hammer" had the distinction of being the most penalized player in the history of the NHL, with 2,294 penalty minutes in just nine years.

Islander right-winger Mike Bossy enjoyed a fantastic season. In a game against Quebec, he became only the second player in history to score 50 goals in 50 games. His 50th goal, his second of the game, came with less than two minutes left in regulation time. The only other player to achieve this feat was Montreal's Maurice Richard more than 30 years earlier.

Toward the end of the season, Bossy's Islanders were unstoppable as they swept their last 13 games. Their tally for the year was 110 points, which was three better than St. Louis and seven ahead of the Canadiens. In sharp contrast was Winnipeg's hopeless season, in which they won only nine games.

Wayne Gretzky finished his sophomore season with several more entries in the record book. His final goal of the season gave him a career total of 301, a plateau that he reached faster than anyone else in history. The Great One also topped the record for most points in a season with 164, and established four other NHL marks.

In the preliminary round of the 1981 playoffs, the first-place New York Islanders whipped the Toronto Maple Leafs in three straight games. Bryan Trottier and Mike Bossy teamed up for ten goals in the series.

The North Stars bounced the Bruins, Buffalo ousted Vancouver, and Calgary eliminated Chicago — all in the minimum number of games. The Rangers eliminated the Kings in four games, while St. Louis needed five to stop Pittsburgh. The Philadelphia Flyers defeated the Quebec Nordiques three games to two. In the most exciting preliminary series, the 15th-place Edmonton Oilers stunned the third-place Canadiens by winning the three-game series. Paul Coffey of the Oilers later summed up what the Canadiens were thinking. "I guess the pesky Oilers have come of age," he said. Hab coach Claude Ruel was so appalled at the Oiler victory that he resigned, vowing never to coach again.

The Oilers looked as though they were ready to spring another upset in their best-of-seven quarterfinal series against the Islanders. Despite their inexperience — four 20-year-old forwards, a 19-year-old defenseman, and a 21-year-old goalie (Andy Moog), who was in the Central League a month earlier — Edmonton pushed the series to six games before bowing to the regular-season champs. In other playoff action, the Flames-Flyers matchup went seven games, with Calgary emerging as winners. The Rangers were victorious over the Blues 4–2, and Minnesota breezed by Buffalo 4–1.

In semifinal action the underdog Minnesota North Stars eliminated the seventh-place Calgary Flames 4–2. The battle of the two New York teams resulted in the Islanders outskating the Rangers and winning the series in four straight. "I think you'd have to say we're a great team," said confident Islander Denis Potvin.

The Stanley Cup came down to a contest between the first-place New York Islanders and the ninth-place Minnesota North Stars. The Islanders dominated the first three games, whipping the North Stars 6–3, 6–3, and 7–5. Faced with elimination, the North Stars responded with a 4–2 victory. The mighty Islanders then made short work of the Stars, as they roared to a 5–1 win and their second Stanley Cup in as many years. The ice was covered with confetti as the Islanders rejoiced around the Cup. Bryan

Trottier spoke for them all: "I wish everyone who plays hockey could know the feeling of winning the Stanley Cup. You win it once and you get greedy. You want to keep on winning it over and over again."

The ten playoff goals of Conn Smythe Trophy winner Butch Goring helped lead the Islanders to victory, but they paled in comparison to Minnesota left-winger Steve Payne's feat of 17 goals in the playoffs. Payne was philosophical about the Minnesota defeat, saying, "We need a little more experience and consistency to go all the way. And that will come. The playoffs this year will give us that." Despite his goal production, Payne wasn't the playoff scoring leader. Mike Bossy took top honors with 35 points from 17 goals and 18 assists.

**T**HE **1981–82 SEASON** once again saw changes to the NHL structure, including a revised 80-game schedule, a new playoff format, and a major shuffling of the divisions. When the restructuring was complete, the divisions shaped up as follows:

**Clarence Campbell Conference**

| **Norris Division** | **Smythe Division** |
|---|---|
| Detroit | Calgary |
| Chicago | Edmonton |
| Minnesota | Los Angeles |
| St.Louis | Colorado |
| Toronto | Vancouver |
| Winnipeg | |

**Prince of Wales Conference**

| **Patrick Division** | **Adams Division** |
|---|---|
| New York Islanders | Boston |
| New York Rangers | Montreal |
| Philadelphia | Hartford |
| Pittsburgh | Quebec |
| Washington | Buffalo |

Not only did the teams within each division change, but the makeup of the conferences was altered, as well. In previous seasons the Norris and Adams divisions had made up the Wales Conference. This year the Adams and Patrick divisions made up the new-look Wales Conference, while the Campbell Conference was composed of the Smythe and Norris divisions.

The New York Rangers signed Herb Brooks as new head coach, famous for his United States team's gold-medal victory at the Lake Placid Olympics. Winnipeg recruited Tom Watt, while Colorado signed Bert Marshall. Montreal welcomed Bob Berry, and Parker MacDonald filled the gap in the Kings' organization left by Berry.

The NHL enjoyed an outstanding season from many of its top players. For the first time in league history, ten players had 50-plus goal seasons, while 13 players reached the 100-point plateau. Still, Wayne Gretzky stood out for his amazing personal accomplishments. On December 27 Gretzky surpassed the 50-goal mark in a record 39 games when he scored five times in a 7–5 Oiler triumph over the Philadelphia Flyers. Gretzky's talent continued to shine throughout the season. He tied Phil Esposito's record of 76 goals in a single season, but achieved the plateau in 15 fewer games. In front of a wild hometown crowd, and with less than four minutes left to play, Gretzky scored the record-tying goal against the Detroit Red Wings. Just three nights later, on February 24th, he surpassed the 76-goal mark by belting three goals past the Buffalo Sabres. Gretzky went on to finish the season with 92 goals and 120 assists, both NHL records. His record point total of 212 was an amazing 65 points higher than the 147 accumulated by Mike Bossy of the Islanders.

Even Gretzky's awesome production, however, wasn't enough to lead the Oilers to first place overall. That title went to the Islanders for the second year in a row. The Isles finished with 118 points, seven more than the Oilers. The Winnipeg Jets, under coach Tom Watt, fashioned a record turnaround from the previous season and waltzed into second place in the Norris Division with 80 points.

Abandoned this season was the overall points system as a standard for the playoff format. Instead, the top four teams in each of the divisions qualified for postseason play, meaning that some teams might finish out of the playoffs despite having higher point totals than other teams that qualified. There was much criticism of the new format, especially after upsets occurred in half of the first-round playoff matchups.

The Smythe Division was rocked when second-place (overall) Edmonton was victimized by 17th-place Los Angeles in five games. The clubs set a playoff record of 18 goals in the opener, a game won by the Kings 10–8. Media critics minced no words after the sudden Oiler collapse. Terry Jones, a columnist for the *Edmonton Journal*, wrote: "From today until they've won a playoff series again, they are weak-kneed wimps who thought they were God's gift to the NHL but found out they were nothing but adolescent, front-running good-time Charlies who couldn't handle adversity."

In the other Smythe Division series, the Vancouver Canucks knocked off the Calgary Flames with three straight wins. The Canucks then proved it was no fluke by pasting Los Angeles in four games to win the Smythe title.

There was a bigger surprise in the Norris Division when the Black Hawks, who ended their season a dismal eight games under .500, upset Minnesota in four games. The North Stars had finished 22 points ahead of the Hawks. In the other matchup, the St. Louis Blues ousted the Jets in four games. The Blues' hopes of advancing to the Campbell Conference final were shattered when the Hawks took the division finals 4–2.

The Patrick Division was filled with exciting playoff action. John Tonelli of the Islanders dazzled the Pittsburgh Penguins by scoring the game-tying goal in game five with less than three minutes to play. Tonelli came right back with a sensational overtime goal to cement an Islander victory. In the other division series, the Rangers eliminated the Flyers in four games. The Rangers proved to be formidable opponents in the division finals, but in the end it was the Islanders who gained a trip to the conference championship with a 4–2 series victory.

In the Adams Division, the two teams from La Belle Province squared off with Montreal heavily favored to win. But the Quebec Nordiques pulled off a major upset, winning in five games on an overtime goal by pugnacious Dale Hunter. The division finals pitted the Nordiques against the Boston Bruins after the Bruins clobbered the Buffalo Sabres 3–1. The presence of the Stastny brothers dashed the hopes of the Bruins, as Marian, Peter, and Anton sparkled in game seven, leading the Nords to victory.

The New York Islanders proved to be a much tougher opponent for Quebec in the conference finals. The Isles thrashed the Nords in four straight games.

The Campbell Conference final was a battle between a pair of regular-season stragglers. Vancouver had finished the season three games below .500 while Chicago wound up eight games below the mark. During their lone loss to the Hawks at the Chicago Stadium, coach Roger Neilson and his players on the bench waved white towels in mock surrender after referee Bob Myers disallowed a Vancouver goal. The Canucks faced $11,000 in fines as a result of their actions. Even so, Vancouver, backed by Richard Brodeur's brilliant goaltending, won the series in convincing style by 4–1. Their reward was a first-ever trip to the Stanley Cup finals.

Even "King Richard" Brodeur's miraculous puckstopping couldn't hold off the powerful Islanders in the finals. The Isles captured the first two games by 6–5 and 6–4, and when the Islanders came right back with a 3–0 shutout in game three, the Canuck demise was inevitable. A 3–1 Islander victory in game four completed the sweep and ended the hockey season. The Islanders seized their third consecutive Stanley Cup, the first American team to do so. An Islander dynasty was becoming firmly entrenched.

"This is a team with tremendous desire," said Mike Bossy, "and if we keep that desire, we'll never lose the Cup." Bossy's exceptional postseason play won him the Conn Smythe Trophy as the most valuable player of the playoffs.

**B**EFORE THE START of the 1982–83 season, a 50-year-old tradition ended in Detroit. The Norris family relinquished ownership of the Red Wings, with purchaser Mike Ilitch paying a reported $9 million to acquire the franchise.

A New Jersey-based syndicate was given the go-ahead by the NHL to buy the struggling Colorado Rockies. The deal was believed to have cost John McMullen, co-owner of the Houston Astros, a cool $30 million. The Rockies moved east, became the New Jersey Devils, and joined the Patrick Division, while the Winnipeg Jets were transferred to the Smythe Division to replace the Rockies.

Consistency was the word often used to describe two of the game's finest scorers, Mike Bossy and Wayne Gretzky. Bossy equaled Guy Lafleur's record of six consecutive 50-goal seasons when he scored his 49th and 50th goals in a 6–2 Islander victory over Washington. Bossy became the first NHLer to score 50 or more goals in each of his first six seasons. By the end of the schedule, Bossy had 60 goals, the first player to reach that plateau for three straight seasons.

Wayne Gretzky won the NHL scoring title for the third time in a row with 71 goals and 196 points. He also added another record to the book with 125 assists in 80 games.

At season's end, the Boston Bruins finished atop the NHL standings with 110 points and 50 games won. The Oilers set a record with 424 goals and tied the Flyers for second place with 106 points. The Black Hawks took fourth place with an impressive 32-point improvement over the previous year.

In the playoffs, there was added incentive to skate hard and score often. The NHL offered a bonus of $4,000 to each player on a division-winning team and $2,000 to members of the runner-up club. But the real loot was in making it all the way to the Stanley Cup. An additional $5,000 bonus per winning player sweetened the pot, which upped the total cash to $20,000 for each player on the winning side and $15,000 to members of the defeated club.

The Edmonton Oilers dominated the Smythe Division playoffs. They swept aside the Winnipeg Jets and then downed the Calgary

Flames for the division title with a 4–1 series victory. The 10–2 romp over the Flames in game three gave Gretzky a chance to set new playoff records. His seven points improved the old mark by one. He also tied the short-handed goal record with three, and his four goals equaled the mark for most games with three or more goals. The Oilers scored a record 35 goals in the five games.

In the Norris Division playoffs, the Chicago Black Hawks were easy winners over St. Louis 3–1, while it took the same number of games for the Minnesota North Starts to knock the Toronto Maple Leafs out of contention. In the follow-up series, the Black Hawks, led by Tony Esposito, Tom Lysiak, and Rich Preston, earned a berth in the Campbell Conference finals with a convincing 4–1 victory over the North Stars.

Play in the Patrick Division saw the New York Islanders knock off the Washington Capitals 3–1. The Rangers triumphed, as well, dumping the Flyers in three straight games. However, the Rangers' injury list was lengthy for the division finals and they bowed to the Islanders in six games.

Goaltending proved to be the decisive factor in the Adams Division. The Buffalo Sabres astonished everyone by blowing past Montreal in three games, with netminder Bob Sauve shutting out the Habs in two of the games. The other matchup saw the Nordiques eliminated by the Bruins. The outstanding goaltending of Pete Peeters was the difference. The best-of-seven follow-up series versus Buffalo was a dramatic affair. The Bruins needed an overtime goal from defenseman Brad Park in game seven to win the series and the division crown.

The Campbell Conference final was a one-sided affair. The Black Hawks bowed meekly to the high-scoring Oilers, who won four straight games. In the Wales Conference final, the defending champion Islanders needed six games to eliminate the Boston Bruins. Mike Bossy broke loose for four goals in game six, an 8–4 Islander victory.

There was great anticipation that the Stanley Cup finals would be a fantastic series. It was billed as the Dream Series. Both the Oilers and the Islanders had the depth and the talent to go all the way. By the time it was over, however, the Oilers' dream finish had become a nightmare, and the Isles captured their fourth Stanley Cup with a stunning four-game triumph.

Game one was a classic case of defense beating offense as the Islanders outplayed the Oilers 2–0. In game two, the Oilers were knocked off balance when the Isles scored three first-period goals. Edmonton lost 6–3. The Islanders breezed through game three and emerged with a 5–1 victory, and in game four, they took their place in NHL history with a 4–2 win and a series sweep. They became only the third team ever to win four consecutive Cups.

Billy Smith's outstanding series — he held the Oilers to only seven goals and shut out Wayne Gretzky completely — made him a worthy recipient of the Conn Smythe Trophy. It was the first time the MVP award was awarded to a goalie since 1975, when Bernie Parent of the Flyers captured it.

**T**HE 1983 84–SEASON began with a record 63 American-born players selected in the entry draft. Five of them were first-round choices with 18-year-old Brian Lawton selected number one by Minnesota. Pat LaFontaine, a Detroit native, was picked third overall by the Islanders, and goalie Tom Barrasso of Boston was the number five selection. He went to Buffalo.

The season began with only four coaching changes, the fewest in more than a decade. Lou Angotti popped up in Pittsburgh, Bill Mahoney signed on with the North Stars, Jack Evans was the new coach in Hartford, and talkative Jacques Demers injected some of his famous enthusiasm into the St. Louis Blues. In midseason, John Ferguson replaced Tom Watt in Winnipeg, even though Watt had helped improve the Jets' record by 48 points the previous year. Watt was another victim in a trend that saw about 160 NHL coaches lose their jobs in a ten-year period — one of the worst records in professional sports.

Overtime was finally approved. It had been removed from the game during World War II because of travel restrictions. A five-minute sudden-death period had been proposed in 1980, and after much foot-dragging it became official for the 1983–84 season.

Once again the Edmonton Oilers were the class of the league. The Oilers registered 57 wins for a point total of 119, while the Islanders and the Bruins finished in a deadlock for second place overall, both with 104 points. The Oilers' Wayne Gretzky and Paul Coffey posted remarkable totals. Gretzky's 205 points placed the superstar center at the top of the scoring race, while Coffey's 126 points were good enough for the runner–up position. The Oiler rearguard surpassed by six Bobby Orr's 1969–70 record of most points by a defenseman.

At playoff time, the Winnipeg Jets found themselves facing off against the Oilers, their old nemesis, in a Smythe Division matchup. As usual, the Jets bowed quietly in three straight games, leaving them with a postseason futility record against the Oilers of 0–15. The Oilers advanced against the Calgary Flames for the division title after the Flames ousted Vancouver in four games. The Alberta series went seven games, but the Flames simply couldn't muster enough offense to stay with the explosive Oilers.

In the Norris Division, St. Louis swept past Detroit in four games. Blues' coach Jacques Demers admitted his club was out-played by Detroit and attributed the series win to the heroic goal-tending of Mike Liut. "He played like Ken Dryden," said Demers. In the other Norris matchup, the Chicago Black Hawks were hoping to muzzle Minnesota as they had in the past two playoff meetings. But this time the Hawks came up short. Minnesota won 4–2 and then went on to eliminate Liut and the Blues to take the Norris crown.

Goalie Steve Penney was the talk of the Adams Division playoff between Montreal and Boston. He allowed just two goals in three games as the Habs pushed the Bruins aside. Penney's puckstopping was remarkable considering he had played only four games during the regular season. Quebec's regular-season domination of Buffalo continued into the playoffs, and the Nords won easily 3–0.

The division finals involving Montreal and Quebec included one of the biggest brawls in playoff history. As the teams were leaving the ice at the end of the second period in game three, hostilities broke out, the ice was transformed into a battleground, and a 40-minute free-for-all ensued. When peace was restored, 12 players had been ejected with misconduct penalties. The incident was rekindled in the third period when two Nordiques, Dale Hunter and Randy Moller, returned to the ice after game officials failed to notify them of their ejection from the game. The Quebec players were eventually thrown out. NHL supervisor of officials John McCauley shouldered the blame, saying, "It was the worst mistake I ever made." The long brawl worked in favor of the Habs, as they stormed back in the third period to make up a two-goal deficit. They scored three more goals to win the game 5–3 and the series 4–2.

The Washington Capitals posted an easy playoff victory over the Philadelphia Flyers to advance to the finals in the Patrick Division. The Islanders prevailed over the Rangers and their series finale was described as one of the best playoff games ever. A goal in overtime by defenseman Ken Morrow clinched game five and the series for the Isles. Morrow's marker pushed the Islanders' overtime record over ten years of playoff activity to 21–5. The team went on to capture the Patrick Division title with a convincing five-game triumph over the Washington Capitals.

In the Wales Conference finals, the Islanders staged a remarkable comeback to stun the Canadiens. After losing the first two games at the Montreal Forum, the Islanders regrouped and ran off four straight victories. How good were they? Montreal coach Jacques Lemaire stated emphatically, "They are the best team in North America. I think they'll win the Cup."

The Edmonton Oilers had an easy time of it in the Campbell Conference finals. They outscored the Minnesota North Stars 22–10 in a four-game sweep.

The Stanley Cup brought together two fascinating finalists. In the East, the Islanders were tough, experienced, and hungry to complete their "Drive for Five" and tie Montreal's record of five consecutive Cup victories. In the West, the Edmonton Oilers were young, aggressive, and packed with great individual talent. They were further motivated by owner Peter Pocklington's brash prediction in 1979: "Within five years the Oilers will hold the Stanley Cup."

Game one featured goalie Grant Fuhr's marvelous talents as he fashioned a 1–0 shutout over the defending champs. The Isles bounced back to bury the Oilers 6–1 in game two. Mark Messier dominated games three and four with his speed and strength. Both games went to the Oilers by 7–2 scores.

Wayne Gretzky provided the spark in game five, scoring twice and setting up a third goal in Edmonton's 5–2 series-ending victory at the Northlands Coliseum. The Oilers' Cup triumph also depended on the skills and consistency of Kevin Lowe, Paul Coffey, Kevin McClelland, Pat Hughes, Ken Linesman, and Dave Semenko.

Mark Messier pushed aside the Conn Smythe Trophy he'd won and said, "Gretz made a great little speech before the final game.

*The Great One, Wayne Gretzky, a hockey giant in any era.* (Action Photographics)

He stood up and said all the individual trophies he's won could never compare with winning the Stanley Cup. That really got all of us going. It made us all realize how much it means to win the Cup."

**T**HERE WERE SEVERAL new faces behind NHL benches for the opening of the 1984–85 season. Dan Maloney replaced Mike Nykoluk in Toronto, Bob Berry lost his job as Montreal coach, then succeeded Lou Angotti in Pittsburgh. Doug Carpenter signed on with New Jersey, and Mike Keenan took charge of the Philadelphia Flyers under new general manager Bobby Clarke. Pat Quinn went from the Flyers to the Kings, and Bill LaForge was hired by Harry Neale, general manager of the Canucks.

Some familiar faces — and voices — moved away from the spotlight. Danny Gallivan, 67, whose colorful play-by-play commentary on radio and television had thrilled millions during hundreds of Stanley Cup games, announced his retirement, as did Guy Lafleur, one of Montreal's greatest scorers.

In June, Clarence Campbell, who had been league president for 31 years, died of pneumonia. He had figured prominently in many Stanley Cup controversies, including the famous suspension of Rocket Richard for the 1955 playoffs. Richard's dismissal triggered the memorable St. Patrick's Day riot at the Montreal Forum.

A new phenomenon made his NHL debut. Mario Lemieux donned a Pittsburgh jersey and told the media, "I think if the fans are patient with us and give us two or three years, we'll be quite successful."

The Philadelphia Flyers picked up 20 points on the Edmonton Oilers late in the season — thanks to a record 11-game win streak — and nailed down first place overall with 113 points. The Flyers lost a mere four games on home ice during the season. Wayne Gretzky won the scoring title and the Art Ross Trophy with 208 points, 73 more than linemate Jari Kurri.

In the playoffs, Gretzky and the Oilers ousted the L.A. Kings in the Smythe Division semifinals while the Winnipeg Jets celebrated their first-ever series win by dumping the Calgary Flames in four games. In the division finals, the Oilers overpowered the Jets in four games with Gretzky collecting seven points in the final match, tying a record he set in 1983.

In the Norris Division, both first-round series went the minimum three games. Chicago eliminated Detroit and Minnesota knocked off St. Louis. North Stars' goalie Gilles Meloche, who played some amazing hockey against the Blues, was a little more vulnerable against the Black Hawks, who captured the division crown with a 4–2 series victory.

Tim Kerr had a fantastic first-round playoff series as he led the Philadelphia Flyers to a three-game sweep over the Rangers. Kerr rewrote the record books in game three when he scored three power-play goals in one period. He also tied the league record for power-play goals in one playoff game. The New York Islanders dropped their first two games to the Washington Capitals but battled back to win the series. In doing so, they became the first NHL team to come back from a two-game deficit and win a best-of-five series. But the Islanders couldn't pull off the same feat in the division finals, as the Flyers walloped them 4–1. "Do me a favor," said a downcast Bob Nystrom when it was over. "Tell the Flyers to beat the hell out of Edmonton for us. I mean that with a passion."

Both matchups in the Adams Division went to five games. The Canadiens won the deciding game against the Bruins by 4–2. The game was a memorable experience for Montreal's Steve Rooney. His wedding in Boston had been arranged several months earlier. It made for a tight schedule on game day. After he tied the knot in the morning, he tied his skate laces later in the day at the Boston Garden. Rooney contributed to Montreal's victory by scoring his first playoff goal.

There was a surprise turnaround in game five in the Quebec–Buffalo matchup. The Sabres were ten minutes away from taking the series when disaster struck. Their 5–3 lead vanished as they gave up three fast goals and lost the game and the series. In the division final, the Nordiques surprised Montreal, the division champs, by capturing game seven in overtime and winning the Battle of Quebec.

The Prince of Wales Conference title went to the Philadelphia Flyers after a six-game battle with Quebec. Dave Poulin's goal — scored while the Flyers were two men short — was the clincher. After game five in Quebec City, coach Michel Bergeron berated the game officials and then showed the media a videotape highlighting some controversial calls. The performance cost him a $5,000 fine.

The Campbell Conference crown was captured by Edmonton, also in six games. The Oilers outscored Chicago 18–5 in winning the first two games, saw the Black Hawks tie the series on home ice, and then thumped the Hawks 10–5 in game five. The sixth game went to the Oilers 6–2.

In the final battle for the Stanley Cup, the injury-riddled Philadelphia Flyers jumped into the lead with a 4–1 victory on Edmonton ice. But the Oilers didn't lose another game, winning 3–1, 4–3, 5–3, and 8–3. The Oilers established a playoff record for goals in a deciding game of a championship series; Detroit had bounced Toronto 7–2 in a deciding championship game in 1948, the previous highest-scoring Cup-winning match.

"We haven't won four or five in a row yet," said defenseman Paul Coffey, "but I think this might be the start of a dynasty."

"All I know," added Wayne Gretzky, "is that 15 years from now I'm going to say, 'Geez, I played on a great team!'"

**BEFORE THE 1985–86 REGULAR SEASON** commenced, Jean Perron took over from Jacques Lemaire behind the Montreal bench. It was the fifth coaching change in Montreal in six seasons. Lemaire was a controversial figure at the Forum. Some of his critics had even accused him of forcing Guy Lafleur into retirement. Lorne Henning was handed the Minnesota coaching job, Tom Watt signed a three-year contract to coach Vancouver, Butch Goring was hired to guide the Bruins, Ted Sator became the new Ranger coach, and Jim Schoenfeld turned up behind the Buffalo bench.

The deaths of two goaltenders rocked the hockey world. On November 10, the Flyers' 26-year-old goalie, Pelle Lindbergh, smashed his car into a retaining wall. While two passengers sustained serious injuries, Lindbergh died later in hospital. In Switzerland, Hall of Fame goaltender Jacques Plante died of cancer at age 57.

The Detroit Red Wings spent millions trying to buy some respectable players. They signed college player Adam Oates, a former star at Rensselaer Polytechnic Institute, to a four-year contract for $1.1 million and then inked highly touted Ray Staszak from the University of Illinois–Chicago for $1.3 million over five years. Staszak's NHL career consisted of four games and one assist. The Wings spent another bundle on Czech defector Petr Klima. After a mere eight wins in 35 games, coach Harry Neale was fired and Brad Park took over. The Wings wound up with an embarrassing 40 points and without a spot in the playoffs.

At the other end of the standings were the powerful Edmonton Oilers, with 56 wins and 119 points. The Oilers' sensational season brought more personal records to Wayne Gretzky and Paul Coffey. Gretzky amassed a record 215 points, three more than his 1981–82 total. His 163 assists broke another NHL mark. Coffey had his sights on a record that was thought to be unbreakable — Bobby Orr's single-season total of 46 goals by a defenseman. On April 2, Coffey slammed the puck into the Vancouver net for goal number 47 — the record breaker — and he finished the season as the new record holder with 48.

Philadelphia and Washington were the only other clubs to break the 100-point barrier. Buffalo fans were unhappy when the Sabres' 80-point season wasn't good enough to get them into the playoffs in the tough Adams Division, although they would have been playoff-bound in any other division. Buffalo's failure marked the first time Scotty Bowman hadn't coached his team to a playoff spot.

When postseason play began, the Oilers, as expected, made short work of the fourth-place Vancouver Canucks in the Smythe Division, sweeping them aside in three games. It was the Oilers' ninth consecutive playoff-series win. The Calgary Flames, led by veterans Doug Risebrough, John Tonelli, and Lanny McDonald, overpowered the Winnipeg Jets in three games. Then, in one of the most stunning upsets of the decade, the Flames eliminated the Edmonton Oilers by winning game seven 3–2. Perry Berezan's series-winning goal in the third period was one of the most bizarre in Stanley Cup history. Berezan dumped the puck into the Oiler zone where defenseman Steve Smith picked it up. Smith banked a clearing shot off goaltender Grant Fuhr's pad and the puck skipped into the Oiler net.

The Norris Division featured another major upset. The Toronto Maple Leafs, making their first playoff appearance of the 1980s, ousted Chicago (now known as the Blackhawks), the division champions, in three straight games. In other Norris action, the Blues and North Stars went five games before St. Louis advanced to the finals. Toronto goaltender Ken Wregget was outstanding against St. Louis in a seven-game battle for the Norris title. St. Louis won the final game 2–1. It was a good showing for the Leafs, considering they had the second-worst regular-season record. "Now we'll be able to walk down the street this summer and not be ashamed to meet someone," quipped Leaf winger Rick Vaive.

The New York Rangers were responsible for another surprise in the Patrick Division when they eliminated the Philadelphia Flyers in five games. Washington swept past the Islanders but couldn't stop the red-hot Rangers in the division finals. New York won in six games.

*Rookie goal-tender Patrick Roy was one of the principal reasons the Canadiens won their 23rd Cup in 1986.* (Norman James)

A rookie goaltender was the big story in the Adams Division playoffs. Montreal's Patrick Roy gave up a mere six goals in the Canadiens' sweep of the Boston Bruins. The win was no surprise. The Bruins hadn't won an opening-round playoff series against Montreal since 1943. The other Adams series saw the Hartford Whalers oust the Quebec Nordiques in three games. The division final was a tense, hard-fought battle that went to overtime in the seventh game before Claude Lemieux's goal ended it. Once again, Patrick Roy sparkled in goal. "I haven't seen netminding like that in 14 years," said the Habs' Larry Robinson, comparing Roy to Hall-of-Famer Ken Dryden.

Finalists in both the Wales and Campbell conferences were teams that had struggled during the regular season. In the Wales, Montreal, seventh overall, met the Rangers, who had finished a lowly 14th. However, the series was a slam-bang affair until the Canadiens ended it in five games. There was only one more obstacle between the Habs and their 23rd Stanley Cup.

In the battle for Campbell Conference honors, the Calgary Flames, sixth overall, faced the St. Louis Blues, 12th-place finishers. The Flames, their confidence buoyed by the Oiler upset, knocked out the Blues in seven games. A little-known coaching ploy was revealed during this series. Blues' coach Jacques Demers was caught throwing pennies on the ice to force a break in the action and give his players a brief rest. There was speculation that Demers had learned the trick from Philadelphia coach Mike Keenan.

The Stanley Cup finals between the two Canadian finalists in the spring of 1986 were filled with thrills. Game one was a lopsided 5–2 victory for the Flames in Calgary. Montreal evened the series two nights later when Brian Skrudland whipped in the fastest overtime goal in Cup history, nine seconds into the extra period. Many fans at the Saddledome missed the shocking ending because they were just returning to their seats. Back at the Forum, the Canadiens won games three and four by 5–3 and 1–0. The shutout in game four was Patrick Roy's first in the NHL, and the first playoff shutout recorded by a rookie in 31 years. Game five at the Saddledome ended on a spectacular note. With 14 seconds to play, Roy made an incredible toe save on a Jamie Macoun shot and preserved a 3–2 Montreal victory. After a seven-year drought, the Habs were back on top of the hockey world with their 23rd championship — more titles than any team in any pro sport had ever achieved. And they were led to the pinnacle by a rookie coach and a rookie goaltender. For his dazzling play-off performances, Patrick Roy was awarded the Conn Smythe Trophy.

But the playoffs ended on an ugly note. A victory celebration in Montreal following the final game quickly got out of control. Cars were toppled, store windows smashed, and looters ran off with stolen goods. When a fire truck was called to put out a huge bon-fire in the city center, drunken fans hampered the efforts of the fire fighters to extinguish the blaze. A huge number of riot police were needed to quell the disturbance.

**IN THE SUMMER** of 1986, more changes took place in Detroit. The Wings selected Michigan State's Joe Murphy as the number one draft choice overall, the first college play-er to be chosen first. Murphy would be coached by Jacques Demers, lured away from St. Louis by a huge contract. Demers soon found himself in several heated debates with new Leaf coach John Brophy. Both were successful in guiding their teams into the playoffs.

Phil Esposito realized a long-held dream when he was hired as general manager of the New York Rangers. The former scoring champion became the fourth straight Ranger manager with no previous experience in the position.

Three star players retired prematurely. Gilbert Perreault walked away from the Buffalo Sabres, forfeiting three-quarters of his esti-mated salary of $400,000 plus a onetime pension bonus of $250,000. To earn it he would have had to play another 40 games. Barry Beck quit the Rangers, saying he could no longer play for coach Ted Sator, and Mario Tremblay retired from the Canadiens at age 30 because of nagging shoulder problems.

Scotty Bowman turned over the coaching job in Buffalo to Craig Ramsey. A few weeks later, Bowman was fired as general manager and replaced by former Sabre Gerry Meehan. Meehan then fired Ramsey and brought in Ted Sator, who had been dismissed in New York. Butch Goring was replaced in Boston by popular Terry O'Reilly.

Pat Quinn, coach of the Kings, found himself in hot water when it was revealed he'd accepted money from the Vancouver Canucks (for a future position in the Canucks' organization) while still in the employ of the Kings. NHL president John Ziegler suspended Quinn from coaching until the 1990–91 season and levied hefty fines against both the Canucks and the Kings. And a change in the playoff format was introduced, the best-of-five preliminary round becoming a best-of-seven series.

Once again, the Edmonton Oilers finished in first place overall with 106 points. The only other club to reach the 100-point plateau was Philadelphia, with an even 100. While two rookies made big impressions — goalie Ron Hextall of the Flyers had the most wins (37) and the Kings' Luc Robitaille scored 42 goals — it was Wayne Gretzky who captured the scoring title for the seventh time with 183 points.

Gretzky and the Oilers ran into a bit of a scare in the first round of the Smythe Division playoffs, losing game one to the Los Angeles Kings. But in game two, Gretzky collected a goal and six assists in a 13–3 Oiler rout, tying his own record for most points in a playoff game. When the Calgary Flames met the Winnipeg Jets in the other Smythe matchup, injuries to key players hurt the Flames and they bowed out in six games.

In the Norris Division, the Leafs' John Brophy had the last laugh on Jacques Demers after Demers stated: "It will take a miracle for Toronto to make the playoffs." Toronto not only grabbed fourth place but went on to upset St. Louis, the division champs, in six games. Demers had his Red Wings in high gear for their playoff battle with the Blackhawks. The Wings won four straight games. Demers could thank his goalie, Glen Hanlon, for some miraculous work in the division finals against Toronto. After the

Leafs grabbed a 3–1 series lead, Hanlon blanked them twice in the next three games. Hanlon's 3–0 shutout in game seven sent the Red Wings into the Campbell Conference finals.

In the Patrick Division, the longest playoff game in 44 years didn't end until early Easter Sunday morning when the Islanders and the Capitals tangled in game seven in Washington. Six hours and 15 minutes after the opening faceoff — in the fourth overtime period — Pat LaFontaine's screened shot eluded Bob Mason, and the Islanders came away with a victory in the dramatic series. The contest was the fifth longest in NHL history. "It was like playing in a dream," said an exhausted Kelly Hrudey, the winning goalie, at the end of the game. "I never thought I could face 75 shots and allow just two goals. Don't expect me to do that again. This is a once-in-a-lifetime thing." In the other Patrick matchup, the Philadelphia Flyers and the New York Rangers came down to the seventh game tied 3–3. Hextall shut out the Rangers 5–0 in the deciding game. The number of Ranger seasons without a Stanley Cup victory stretched to 47.

The playoff story in the Adams Division had a familiar ring: the Boston Bruins met the Montreal Canadiens and the Canadiens won. The Bruins failed to win a game, and Montreal's monopoly on postseason battles between the two clubs rose to 18 consecutive victories. Meanwhile, Quebec Nordique goalie Mario Gosselin brashly predicted a Quebec victory over Hartford in the other semifinal series — after his club lost the first two games. With Gosselin stopping everything the Whalers threw at him from then on, the Nords stormed back and won four in a row, ending the series on Peter Stastny's overtime goal.

When the battle between the Nordiques and the Canadiens for the Adams title ended, there were scars and bitter feelings. Montreal's 5–3 victory in game seven sent the Canadiens into the Wales Conference final but left Quebec City fans fuming. Most of the anger and bitterness stemmed from an incident in game five at the Forum. That night a goal by the Nordiques at 17:07 of the third period was disallowed by referee Kerry Fraser after Paul Gillis of the Nords became entangled with the Habs' Mats

Naslund. Between them they managed to jostle goalie Brian Hayward out of position, allowing Alain Cote to score. Seventeen seconds later the Habs scored a goal to win the game.

Coach Michel Bergeron was incensed when Fraser waved off Cote's goal, and accused the league of being anti-Quebec. Irate team president Marcel Aubut said, "We can't let one man [Fraser] ruin careers and make a team lose millions of dollars simply by blowing a call on the ice. Things have to change. Millions of people saw this disgrace on television." When the series ended, Bergeron refused to shake hands with Perron. "Why should I?" he snapped. "We didn't lose that series. I'll never accept the outcome. It's the first time in history the Canadiens took a four-out-of-seven series by winning only three times."

With the fireworks behind them, the Canadiens went on to meet the Philadelphia Flyers for the Wales Conference championship. After the teams split a pair of games in Philadelphia, the Canadiens fell apart on home ice, losing two in a row. Montreal fought back to win game five, but back at the Forum for game six an astonishing thing happened. Two of the Flyers, rugged Ed Hospodar and backup goalie Chico Resch, objected to the Habs' pregame ritual of shooting one of the warm-up pucks into the Flyers' empty net. When Shayne Corson tried it at the end of the warm-up period, Hospodar rushed over and hooked his stick while Resch tossed his big goal stick at the puck. That did it! Players who had left the ice came racing back and engaged in a mammoth brawl. The game that followed was tame by comparison. The Flyers fell behind but rallied for a series-ending victory and stymied Montreal's plans to win their 24th Stanley Cup. Lord Stanley's trophy would go to either Philadelphia or the survivor of the Campbell Conference playoffs.

To no one's surprise, the Edmonton Oilers skated off with the Campbell Conference title, demolishing the Red Wings in five games. On home ice in game five, the Oilers' Mark Messier paced his team to a 6–3 triumph. Despite the loss, the Red Wings were accorded a great deal of respect. Demers had brought them a long way — from last place overall to the final four — in one season.

When the final series for the Stanley Cup got under way, Wayne Gretzky was reminded that he hadn't scored a goal since the Oilers eliminated the Jets. Perhaps that was all the incentive Gretzky needed, for he engineered some dazzling plays in game one, scored a goal, and set up the winner by Paul Coffey. In game two, he scored again and set up the game winner — an overtime marker by Jari Kurri. Back at the Spectrum, the Flyers displayed some good hockey in game three and won 5–3, but in game four, three assists by Gretzky led to a 4–1 Oilers win. During this game, Ron Hextall, the temperamental Flyer netminder, slashed Oiler Kent Nilsson across the legs with his goal stick, an infraction that wasn't penalized with a suspension until the following season when Hextall sat out eight games. Thanks to Hextall's superb goaltending, the Flyers captured game six 3–2. But in game seven, the Oilers drilled 43 shots at Hextall and won the game 3–1. Glenn Anderson's 30-footer with 2:24 remaining was the insurance marker Edmonton was looking for. At the final buzzer the Oilers spilled across the ice to celebrate their third Stanley Cup championship in four years.

No player enjoyed the excitement more than defenseman Steve Smith, whose bank shot into his own team's net had ended the Oilers' Cup bid the previous season. "I was in tears last year and I'm in tears this year," said, Smith, smiling. "The difference is, this year they're tears of joy."

**S**INCE THE EXPANSION of 1979–80, an average of eight NHL coaches failed to survive from one season to the next. The 1987–88 campaign was no exception as seven coaches were replaced before training camp began.

The New York Rangers paid big money to entice Michel Bergeron away from Quebec. He signed a five-year, million-dollar deal and the Rangers even threw in a first-round draft choice. Former Ranger coach Herb Brooks turned up in Minnesota, Bob Murdoch was hired by Chicago, Terry Crisp became the new skipper of the Flames, the Canucks recruited Bob McCammon, Andre Savard signed with Quebec, and Pierre Creamer became the new coach in Pittsburgh.

In October, Doug Jarvis of Hartford saw his amazing iron man streak of 964 games come to an end, and two months later Philadelphia's Ron Hextall became the first NHL goalie to score a goal in a game. He did it against Boston, slapping the puck 170 feet and bouncing it into the empty net.

For the first time since his rookie season nine years earlier, Wayne Gretzky had some real competition for the scoring crown. Mario Lemieux proved to be a formidable scorer and collected 70 goals and 98 assists for 168 points, beating Gretzky for the Art Ross Trophy by 19 points.

But Lemieux's heroics weren't enough to get Pittsburgh into the playoffs. The Penguins compiled an above-.500 record and collected 29 more points than the Norris Division's playoff-bound Toronto Maple Leafs but still missed the postseason fun.

The Calgary Flames, coached by Bob Johnson and paced by sharpshooting Hakan Loob, Mike Bullard, and Joe Nieuwendyk, captured first place overall with 105 points. The Montreal Canadiens were right behind with 103.

For the first time in 15 years, there were no sweeps in the first round of the playoffs. In the Smythe Division, the defending champion Edmonton Oilers took five games to eliminate Winnipeg, while Calgary was ousting Los Angeles, also in five. Bruce McNall, the new owner of the Kings, vowed to strengthen his club. At the same time, he gave general manager Rogie Vachon a vote of confidence. In the division finals, Calgary's high scorers were frustrated by the persistent checking of the Oilers. The result was a stunning sweep as the regular-season champions were sent reeling to the sidelines.

Toronto, coached by John Brophy, entered the 1988 playoffs with the worst winning percentage (.325) of any team in playoff history. Detroit polished them off in six games. Then the verbal fireworks erupted. Leaf winger Mirko Frycer, benched for the final three games of the series, said of Brophy, "He's completely nuts and everybody hates him. Nobody wants to play for him." Brophy's retort was equally harsh. "Every time Frycer came back on the ice this year he fell down and got injured. He's the last guy who should say anything. They can't dig up enough plastercast in Toronto to keep him together."

Meanwhile, in the other Norris Division semifinal, the St. Louis Blues disposed of a slump-ridden Chicago team in five games. The Hawks' record in the past three playoff seasons went to 1–11. In the division final, the Red Wings put an end to the Blues' season in six games.

In the Patrick Division, the heavily favored Philadelphia Flyers bowed to a disciplined Washington Capital club. The Caps were down 3–1 in the series but rebounded, and won game seven on an overtime goal by Dale Hunter. When the New Jersey Devils made their first-ever playoff appearance against the Islanders, they were the victims in game four of a bizarre winning goal in overtime scored short-handed by Brent Sutter. But it was the Devils who ultimately prevailed, sinking the Isles in six games. In the division finals against Washington, the Devils came through with a dramatic victory in game seven to advance to the conference finals. In game three, a 10–4 rout of the Caps, the Devils' Patrik Sundstrom set a playoff record with three goals and five assists.

In the Adams Division, the Montreal Canadiens eliminated the Hartford Whalers while the Boston Bruins sent the Buffalo Sabres to the sidelines; both series went six games. The Bruins entered the finals against Montreal with the media reminding them they hadn't captured a playoff series from the Habs in 45 years. So it was a major surprise when the Bruins shut down Montreal's awesome power play and broke the long-standing jinx with a five-game series victory.

The Wales Conference finals went to the wire before Boston was able to beat back the stubborn New Jersey Devils. But much of the drama of the confrontation took place behind the scenes. At the end of game three, Devils' coach Jim Schoenfeld, incensed over the refereeing of Don Koharski, accosted the official in the hallway. Angry words were exchanged, and Koharski was either pushed or lost his balance. He told Schoenfeld, "You'll never coach again."

Schoenfeld replied, "You're full of shit. You fell, you fat pig. Have another doughnut."

NHL executive vice president Brian O'Neill suspended Schoenfeld for abuse of officials. But the Devils, in a surprise move, went to the courts and secured a judge's order that bound the NHL to allow Schoenfeld to coach the Devils in game four.

Before the game, the officials decided they couldn't perform their duties under the circumstances and a frantic search for substitutes was undertaken. The amateurs hired to control the game were referee Paul McInnis, a 52-year-old Devils' off-ice official, who borrowed a pair of Aaron Broten's skates for his NHL debut; linesman Vin Godleski, a 51-year-old Devils' off-ice official; and 50-year-old linesman Jim Sullivan, an Islanders' off-ice official. At first only McInnis wore a striped shirt while the linesmen were attired in green sweatpants, yellow shirts, and white helmets. Later, they changed to regulation stripes. Throughout this bizarre episode in Cup competition, participants in the dispute expressed their frustration at not being able to contact NHL president John Ziegler for guidance. When Ziegler surfaced a day or two later, he refused to discuss his whereabouts. The Devils won the game 3–1 but wound up losing the series 4–3.

Meanwhile, Detroit fans thought the return of Steve Yzerman from a knee injury significantly increased the Red Wings' chances of advancing to the Stanley Cup finals when they met Edmonton in the Campbell Conference finals. But even Yzerman's presence in the Wing lineup wasn't enough, and the Oilers pushed Detroit aside in five games. Red Wing coach Jacques Demers was livid when he discovered six of his players out well past the team curfew on the night before the final game. As punishment, the revelers were denied the $16,000 bonus each expected to receive from team owner Mike Ilitch.

In the preseason, the Edmonton Oilers were selected by 16 of 22 hockey writers to win the Stanley Cup. The majority opinion proved to be the right one as the Oilers breezed past Boston to win their fourth Cup in five years. The Oilers gave up only nine goals in their four-game sweep of the Bruins, winning by scores of 2–1, 4–2, 6–3, and 6–3. The final game, played in Edmonton, was a replay of a game terminated by a power failure at the Boston

Garden two days earlier. With the score tied 3–3 late in the second period, heat, humidity, and ancient electrical equipment had conspired to produce a blacked-out arena. Although the game was never completed, the statistics remained valid, which meant Boston's Greg Hawood scored his first NHL goal and Rick Middleton picked up his 100th career playoff point.

Wayne Gretzky, the Conn Smythe Trophy winner, soared to new heights with 12 goals and 31 assists for 43 points in the playoffs, breaking his own points record for a single playoff season. Boston coach Terry O'Reilly acknowledged Gretzky's superiority in the series, stating, "There should be a rule that he [Gretzky] has to be passed around from team to team every year." Gretzky deflected the limelight to teammate Kevin Lowe. "You know what it takes to win Stanley Cups?" he asked. "Guys like Kevin Lowe. Not only did he play the entire series with a cast on his wrist, but he played the last two games with broken ribs."

With just two losses in 18 playoff games, the Oilers boasted the second-highest winning percentage (.889) since the NHL expanded from six teams. Only Montreal, with 12–1 records in 1968 and 1976, had been more dominant during the playoffs.

**W**AYNE GRETZKY CONTINUED to make headlines during the off season. He captured the world spotlight with his fairy-tale marriage to Hollywood actress Janet Jones. Then, less than a month later, he was the central figure in the biggest trade in sports history. Oiler fans sobbed in disbelief when they learned that Gretzky, a player with talents unmatched by anyone past or present, had been dealt to Bruce McNall and the Los Angeles Kings. In the controversial deal, the Kings received Gretzky, Mike Krushelnyski, Marty McSorley, minor-leaguer John Miner, and $15 million U.S. Peter Pocklington and the Oilers picked up Jimmy Carson, Martin Gelinas, minor-leaguer Craig Redmond, and three first-round draft picks.

At a tearful news conference, Gretzky told the world, "After spending some time with Mr. McNall, I decided for the benefit of myself, my wife, and our expected child in the new year, that it would be beneficial for everyone involved to let me play for the Los Angeles Kings."

Despite one of the best coaching records in the NHL, Mike Keenan was let go by Philadelphia. Within days he signed on with the Chicago Blackhawks. Minnesota fired Herb Brooks and hired Pierre Page, their sixth coach in as many years. Jean Perron resigned from the Canadiens, citing "pressures from within the organization" as the reason for leaving. The Canadiens signed former policeman Pat Burns as their coach, partly on the recommendation of Wayne Gretzky. All coaching salaries paled in comparison to that of Detroit's Jacques Demers, whose contract ballooned from $50,000 to $250,000.

Islanders' superstar Mike Bossy was forced into retirement because of a chronic back problem, while Guy Lafleur decided to unretire and signed on with the New York Rangers. A Canadian Gallup poll revealed that hockey fans considered Wayne Gretzky to be the best hockey player in the past half century. Gretzky's 48 percent topped the 15 percent received by Maurice Richard. Gordie Howe trailed by 10 percent.

Mario Lemieux, destined to compete favorably with Gretzky in some future poll, added to his splendid reputation during 1988–89. He scored his 50th goal in his 44th game and by season's end had figured in 109 of his team's total of 347. This meant Lemieux had helped out on 57.3 percent of them, breaking Gretzky's unofficial record of 51.8 percent.

As predicted, Soviet players were wearing NHL uniforms late in the season. Sergei Priakin became the first Soviet national team member to play in the NHL when he signed with Calgary.

Winnipeg fired general manager John Ferguson in midseason and replaced him with Mike Smith. In New York, Phil Esposito dismissed coach Michel Bergeron in the final week of the regular season — a move that proved to be unpopular with Ranger fans — and took over the coaching duties himself.

The schedule ended with some dramatic changes in overall positions from the previous season. The Calgary Flames moved up the ladder, jumping from 13th spot to number one, with 54 wins and 117 points. The Flames' Joey Mullen collected 110 points and broke Jimmy Carson's record for most points in a season by an American player. The Canadiens, despite a rookie coach and no scorers in the top 25, managed to place second, Washington placed third, and the L.A. Kings leapfrogged from 18th position to fourth overall. Their 376 goals were the most scored by any team.

The playoffs began with an outstanding series in the Smythe Division. The Vancouver Canucks gave first-place Calgary a fright when they stretched the series to overtime in game seven. Goalie Mike Vernon saved the Flames by making 11 saves in the overtime and holding the Canucks at bay until Joel Otto scored the winner. In the other Smythe matchup, the Edmonton Oilers ran up a three-games-to-one lead over Los Angeles only to see the Kings storm back with four straight wins. In the series, Gretzky set a career playoff record with his 86th goal. But the Kings were no match for Calgary in the Smythe Division finals. They were outscored 22–11 and were swept aside in four straight games.

Goaltending was a major story in the Norris Division playoffs as netminder Alain Chevrier led the Chicago Blackhawks to a stunning victory over Detroit in six games. Elsewhere, the hot sticks of Brett Hull and Peter Zezel, who scored four and six goals respectively, enabled the St. Louis Blues to triumph over the Minnesota North Stars. In the division finals, the Blackhawks ousted the Blues in five games. The final match was memorable for Chicago's Jeremy Roenick. The 19-year-old rookie with only 20 games of NHL experience scored the winning goal.

The Pittsburgh Penguins had little difficulty sweeping aside Phil Esposito's New York Rangers in the Patrick playoffs. Just as the Penguins relied on Tom Barrasso's puckstopping against New York, the Philadelphia Flyers counted on Ron Hextall to see them through their series with Washington. Hextall performed brilliantly and even scored his second goal to create a playoff "first" in game five. Then he went down with an injured knee in the finals versus Pittsburgh. Ken Wregget stepped in and performed like a Hextall clone, helping the Flyers capture the series 4–2. In game six, Mario Lemieux tied an NHL record with five goals and three assists in a 10–7 shootout.

The Montreal–Hartford series in the Adams Division turned out to be a heartbreaker for Whaler fans. The Habs won the series in four games, but only one goal separated the two teams in three games, and the last two were won by Montreal in overtime. The Boston Bruins bounced the Sabres in five games in the other Adams matchup. Two Sabres, Mike Foligno and Larry Playfair, criticized coach Ted Sator when it was over. "We were out-coached," said Foligno. Playfair supported Foligno, adding, "A lot of players can't play for him [Sator]." The division finals saw the Canadiens prevail over Boston. One goal separated the two clubs in each of the five games played. At the end of the series, Bruin coach Terry O'Reilly announced his retirement.

The Canadiens and the Flyers put on an entertaining show in the Wales Conference finals. In winning, Montreal shut down the Flyers' power play with a perfect 0–24 mark. The Flyers' Brian Propp suffered a concussion in game one after being checked hard by the Habs' Chris Chelios. In retaliation, goalie Ron Hextall — with less than two minutes to play in game six — crashed his stick and blocker pad into Chelios. Hextall was banished with a match penalty and later handed a 12-game suspension.

The Campbell Conference title was captured by Calgary in five games. The first place (overall) Flames outclassed the Blackhawks, 16th-place finishers, throttling the Chicago power play, which went a dismal three for 31.

Hockey's smallest player, former altar boy Theoren Fleury, was a huge presence on the ice in game one of the Stanley Cup finals. The five-foot-five, 150-pound speedster scored the winning goal for the Flames against the Canadiens in a 3–2 victory. The Canadiens squared the series by winning game two 4–2, a game in which Hab coach Pat Burns benched Claude Lemieux for failing to stop taking dives when checked. Montreal's famous hockey writer Rejean Tremblay stirred up a controversy by suggesting that Burns's strict treatment of Lemieux was because of his antifrancophone attitude. The Canadiens' hierarchy wasn't amused and banned Tremblay from the Habs' charter flight back to Montreal.

Game three at the Montreal Forum turned into a marathon and wasn't settled until well into the second overtime period when Ryan Walter's goal won the contest 4–3. But the Flames roared back to win games four and five by 4–2 and 3–2 scores. By then the momentum was all Calgary's, and in game six at the Forum, where no visiting team had ever won the Stanley Cup, the Flames held on for a 4–2 decision and their first Cup victory. The win was especially sweet for veteran right-winger Lanny McDonald, who was inserted into the Calgary lineup after missing the previous three games. McDonald responded by scoring a goal that put the Flames ahead 2–1. Doug Gilmour, one of the hottest Flames in the series, scored the eventual winner at 11:02 of the third period, then dumped one into the empty net to clinch the victory.

Coach Terry Crisp became the 12th person to win the Cup both as a player and a coach, and defenseman Al MacInnis, with a 30-point playoff performance, was awarded the Conn Smythe Trophy as the series' MVP. Back in Calgary two days later, a crowd of close to 50,000 ignored a freezing drizzle to honor the Flames in a victory parade. When asked about the weight of the Stanley Cup, Lanny McDonald replied, "There's no weight to it when you win it. A guy could carry it forever."

**A NUMBER OF SOVIET PLAYERS** joined the NHL for the 1989–90 season. Sergei Makarov joined his countryman Sergei Priakin in Calgary, Igor Larionov and Vladimir Krutov were signed by Vancouver, while Viacheslav Fetisov and Sergei Starikov went to New Jersey. Netminder Sergei Mylnikov became a Quebec Nordique, and defector Alexandr Mogilny was added to the Buffalo roster.

Mats Sundin became the first European to be drafted first overall in the entry draft. The 18-year-old Swede became the property of the Nordiques, but they were forced to be patient. Sundin had commitments at home that delayed his NHL debut by several months.

Another teenage star, 16-year-old Eric Lindros of Toronto, was making waves in the world of junior hockey. "I think he could play in the NHL right now," said Flyer general manager Bobby Clarke of the six-foot-four, 217-pound phenomenon.

Hockey fans had difficulty keeping track of the managing and coaching changes. Rick Dudley replaced Ted Sator in Buffalo, Rick Ley took over from Larry Pleau in Hartford, Glen Sather said he'd had enough bench work in Edmonton and turned the coaching chores over to John Muckler. Gone from Los Angeles was Robbie Ftorek, replaced by Tom Webster. Phil Esposito was fired by the Rangers and replaced by Neil Smith as general manager and Roger Neilson as coach. Gord Stellick quit the Leafs as general manager and surfaced as assistant to Neil Smith in New York. Floyd Smith took over Stellick's job, fired George Armstrong as coach, and brought in Doug Carpenter. The Winnipeg Jets recruited Bob Murdoch as coach, and the Boston Bruins signed Mike Milbury.

Guy Lafleur came back for a final NHL fling — this time with the Quebec Nordiques, Marcel Dionne was released by New York after an outstanding career that was highlighted by 731 goals, and Hall-of-Famers Doug Harvey, 65, Hap Day, 88, and Harold Ballard, 86, passed away. In the 1980s, Ballard often promised Leaf fans a Stanley Cup "in a season or two." The truth was, his teams never finished above .500 in the decade and missed the playoffs four times.

In mid-October, during a game in Edmonton, Wayne Gretzky broke Gordie Howe's illustrious career points record of 1,850. The occasion was marked with the red-carpet treatment for Gretzky, complete with gifts and speeches, including words of congratulation from Howe himself. "This is the greatest feeling in the world," said Gretzky. "It will be the highlight of my life."

After a December governor's meeting in Florida, NHL president John Ziegler announced that seven new teams would be joining the league — and the annual Stanley Cup hunt — by the year 2000. Two of the seven new franchises would begin play in the 1992–93 season. Membership would cost each new franchise holder a staggering $50 million.

Mario Lemieux ran off a consecutive-game point-scoring streak of 46 games, then was forced to miss several games due to back problems. The injury cost him a chance to break Gretzky's record of 51. Brett Hull scored a pair of goals in his final game for a total of 72 — a record for right-wingers. Wayne Gretzky missed several games with a groin injury but still won the scoring title with 142 points.

The 1989–90 season ended with the Calgary Flames holding first place overall for the second year in a row. The Flames accumulated 117 points, two more than second-place Montreal. But the Flames ran aground in the first round of the Smythe Division playoffs, losing to the Kings 4–2. Goalie Kelly Hrudey was the Flame killer, playing superbly in all six games. Prior to the series, Hrudey's record against Calgary was 1–10–3. In the division's other matchup, the Edmonton Oilers turned things around in the fourth game of their battle with Winnipeg, coming back from a 3–1 deficit to oust the Jets. In the follow-up series with the injury-riddled Kings, the Oilers had an easy time of it and rolled to four straight victories.

In the Norris Division, the Maple Leafs were favored over St. Louis because their regular-season record against the Blues was 7–1. But the Leafs failed to stop Brett Hull, who registered five goals and ten assists as the Blues prevailed in five games. The Chicago Blackhawks needed seven games to eliminate the Minnesota North Stars. In the division finals, the Hawks struggled through another seven games against St. Louis before ending the series with a 8–2 trouncing of the Blues in the deciding match.

The Patrick Division playoffs featured a bruising battle between the Rangers and the Islanders. In game one, Ranger defenseman James Patrick smashed Islander star Pat LaFontaine to the ice, knocking him unconscious. A predictable brawl broke out with two seconds to play, instigated by Islander coach Al Arbour, who wanted revenge. Arbour was fined $5,000 and his team fined $25,000. The Rangers won the series in five games. Meanwhile, the Washington Capitals overpowered the New Jersey Devils in six games. An unlikely hero for the Caps was little-known John

Druce, who scored three goals in the series, two of them game winners.

In the division finals against New York, Druce scored nine times, once more than he had during regular-season play. Washington defenseman Rod Langway shattered his 92-game scoreless streak in dramatic fashion when he scored the series-clinching goal in overtime in game five.

The Hartford Whalers pushed Boston all the way to seven games in their Adams Division series. But the Whalers were held back by a dismal power play and lost the series, prompting coach Rick Ley to call his charges "spoiled and pampered." The Montreal Canadiens, with injured defense star Chris Chelios missing from the lineup, knocked off the Buffalo Sabres in six games. In the finals the Habs had history on their side — 18 consecutive series wins over Boston up to 1988. But the Bruins were buoyed by more recent stats — like two Bruin wins in the past three meetings. Montreal's power play failed miserably against the Bruins — an anemic 2 for 51 — and it was a major factor in their five-game defeat. It was rather obvious the Habs missed the leadership of departed stars Bob Gainey and Larry Robinson.

In the Wales Conference finals, the Bruins were surprised at how easily they disposed of Washington. Goalie Andy Moog held the Caps to just six goals as the Bruins ran off a four-game sweep. Washington's John Druce completed his playoff heroics with 14 goals in 15 games.

The Campbell Conference finals saw Denis Savard of Chicago play a leading role early in the series. Games two and three featured Savard's wizardry as he guided the Blackhawks to a 2–1 series lead over Edmonton. But for the rest of the series Savard was effectively shut down by Esa Tikkanen, who said, "Savard is a hell of a player, an unbelievable skater." Prominent in the Oilers' 4–2 series triumph was the youthful line of Adam Graves, Joe Murphy, and Martin Gelinas.

Even though many Oiler fans still blistered Peter Pocklington 21 months after the Wayne Gretzky trade, they were pacified somewhat when the Oilers skated their way into the 1990 Stanley

Cup finals against the Bruins. In every category — offense, defense, goal, team speed, and power plays — the Oilers dominated the series, which lasted five games. The Oilers' Stanley Cup win — their fifth in seven years, left many of the winning players wishing their former teammate Wayne Gretzky could have been part of it. During the traditional postseries television interviews, Mark Messier said to the camera, "This one's for you, Gretz."

# 12 Into the Nineties

**I**N JULY 1990, Sergei Fedorov, one of the best 20-year-old hockey players in the world, slipped away from his Soviet teammates during the Goodwill Games in Seattle and surfaced a few days later in Detroit, holding a signed NHL contract. He would prove to be an outstanding acquisition for the Red Wings — the best since Steve Yzerman.

The Vancouver Canucks figured Pavel Bure, another young Soviet who starred at the Goodwill Games, was ready for NHL combat, and Pittsburgh welcomed number one draft choice Jaromir Jagr, who left his home in Czechoslovakia unannounced and landed in the Steel City. The Penguins also signed veteran Bryan Trottier after the former Ross, Smythe, and Calder trophy winner ended a long relationship with the Islanders. Another veteran, Denis Savard, was traded from Chicago to Montreal in return for Chris Chelios. Savard received a hero's welcome from Hab fans. The deal came a month after Mike Keenan was promoted to general manager and coach of the Blackhawks. In a surprise deal, Dale Hawerchuk went from Winnipeg to Buffalo for Phil Housley.

Edmonton goalie Grant Fuhr was handed a one-year suspension for admitting to substance abuse, prompting teammate Mark Messier to call out for a Players' Association drug policy. Messier thought it unfair that Fuhr, who sought help for his problem, was suspended for the same length of time as players like Don Murdoch and Bob Probert, who were caught trying to smuggle cocaine across the Canadian border. In midseason, NHL president John Ziegler announced that Fuhr's suspension had been commuted to 60 games.

In other off-season moves, the Penguins hired former Calgary coach Bob Johnson, the Red Wings fired Jacques Demers and signed Bryan Murray as general manager and coach, Norman Green bought the Minnesota North Stars and hired Bobby Clarke as his general manager, and Clarke, in turn, signed Bob Gainey as his coach. But the North Stars' attendance figures would fall with a thud and the team would average just over 6,200 for its first ten home games. Pierre Page left the Stars, signed on as general manager of the Quebec Nordiques, and surprised everybody by hiring a unilingual coach, Dave Chambers. Toronto hired coach Tom Watt, and Calgary fired coach Terry Crisp and replaced him with Doug Risebrough. Almost everyone called the Flames to regain number one status in the NHL. Meanwhile, in a league shocker, the St. Louis Blues gave free agent defenseman Scott Stevens $5.145 million to sign a four-year deal, plus a signing bonus of $1.4 million, and they further shed their tightwad image by handing Brett Hull a $7-million contract for four years.

In December, the NHL governors made a monumental decision by voting two additional franchises to the cities of Tampa Bay in Florida and Ottawa, Ontario. The announcement stunned many observers. Tampa Bay's bid, only weeks earlier, had appeared to be lacking the $50-million franchise fee and a suitable arena. Ottawa, too, had been viewed as a much weaker bet than another Canadian rival, Hamilton, Ontario.

Five NHL clubs engaged in a late-season run to the wire with Chicago nosing out St. Louis, Los Angeles, Calgary, and Boston for first place overall. Wayne Gretzky of the Kings won a record ninth scoring title with 163 points, while runner-up Brett Hull of the Blues was the deadliest goal scorer with 86.

There was a stunning upset in the first round of the Norris Division playoffs. Weak goaltending by Calder Trophy favorite Ed Belfour of Chicago allowed the Minnesota North Stars, 16th-place finishers, to knock off the Hawks in six games. It was one of the biggest upsets in playoff history. Belfour, who led the league in wins with 43, was yanked in three consecutive games by coach Mike Keenan. The St. Louis Blues finished the season with 105 points and then rallied from a 3–1 series deficit to oust the Detroit Red Wings in seven games. It marked the eighth time in Stanley Cup history that a team had come back after trailing 3–1.

In the Smythe Division semifinals, the Edmonton Oilers eliminated Calgary in overtime in game seven on Esa Tikkanen's goal. TV analyst Don Cherry called the series "the best I've ever seen." In the division's other semifinal, Los Angeles knocked off Vancouver 4–2. The Oilers went on to eliminate the Kings, also in seven games, with Craig MacTavish scoring the winner in sudden-death overtime.

But the Oilers' hopes for another Stanley Cup party were dashed by the amazing Minnesota North Stars in the battle for the Campbell Conference title. After the North Stars pushed aside the injury-riddled Oilers in five games, Minnesota owner Norman Green said, "This is the greatest story in sports." Early in the season, Green had predicted a turnaround for his team — but not in six months. He anticipated it would take at least a year. Two North Star veterans, Brian Bellows and Neal Broten, were equally thrilled. "Neal and I have been together for nine years," bellowed Bellows, "and we're finally going for the Cup. It's incredible."

The Buffalo Sabres made yet another premature exit from postseason play, giving up 29 goals in six games to Montreal, while the Boston Bruins advanced to the Adams Division final with a win over Hartford, 4–2 in games. The Bruins battled Montreal through seven games for the Adams Division crown and somehow were able to cling to a 2–1 lead in the seventh game, while the Habs stormed around their goal trying to force overtime. Montreal's all-time playoff-series record against the Bruins went to 21–5.

Pittsburgh goalie Frank Pietrangelo, a playoff substitute for the injured Tom Barrasso, was brilliant against the New Jersey Devils in a Patrick Division semifinal, won by the Penguins four games to three. After the Rangers lost to Washington in six games, general manager Neil Smith blistered Mike Gartner for his poor goal production (he produced one). Gartner said, "I'll take my share of the responsibility, but no more than my share."

The Penguins' Tom Barrasso shrugged off his sore shoulder in the Patrick Division final with Washington and stopped 97 of 100 shots in the final three games. Pittsburgh, for the first time in franchise history, advanced to the Wales Conference final against Boston.

The Bruins bowed to the bigger, faster Penguins four games to two, amid charges of goonism from losing coach Mike Milbury. Milbury was incensed in game three when Penguins' defenseman Ulf Samuelsson sent Bruin star Cam Neeley limping off after a questionable check. Neeley's thigh injury would prove to be much more serious than anticipated and would keep him out for most of the following season.

On May 25, at the Met center in Minnesota, the Pittsburgh Penguins finally added their roster of names to the coveted Stanley Cup after destroying the Minnesota North Stars in game six by an 8–0 score. The Penguins captured the series — and the Stanley Cup — four games to two, ending 24 years of failure and frustration. The score was the largest margin of victory for a final game in this century.

"To see and feel the Cup, to pick it up, to hold it — that's the greatest feeling I've ever had," the delirious Phil Bourque told reporters. "I can't think of anything I'd rather do than skate around with the Cup over my head."

A day later, the Cup sat in all its glory on the front lawn of goaltender Tom Barrasso's house. Later, it wound up at the bottom of Mario Lemieux's swimming pool. But Lemieux, the Conn Smythe Trophy winner, made sure it was dry and shiny for a civic reception in Pittsburgh on May 27. As an estimated 80,000 fans looked on, he held the trophy high and shouted, "This Cup is for you!"

*The Pittsburgh Penguins' Mario Lemieux — at long last a Stanley Cup!*
(Norman James)

**I**N 1991–92, the NHL skated through its 75th season, attempting to deal with a number of major problems. Eric Lindros refused to join Quebec, there was no collective bargaining agreement in place, no satisfactory television deal for hockey in the U.S., the FBI was taking a close look at the league and the business affairs of Alan Eagleson, and a number of headaches, most of them financial, were created by the two conditional franchises in Tampa Bay and Ottawa.

Prior to the season, collective bargaining talks were initiated between the league and the NHLPA. The first round of talks ended with Philadelphia Flyer owner Ed Snider challenging Jim Quinn, an aggressive New York-based antitrust lawyer to a fistfight. It quickly became obvious that negotiating with Bob Goodenow, the new executive director of the NHLPA, would be much more difficult than dealing with his predecessor, Alan Eagleson, and that a strike or lockout might have to be faced, possibly prior to the Stanley Cup playoffs.

Eagleson, meanwhile, orchestrated another Canada Cup tournament, which was won by Canada over the United States in

Hamilton on September 16. Until he was knocked out of the tournament by a Gary Suter check in game one of the finals, Wayne Gretzky was the dominant forward in the tournament and Bill Ranford the top goalie. Pittsburgh's Bob Johnson, coach of Team U.S.A., was dealt some devastating news on the eve of the tournament. He was diagnosed as having brain tumors, and within a few weeks the popular coach was dead.

Eric Lindros, drafted first overall by the Nordiques in the June entry draft and a star with Team Canada in September, stubbornly refused to sign with the Quebec City club. "It's just not a place where I want to spend my career," he said. "I have nothing against the city of Quebec, nothing against the French people, and nothing against the Nordiques. It's just that I think I should be able to decide where I spend my career."

The Edmonton Oilers made another blockbuster deal when they dealt Mark Messier and "future considerations" to New York in return for Bernie Nicholls, Louie DeBrusk, Steven Rice, and a reported $5 million.

The San Jose Sharks became the newest member of the NHL, while the Tampa Bay Lightning and the Ottawa Senators, scheduled to begin play in 1993, both had problems raising the money for their franchise fee payments. On December 20, four days past the deadline, NHL president John Ziegler announced that both clubs had met the terms for expansion and they were officially recognized as league members. Tampa Bay was placed in the Norris Division and Ottawa found a berth in the Adams Division.

There were some familiar faces in new places. Cliff Fletcher left Calgary to take on the challenge of rebuilding the Leafs. One of his first moves was to acquire goalie Grant Fuhr and winger Glenn Anderson in a deal with the Oilers. Later he picked up Doug Gilmour, Ric Nattress, Jamie Macoun, Rick Wamsley, and Kent Manderville from the Flames in return for Gary Leeman, Craig Berube, Michel Petit, Alexander Godynyuk, and Jeff Reese. John Muckler left Edmonton to join the Buffalo Sabres as director of hockey operations. Jari Kurri returned from Europe to join the L.A. Kings, and Pat LaFontaine became a Sabre while Pierre

Turgeon and a package of players went to the Islanders in return. Kevin Dineen was traded by Hartford to Philadelphia for Murray Craven, and by midseason Adam Oates went from the Blues to the Bruins in return for Craig Janney and Stephane Quintal.

On April 1, the NHLPA voted 560–4 to stage the first strike in NHL history, one that directly threatened the 1992 playoffs. There were six or seven issues that couldn't be settled, including trading card revenues, free agency, length of contract, and control of a 1986 pension surplus. The Whalers' Pat Verbeek was more vocal than most players when asked about the strike. "Obviously, the owners don't want any playoffs," he said. "Absolutely in our minds we're doing the right thing. We've had the raw end of the stick for a long time. If we don't do what we say, we're a laughing stock. It's time to face up to the fight and the fight is at hand."

The ten-day strike was settled on April 10 when a tentative truce was reached in New York. Crucial to the settlement was the NHLPA's acceptance of what amounted to a one-year deal and the owners' acknowledgment that the players had full rights to trading card revenues. John Ziegler said the league would lose $9 million in the 1991–92 season, $52 million in 1992–93, and $102 million in 1993–94.

The New York Rangers finished first overall with 104 points. Washington and Detroit tied for second with 98 points, while Vancouver was a surprise fourth with 96. Two Rangers, Mark Messier and Brian Leetch, finished among the top ten scorers with 107 and 102 points respectively. Mario Lemieux, who missed several games with back problems, captured the Art Ross Trophy as scoring champion with 131 points in 64 games. Teammate Kevin Stevens was second with 123.

In the Smythe Division playoffs, the Vancouver Canucks flirted with disaster when they fell behind Winnipeg three games to one. Then they rebounded with three straight wins to become one of only 11 teams to accomplish such a feat. When the L.A. Kings met the Edmonton Oilers in the other Smythe matchup, it was a battle of youth versus age and youth triumphed. The Kings, with a payroll of $13.5 million, the highest in league history, spent the money on veterans, and with 11 players over 30 they couldn't keep pace with the much younger Oilers, who won the series in six games. Six days after the series, Kings' coach Tom Webster was fired. In the division finals, the pumped-up Edmonton Oilers, playing on home ice under five Stanley Cup banners, ousted the Vancouver Canucks four games to two.

In the Norris Division, the Detroit Red Wings, despite some shabby goaltending and trailing 3–1 in the series with Minnesota, bounced back to dispose of the North Stars in seven games. Meanwhile, the Chicago Blackhawks ousted the St. Louis Blues four games to two. The Blues' defeat cost coach Brian Sutter his job, even though he had piloted the Blues to more wins (153) than any coach in Blues' history. Sutter was replaced by Bob Plager, an original Blue.

During the regular season, the Red Wings outscored the Chicago Blackhawks by an average of almost a goal a game. But they couldn't find that goal when they needed it in the Norris Division finals and were bowled over in four straight games. Jeremy Roenick, with eight stitches in his mouth and a badly bruised cheek and nose, scored both Chicago goals in the Hawks' 2–1 win in game four.

In the Patrick Division, Washington had Pittsburgh on the brink, leading three games to one. But Mario Lemieux, nursing a sore back, scored 17 points in leading the Pens to a seven-game series victory. The Rangers–Devils series also went the distance and ended with the Rangers' big line of Mark Messier, Adam Graves, and Tony Amonte exploding for nine points in an 8–4 victory in the final game. The Rangers, suffering through five decades of Stanley Cup disappointment, appeared to be shoo-ins against Pittsburgh in the finals. The Pens were missing Joey Mullen, and in game two they lost Mario Lemieux, who was viciously slashed by New York's Adam Graves and suffered a broken hand. When Graves was handed a mere four-game suspension, Lemieux talked of retiring from the game at age 26 and at the peak of his career. Earlier, he had ridiculed the league for the way discipline was maintained and called the NHL a "garage league." With flashy Jaromir Jagr and Ron Francis picking up the slack, the Penguins eliminated the Rangers, 18 points their superiors, in six games. After the series, Mario Lemieux said he thought the Rangers had a "contract" out on him.

Montreal fans were ecstatic when Russ Courtnall scored in the second overtime period to give the Habs a 3–2 seventh-game victory over Hartford in the Adams Division semifinals. Only 5,600 fans turned out in Hartford for game three. In the other Adams matchup, Andy Moog's goaltending was the difference as the Boston Bruins shaded Buffalo, also in seven games. Montrealers had nothing to cheer about in the finals. The Canadiens scored only four goals in the final three games and lost four straight to the Bruins. It marked the first time in 40 years that the Habs were tossed aside so easily.

The Bruins' hot streak came to an end in the Wales Conference finals against Pittsburgh. After losing the opener 4–3, the Bruins were manhandled by the Pens in the next three games. Mario Lemieux made a stunning return to the Pittsburgh lineup, coming back from his hand injury much earlier than anyone anticipated. "All of a sudden we were in awe of Lemieux, and it changed the whole series around," said Bruin coach Rick Bowness. In the final game, Lemieux scored a goal of breathtaking brilliance, deliberately pushing the puck into the skates of a backpedaling Ray Bourque, then retrieving the disc and burying it over Andy Moog's catching glove. "If I ever write a book, that goal will get an entire chapter," said Lemieux's astonished teammate Ron Francis.

In the Campbell Conference showdown, the Chicago Blackhawks recorded their second straight playoff sweep by dismantling the Edmonton Oilers and earning a berth in the Stanley Cup finals for the first time in 19 years. "Too much Chelios, too much Smith, too much Larmer, and too much Roenick" was Oiler Kevin Lowe's explanation for the swift defeat. Stressing defense, the Blackhawks throttled the Edmonton power play, which went 0-for-19.

Most Stanley Cup finals in the past two decades were one-sided confrontations, with only one, the Oilers versus the Flyers in

1987, lasting seven games. The 1992 matchup between the Penguins and the Blackhawks promised to be spectacular, a fitting finale to the strike-marred 75th anniversary season. And it started out that way when Chicago jumped into a 3–0 lead in game one and were ahead 4–1 in the second period. Then the Penguins scored twice in less than a minute to get back into the game. With 4:55 left in the third period, Jaromir Jagr scored one of the prettiest goals ever seen. He fooled Sutter with a between-the-skates move, waltzed around Kucera, and backhanded the puck past Ed Belfour. Mario Lemieux's game winner came with only 12 seconds left on the clock. The 5–4 triumph ended Chicago's record playoff streak of 11 consecutive victories.

The Penguins ran off three more wins to tie the Blackhawks' 11-game streak, and they captured their second straight Stanley Cup with a thrilling 6–5 victory at the Chicago Stadium on June 1. When it was over, most of them dedicated the victory to their former coach Bob Johnson. "He was always on our minds," said Mario Lemieux. "He taught us how to win." Scotty Bowman, who stepped in reluctantly for Johnson early in the season, was credited with convincing the Penguins to play a more defensive style in the playoffs, a major factor in their victory.

The series was too one-sided to be called a spectacle. Pittsburgh was simply too dominant. Mario Lemieux was magnificent, and goaltender Tom Barrasso frustrated the Hawks on countless occasions. Despite missing five games with a broken hand, Lemieux was the leading playoff scorer with 34 points, including five game-winning goals in only 15 games. When Lemieux was awarded the Conn Smythe Trophy, teammate Phil Bourque said, "He's definitely the best player in the world."

*Scotty Bowman, the coach with the Stanley Cup touch, won his sixth in 1992.*

# Afterword

**A** **FEW DAYS AFTER** the 1992 playoffs, I journeyed to New York to act as master of ceremonies — for the 15th consecutive time — at the annual Canadian Society Hockey Dinner held at the Waldorf Astoria. It's one sports dinner I really look forward to each year, and this time Guy Lafleur was the honored guest. In the past, the Canadian Society has honored such notables as Rocket Richard, Gordie Howe, Red Kelly, Ken Dryden, Bobby Hull, Jean Beliveau, Vladislav Tretiak, Clarence Campbell, and Denis Potvin.

On the night before the dinner, chairman Paul Levesque invited the hockey celebrities and their wives to a posh French restaurant. There, gathered around a single long table, was Jean Beliveau, Yvan Cournoyer, Red Kelly, Scotty Bowman, Ken Dryden, Vladislav Tretiak and, of course, Guy Lafleur. Over the wine, someone — I think it was Cournoyer — suggested that each player get up and relate a Stanley Cup experience. Somebody else counted the number of Stanley Cups represented by the celebrities in the room and arrived at the figure 47.

Cournoyer, who played on ten Stanley Cup winners, all with the Canadiens, said he is often asked who was the best player on those championship teams. "I tell them I can't say who was best," he said with a grin. "With the Canadiens, nobody was the best.

We were taught it was a team game, a team effort. When I joined the Canadiens, Jean Beliveau took me aside and told me not to think about winning scoring titles or scoring 50 goals or making the all-star team. 'Just remember,' he said, 'at the end of the season we'll win the Stanley Cup, and that's all that matters.'"

Beliveau, whose brilliance helped bring ten Stanley Cup championships to Montreal, recalled a couple of losses, one to Detroit in 1954 on Tony Leswick's fluke goal off Doug Harvey's glove in the seventh game, and another to the Leafs in 1967. "I think we had a better team than Toronto that year," he said, smiling across the table at Red Kelly, "but Red, you had Bower and Sawchuk in goal and that, I believe, was the difference."

Beliveau also praised Ken Dryden for his remarkable debut in the Stanley Cup playoffs in 1972. "He joined us late in the season, just in time to be eligible for postseason play, and he performed miracles against the Bruins in the first round. Believe me, the Bruins had a great year, but Dryden made one sensational save after another. I can still see Phil Esposito standing beside Dryden's net and glaring at him in anger and frustration and disbelief."

Dryden reflected on that same series, his initial rise to NHL prominence, and said he wasn't at all nervous in those games against the Bruins. "It wasn't as though I was a stranger to the Boston Garden," he said. "I had played many games in Boston in college hockey before full houses and screaming fans, and I reveled in it. Even as a rookie, I felt perfectly comfortable in the Montreal goal that year."

Tretiak rose to say, through an interpreter, that he had often dreamed of playing on a Stanley Cup team and came close at the end of his career when he almost joined the Montreal Canadiens. But alas, in those days it was difficult to gain permission from Soviet authorities to play for an NHL team, and the opportunity to compete in the Stanley Cup playoffs was denied him.

Red Kelly told a story about a Toronto Stanley Cup win and how he suffered a leg injury in the final match. After the game, he collapsed in the shower and was rushed to hospital. As a result, he missed all the postgame excitement. The next day, he was required to be in Ottawa where he was a Member of Parliament, representing Lester Pearson's Liberals. Kelly managed to get to Ottawa and the House of Commons where "I sat all afternoon with my sore leg sticking out in the aisle. I could hardly bend it, and other members kept stepping over it."

At the end of the day, he flew back to Toronto to discover that Leaf owner Harold Ballard had been a visitor to his house. "Harold came around with some champagne under one arm and the Stanley Cup under the other," Red said, chuckling. "He even had a cameraman in tow. He knew that I'd missed the postgame party the night before and he wanted to make sure I tasted champagne from the Cup. When he found out I was away, he grouped the kids around the Cup and placed my three-month-old son Conn right in the bowl. While the cameraman was taking his photos, Conn broke out in a wide grin. My wife Andra knew what that meant. Sure enough, Conn made a big dump right in the Cup. I think of that every time I see players drinking out of that bowl each spring."

Scotty Bowman, fresh from his Stanley Cup victory party in Pittsburgh, said his son was named after his first Cup triumph in Montreal. "I not only called him Stanley, but I got in the habit of calling him Stanley Cup," said Scotty, "even though his middle name was Glenn — after my goalie in St. Louis, Glenn Hall. One time I had to register my son for something at school, and I told the man his name was Stanley Glenn. On the way home in the car, Stanley started to cry. When I asked what was wrong, he whimpered, 'You mean my name isn't really Stanley Cup?' He was really upset. I told him, 'Stanley, you'll always be Stanley Cup to me.'"

Scotty also mentioned how the 1992 victory celebrations in Pittsburgh almost got out of hand when a group of players brought the Cup to Mario Lemieux's house. One of the players impulsively climbed a steep incline behind the Lemieux swimming pool and, from his lofty perch, hoisted the Cup high over his head and heaved it in the general direction of the pool.

"Fortunately, his aim was true and the Cup hit the water with a great splash," said Scotty. "I shudder to think of what might have happened if the Cup had hit the concrete patio surrounding the pool."

Finally, Guy Lafleur stood and reminisced about the first of his five Cup wins with the Canadiens. "When I arrived, I was in awe of such greats as my idol Jean Beliveau, and Frank Mahovlich and so many other Montreal stars," said Lafleur. "They talked about past Cup wins, and it seemed to me there were so many of them. I wondered if there would be any left for me. I knew I wouldn't be happy until I was on a Stanley Cup team and I was afraid it might not happen. When it did, it was in Chicago. I was so happy I began mixing beer with champagne, and soon I was pretty drunk. That was the year, you remember, when Claude Larose broke his leg in the last game in Chicago and he came home on the charter flight on a stretcher. When we landed in Montreal, I couldn't move from my seat. So Butch Bouchard threw Larose off the stretcher, picked me up, and tossed me onto it. Poor Claude had to be helped off the flight while I was carried off on the stretcher."

It was another in a thousand stories about hockey's most famous trophy — the Stanley Cup.

# Statistics

## Stanley Cup Winners

| Season | Champions | Manager | Coach |
|---|---|---|---|
| 1991-92 | Pittsburgh Penguins | Craig Patrick | Scotty Bowman |
| 1990-91 | Pittsburgh Penguins | Craig Patrick | Bob Johnson |
| 1989-90 | Edmonton Oilers | Glen Sather | John Muckler |
| 1988-89 | Calgary Flames | Cliff Fletcher | Terry Crisp |
| 1987-88 | Edmonton Oilers | Glen Sather | Glen Sather |
| 1986-87 | Edmonton Oilers | Glen Sather | Glen Sather |
| 1985-86 | Montreal Canadiens | Serge Savard | Jean Perron |
| 1984-85 | Edmonton Oilers | Glen Sather | Glen Sather |
| 1983-84 | Edmonton Oilers | Glen Sather | Glen Sather |
| 1982-83 | New York Islanders | Bill Torrey | Al Arbour |
| 1981-82 | New York Islanders | Bill Torrey | Al Arbour |
| 1980-81 | New York Islanders | Bill Torrey | Al Arbour |
| 1979-80 | New York Islanders | Bill Torrey | Al Arbour |
| 1978-79 | Montreal Canadiens | Irving Grundman | Scotty Bowman |
| 1977-78 | Montreal Canadiens | Sam Pollock | Scotty Bowman |
| 1976-77 | Montreal Canadiens | Sam Pollock | Scotty Bowman |
| 1975-76 | Montreal Canadiens | Sam Pollock | Scotty Bowman |
| 1974-75 | Philadelphia Flyers | Keith Allen | Fred Shero |
| 1973-74 | Philadelphia Flyers | Keith Allen | Fred Shero |
| 1972-73 | Montreal Canadiens | Sam Pollock | Scotty Bowman |
| 1971-72 | Boston Bruins | Milt Schmidt | Tom Johnson |
| 1970-71 | Montreal Canadiens | Sam Pollock | Al MacNeil |
| 1969-70 | Boston Bruins | Milt Schmidt | Harry Sinden |
| 1968-69 | Montreal Canadiens | Sam Pollock | Claude Ruel |
| 1967-68 | Montreal Canadiens | Sam Pollock | Toe Blake |
| 1966-67 | Toronto Maple Leafs | Punch Imlach | Punch Imlach |
| 1965-66 | Montreal Canadiens | Sam Pollock | Toe Blake |
| 1964-65 | Montreal Canadiens | Sam Pollock | Toe Blake |
| 1963-64 | Toronto Maple Leafs | Punch Imlach | Punch Imlach |

| Season | Champions | Manager | Coach |
|--------|-----------|---------|-------|
| 1962-63 | Toronto Maple Leafs | Punch Imlach | Punch Imlach |
| 1961-62 | Toronto Maple Leafs | Punch Imlach | Punch Imlach |
| 1960-61 | Chicago Black Hawks | Tommy Ivan | Rudy Pilous |
| 1959-60 | Montreal Canadiens | Frank Selke | Toe Blake |
| 1958-59 | Montreal Canadiens | Frank Selke | Toe Blake |
| 1957-58 | Montreal Canadiens | Frank Selke | Toe Blake |
| 1956-57 | Montreal Canadiens | Frank Selke | Toe Blake |
| 1955-56 | Montreal Canadiens | Frank Selke | Toe Blake |
| 1954-55 | Detroit Red Wings | Jack Adams | Jimmy Skinner |
| 1953-54 | Detroit Red Wings | Jack Adams | Tommy Ivan |
| 1952-53 | Montreal Canadiens | Frank Selke | Dick Irvin |
| 1951-52 | Detroit Red Wings | Jack Adams | Tommy Ivan |
| 1950-51 | Toronto Maple Leafs | Conn Smythe | Joe Primeau |
| 1949-50 | Detroit Red Wings | Jack Adams | Tommy Ivan |
| 1948-49 | Toronto Maple Leafs | Conn Smythe | Hap Day |
| 1947-48 | Toronto Maple Leafs | Conn Smythe | Hap Day |
| 1946-47 | Toronto Maple Leafs | Conn Smythe | Hap Day |
| 1945-46 | Montreal Canadiens | Tommy Gorman | Dick Irvin |
| 1944-45 | Toronto Maple Leafs | Conn Smythe | Hap Day |
| 1943-44 | Montreal Canadiens | Tommy Gorman | Dick Irvin |
| 1942-43 | Detroit Red Wings | Jack Adams | Jack Adams |
| 1941-42 | Toronto Maple Leafs | Conn Smythe | Hap Day |
| 1940-41 | Boston Bruins | Art Ross | Cooney Weiland |
| 1939-40 | New York Rangers | Lester Patrick | Frank Boucher |
| 1938-39 | Boston Bruins | Art Ross | Art Ross |
| 1937-38 | Chicago Black Hawks | Bill Stewart | Bill Stewart |
| 1936-37 | Detroit Red Wings | Jack Adams | Jack Adams |
| 1935-36 | Detroit Red Wings | Jack Adams | Jack Adams |
| 1934-35 | Montreal Maroons | Tommy Gorman | Tommy Gorman |
| 1933-34 | Chicago Back Hawks | Tommy Gorman | Tommy Gorman |
| 1932-33 | New York Rangers | Lester Patrick | Lester Patrick |
| 1931-32 | Toronto Maple Leafs | Conn Smythe | Dick Irvin |
| 1930-31 | Montreal Canadiens | Cecil Hart | Cecil Hart |
| 1929-30 | Montreal Canadiens | Cecil Hart | Cecil Hart |
| 1928-29 | Boston Bruins | Art Ross | Cy Denneny |
| 1927-28 | New York Rangers | Lester Patrick | Lester Patrick |
| 1926-27 | Ottawa Senators | Dave Gill | Dave Gill |
| 1925-26 | Montreal Maroons | Eddie Gerard | Eddie Gerard |
| 1924-25 | Victoria Cougars | Lester Patrick | Lester Patrick |
| 1923-24 | Montreal Canadiens | Leo Dandurand | Leo Dandurand |
| 1922-23 | Ottawa Senators | Tommy Gorman | Pete Green |
| 1921-22 | Toronto St. Pats | Charlie Querrie | Eddie Powers |
| 1920-21 | Ottawa Senators | Tommy Gorman | Pete Green |
| 1919-20 | Ottawa Senators | Tommy Gorman | Pete Green |
| 1918-19 | No decision.* | | |
| 1917-18 | Toronto Arenas | Charlie Querrie | Dick Carroll |

*In the spring of 1919 the Montreal Canadiens traveled to Seattle to meet Seattle, PCHL champions. After five games had been played — teams were tied at 2 wins and 1 tie — the series was called off by the local Department of Health because of the influenza epidemic and the death from influenza of Joe Hall.

| Season | Champions | Manager | Coach |
|---|---|---|---|
| 1916-17 | Seattle Metropolitans | Pete Muldoon | Pete Muldoon |
| 1915-16 | Montreal Canadiens | George Kennedy | George Kennedy |
| 1914-15 | Vancouver Millionaires | Frank Patrick | Frank Patrick |
| 1913-14 | Toronto Blueshirts | Jack Marshall | Scotty Davidson* |
| 1912-13** | Quebec Bulldogs | M. J. Quinn | Joe Malone* |
| 1911-12 | Quebec Bulldogs | M. J. Quinn | C. Nolan |
| 1910-11 | Ottawa Senators | | Bruce Stuart* |
| 1909-10 | Montreal Wanderers | R. R. Boon | Pud Glass* |
| 1908-09 | Ottawa Senators | | Bruce Stuart* |
| 1907-08 | Montreal Wanderers | R. R. Boon | Cecil Blachford |
| 1906-07 | Montreal Wanderers (March) | R. R. Boon | Cecil Blachford |
| 1906-07 | Kenora Thistles (January) | F. A. Hudson | Tommy Phillips* |
| 1905-06 | Montreal Wanderers | | Cecil Blachford |
| 1904-05 | Ottawa Silver Seven | | A. T. Smith |
| 1903-04 | Ottawa Silver Seven | | A. T. Smith |
| 1902-03 | Ottawa Silver Seven | | A. T. Smith |
| 1901-02 | Montreal AAA | | C. McKerrow |
| 1900-01 | Winnipeg Victorias | | D. H. Bain |
| 1899-1900 | Montreal Shamrocks | | H. J. Trihey* |
| 1898-99 | Montreal Shamrocks | | H. J. Trihey* |
| 1897-98 | Montreal Victorias | | F. Richardson |
| 1896-97 | Montreal Victorias | | Mike Grant* |
| 1895-96 | Montreal Victorias | | Mike Grant* |
| | (December, 1896) | | |
| 1895-96 | Winnipeg Victorias (February) | | J. C. G. Armytage |
| 1894-95 | Montreal Victorias | | Mike Grant* |
| 1893-94 | Montreal AAA | | |
| 1892-93 | Montreal AAA | | |

**Victoria defeated Quebec in challenge series. No official recognition.

*In the early years the teams were frequently run by the Captain. *Indicates Captain

# Team Records

## 1918-1992

**Most Stanley Cup Championships:**
22 — Montreal Canadiens 1924-30-31-44-46-53-56-57-58-59-60-65-66-68-69-71-73-76-77-78-79-86
13 — Toronto Maple Leafs 1918-22-32-42-45-47-48-49-51-62-63-64-67

**Most Final Series Appearances:**
32 — Montreal Canadiens
21 — Toronto Maple Leafs

**Most Years in Playoffs:**
67 — Montreal Canadiens
54 — Toronto Maple Leafs

**Most Consecutive Stanley Cup Championships:**
5 — Montreal Canadiens (1956-57-58-59-60)
4 — Montreal Canadiens (1976-77-78-79)
  — NY Islanders (1980-81-82-83)

**Most Goals Both Teams, One Playoff Series:**
69 — Edmonton Oilers, Chicago Blackhawks in 1985 CF. Edmonton won best-of-seven series 4-2, outscoring Chicago 44-25.

**Most Goals One Team, One Playoff Series:**
44 — Edmonton Oilers in 1985 CF. Edmonton won best-of-seven series 4-2, outscoring Chicago 44-25.

**Most Goals, Both Teams, Two-Game Series:**
17 — Toronto St. Patricks, Montreal Canadiens in 1918 NHL F. Toronto won two-game total goal series 10-7.

**Most Goals, One Team, Two-Game Series:**
11 — Buffalo Sabres in 1977 PR. Buffalo won best-of-three series 2-0, outscoring Minnesota 11-3.
— Toronto Maple Leafs in 1978 PR. Toronto won best-of-three series 2-0, outscoring Los Angeles 11-3.

**Most Goals, Both Teams, Three-Game Series:**
33 — Minnesota North Stars, Boston Bruins in 1981 PR. Minnesota won best-of-five series 3-0, outscoring Boston 20-13.

**Most Goals, One Team, Three-Game Series:**
23 — Chicago Blackhawks in 1985 DSF. Chicago won best-of-five 3-0, outscoring Detroit 23-8.

**Most Goals, Both Teams, Four-Game Series:**
36 — Boston Bruins, St. Louis Blues in 1972 SF. Boston won best-of-seven series 4-0, outscoring St.Louis 28-8.
— Edmonton Oilers, Chicago Blackhawks in 1983 CF. Edmonton won best-of-seven series 4-0, outscoring Chicago 25-11.
— Minnesota North Stars, Toronto Maple Leafs in 1983 DSF. Minnesota won best-of-five series 3-1; teams tied in scoring 18-18.

**Most Goals, One Team, Four-Game Series:**
28 — Boston Bruins in 1972 SF. Boston won best-of-seven series 4-0, outscoring St. Louis 28-8.

**Most Goals, Both Teams, Five-Game Series:**
52 — Edmonton Oilers, Los Angeles Kings in 1987 DSF. Edmonton won best-of-seven series 4-1, outscoring Los Angeles 32-20.

**Most Goals, One Team, Five-Game Series:**

35 — Edmonton Oilers in 1983 DF. Edmonton won best-of-seven series 4-1, outscoring Calgary 35-13.

**Most Goals, Both Teams, Six-Game Series:**

69 — Edmonton Oilers, Chicago Blackhawks in 1985 CF. Edmonton won best-of-seven series 4-2, outscoring Chicago 44-25.

**Most Goals, One Team, Six-Game Series:**

44 — Edmonton Oilers in 1985 CF. Edmonton won best-of-seven series 4-2, outscoring Chicago 44-25.

**Most Goals, Both Teams, Seven-Game Series:**

60 — Edmonton Oilers, Calgary Flames in 1984 DF. Edmonton won best-of-seven series 4-3, outscoring Calgary 33-27.

**Most Goals, One Team, Seven-Game Series:**

33 — Philadelphia Flyers in 1976 QF. Philadelphia won best-of-seven series 4-3, outscoring Toronto 33-23.
— Boston Bruins in 1983 DF. Boston won best-of-seven series 4-3, outscoring Buffalo 33-23.
— Edmonton Oilers in 1984 DF. Edmonton won best-of-seven series 4-3, outscoring Calgary 33-27.

**Fewest Goals, Both Teams, Two-Game Series:**

1 — NY Rangers, NY Americans, in 1929 SF. NY Rangers defeated NY Americans 1-0 in two-game, total-goal series.
— Mtl. Maroons, Chicago Blackhawks in 1935 SF. Mtl. Maroons defeated Chicago 1-0 in two-game, total-goal series.

**Fewest Goals, One Team, Two-Game Series:**

0 — Mtl. Maroons in 1937 SF. Lost best-of-three series 2-0 to NY Rangers while being outscored 5-0.
— NY Americans in 1939 QF. Lost best-of-three series 2-0 to Toronto while being outscored 6-0.
— NY Americans in 1929 SF. Lost two-game total-goal series 1-0 against NY Rangers.
— Chicago Blackhawks in 1935 SF. Lost two-game total-goal series 1-0 against Mtl. Maroons.

**Fewest Goals, Both Teams, Three-Game Series:**

7 — Boston Bruins, Montreal Canadiens in 1929 SF. Boston won best-of-five series 3-0, outscoring Montreal 5-2.
— Detroit Red Wings, Mtl. Maroons in 1936 SF. Detroit won best-of-five series 3-0, outscoring Mtl. Maroons 6-1.

**Fewest Goals, One Team, Three-Game Series:**

1 — Mtl. Maroons in 1936 SF. Lost best-of-five series 3-0 to Detroit and were outscored 6-1.

**Fewest Goals, Both Teams, Four-Game Series:**

9 — Toronto Maple Leafs, Boston Bruins in 1935 SF. Toronto won best-of-five series 3-1, outscoring Boston 7-2.

**Fewest Goals, One Team, Four-Game Series:**

2 — Boston Bruins in 1935 SF. Toronto won best-of-five series 3-1, outscoring Boston 7-2.
— Montreal Canadiens in 1952 F. Detroit won best-of-seven series 4-0, outscoring Montreal 11-2.

**Fewest Goals, Both Teams, Five-Game Series:**

11 — NY Rangers, Mtl. Maroons in 1928 F. NY Rangers won best-of-five series 3-2, while outscored by Mtl. Maroons 6-5.

**Fewest Goals, One Team, Five-Game Series:**

5 — NY Rangers in 1928 F. NY Rangers won best-of-five series 3-2, while outscored by Mtl. Maroons 6-5.

**Fewest Goals, Both Teams, Six-Game Series:**

22 — Toronto Maple Leafs, Boston Bruins in 1951 SF. Toronto won best-of-seven series 4-1 with 1 tie, outscoring Boston 17-5.

**Fewest Goals, One Team, Six-Game Series:**
5 — Boston Bruins in 1951 SF. Toronto won best-of-seven series 4-1 with 1 tie, outscoring Boston 17-5.

**Fewest Goals, Both Teams, Seven-Game Series:**
18 — Toronto Maple Leafs, Detroit Red Wings in 1945 F. Toronto won best-of-seven series 4-3; teams tied in scoring 9-9.

**Fewest Goals, One Team, Seven-Game Series:**
9 — Toronto Maple Leafs, in 1945 F. Toronto won best-of-seven series 4-3; teams tied in scoring 9-9
— Detroit Red Wings, in 1945 F. Toronto won best-of-seven series 4-3; teams tied in scoring 9-9.

**Most Goals, Both Teams, One Game:**
18 — Los Angeles Kings, Edmonton Oilers at Edmonton, April 7, 1982. Los Angeles 10, Edmonton 8. Los Angeles won best-of-five DSF 3-2.

**Most Goals, One Team, One Game:**
13 — Edmonton Oilers at Edmonton, April 9, 1987. Edmonton 13, Los Angeles 3. Edmonton won best-of-seven DSF 4-1.

**Most Goals, Both Teams, One Period:**
9 — NY Rangers, Philadelphia Flyers, April 24, 1979, at Philadelphia, third period. NY Rangers won 8-3 scoring six of nine third-period goals.
— Los Angeles Kings, Calgary Flames at Los Angeles, April 10, 1990, second period. Los Angeles won game 12-4, scoring five of nine second-period goals.

**Most Goals, One Team, One Period:**
7 — Montreal Canadiens, March 30, 1944, at Montreal in third period, during 11-0 win against Toronto.

**Longest Overtime:**
116 Minutes, 30 Seconds — Detroit Red Wings, Mtl. Maroons at Montreal, March 24, 25, 1936. Detroit 1, Mtl. Maroons O. Mud Bruneteau scored, assisted by Hec Kilrea, at 16:30 of sixth overtime period, or after 176 minutes, 30 seconds from start of game, which ended at 2:25 a.m. Detroit won best-of-five SF 3-0.

**Shortest Overtime**
9 Seconds — Montreal Canadiens, Calgary Flames, at Calgary, May 18, 1986. Montreal won 3-2 on Brian Skrudland's goal and captured the best-of-seven F 4-1.

**Most Overtime Games, One Playoff Year:**
16 — 1982. Of 71 games played, 16 went into overtime.

**Fewest Overtime Games, One Playoff Year:**
0 — 1963. None of the 16 games went into overtime, the only year since 1926 that no overtime was required in any playoff series.

**Most Overtime-Game Victories, One Team, One Playoff Year:**
6 — NY Islanders, 1980. One against Los Angeles in the PR; two against Boston in the QF; one against Buffalo in the SF; and two against Philadelphia in the F. Islanders played 21 games.

**Most Overtime Games, Final Series:**
5 — Toronto Maple Leafs, Montreal Canadiens in 1951. Toronto defeated Montreal 4-1 in best-of-seven series.

**Most Consecutive Playoff Game Victories:**
12 — Edmonton Oilers. Streak began May 15, 1984 at Edmonton with a 7-2 win over NY Islanders in third game of F series, and ended May 9, 1985 when Chicago defeated Edmonton 5-2 at Chicago. Included in the streak were three wins over the NY Islanders in 1984, three over Los Angeles, four over Winnipeg and two over Chicago, all in 1985.

**Longest Playoff Losing Streak:**
16 Games — Chicago Blackhawks. Streak started in 1975 QF against Buffalo when Chicago lost last two games. Then Chicago lost four games to Montreal in 1976 QF; two games to NY Islanders in 1977 PR; four games to Boston in 1978 QF and four games to NY Islanders in 1979 QF. Streak ended on April 8, 1980 when Chicago defeated St. Louis 3-2 in the opening game of their 1980 PR series.

**Most Shutouts, One Playoff Year, All Teams:**
8 — 1937. Of 17 games played, NY Rangers had 4. Detroit 3, Boston 1.
— 1975. Of 51 games played, Philadelphia had 5, Montreal 2, NY Islanders 1.
— 1980. Of 67 games played, Buffalo had 3, Philadelphia 2, Montreal, NY Islanders and Minnesota 1 each.
— 1984. Of 70 games played, Montreal had 3, Edmonton, Minnesota, NY Rangers, St. Louis and Vancouver 1 each.

**Fewest Shutouts, One Playoff Year, All Teams:**
0 — 1959. 18 games played.

**Most Shutouts, Both Teams, One Series:**
5 — 1945 F, Toronto Maple Leafs, Detroit Red Wings. Toronto had 3 shutouts, Detroit 2. Toronto won best-of-seven series 4-3.
— 1950 SF, Toronto Maple Leafs, Detroit Red Wings. Toronto had 3 shutouts, Detroit 2. Detroit won best-of-seven series 4-3.

**Most Penalties, Both Teams, One Series:**
219 — New Jersey Devils, Washington Capitals in 1988 DF won by New Jersey 4-3. New Jersey received 98 minors, 11 majors, 9 misconducts and 1 match penalty. Washington received 80 minors, 11 majors, 8 misconducts and 1 match penalty.

**Most Penalty Minutes, Both Teams, One Series:**
656 — New Jersey Devils, Washington Capitals in 1988 DF won by New Jersey 4-3. New Jersey had 351 minutes; Washington 305.

**Most Penalties, One Team, One Series:**
119 — New Jersey Devils in 1988 DF versus Washington. New Jersey received 98 minors, 11 majors, 9 misconducts and 1 match penalty.

**Most Penalty Minutes, One Team, One Series:**
351 — New Jersey in 1988 DF versus Washington. Series won by New Jersey 4-3.

**Most Penalty Minutes, Both Teams, One Game:**
298 Minutes — Detroit Red Wings, St Louis Blues, at St. Louis, April 12, 1991. Detroit received 33 penalties for 152 minutes; St. Louis 33 penalties for 146 minutes. St. Louis won 6-1.

**Most Penalties, Both Teams, One Game:**
66 — Detroit Red Wings, St. Louis Blues, at St. Louis, April 12, 1991. Detroit received 33 penalties; St. Louis 33. St. Louis won 6-1.

**Most Penalties, One Team, One Game:**
33 — Detroit Red Wings, at St. Louis, April 12, 1991. St. Louis won 6-1.
— St. Louis Blues, at St. Louis, April 12, 1991. St. Louis won 6-1.

**Most Penalty Minutes, One Team, One Game:**
152 — Detroit Red Wings, at St. Louis, April 12, 1991. St. Louis won 6-1.

**Most Penalties, Both Teams, One Period:**
43 — NY Rangers, Los Angeles Kings, April 9, 1981, at Los Angeles, first period. NY Rangers had 24 penalties; Los Angeles 19. Los Angeles won 5-4.

**Most Penalty Minutes, Both Teams, One Period:**
248 — NY Islanders, Boston Bruins, April 17, 1980, first period, at Boston. Each team received 124 minutes. Islanders won 5-4.

**Most Penalties, One Team, One Period: (And) Most Penalty Minutes, One Team, One Period:**
24 Penalties; 125 Minutes — NY Rangers, April 9, 1981, at Los Angeles, first period. Los Angeles won 5-4.

**Fewest Penalties, Both Teams, Best-Of-Seven Series:**
19 — Detroit Red Wings, Toronto Maple Leafs in 1945 F, won by Toronto 4-3. Detroit received 10 minors. Toronto 9 minors.

**Fewest Penalties, One Team, Best-Of-Seven Series:**
9 — Toronto Maple Leafs in 1945 F, won by Toronto 4-3 against Detroit.

**Most Power-Play Goals By All Teams, One Playoff Year:**
199 — 1988 in 83 games.

**Most Power-Play Goals, One Team, One Playoff Year:**
35 — Minnesota North Stars, 1991, in 23 games.
31 — NY Islanders, 1981, in 18 games.

**Most Power-Play Goals, One Team, One Series:**
15 — NY Islanders in 1980 F against Philadelphia. NY Islanders won series 4-2.
— Minnesota North Stars in 1991 DSF against Chicago. Minnesota won series 4-2.

**Most Power-Play Goals, Both Teams, One Game:**
8 — Minnesota North Stars, St. Louis Blues, April 24, 1991 at Minnesota. Minnesota had 4, St. Louis 4, Minnesota won 8-4.

**Most Power-Play Goals, One Team, One Game:**
6 — Boston Bruins, April 2, 1969, at Boston against Toronto. Boston won 10-0.

**Most Shorthand Goals By All Teams, One Playoff Year:**
33 — 1988, in 83 games.

**Most Shorthand Goals, One Team, One Playoff Year:**
10 — Edmonton Oilers, 1983, in 16 games.

**Most Shorthand Goals, Both Teams, One Series:**
7 — Boston Bruins (4), NY Rangers (3), in 1958 SF, won by Boston 4-2.
— Edmonton Oilers (5), Calgary Flames (2), in 1983 DF won by Edmonton 4-1.

**Most Shorthand Goals, One Team, One Series:**
5 — Edmonton Oilers in 1983 against Calgary in best-of-seven DF won by Edmonton 4-1.
— NY Rangers in 1979 against Philadelphia in best-of-seven QF, won by Rangers 4-1.

**Most Shorthand Goals, Both Teams, One Game:**
4 — NY Islanders, NY Rangers, April 17, 1983 at NY Rangers, NY Islanders had 3 shorthand goals, NY Rangers 1. NY Rangers won 7-6.
— Boston Bruins, Minnesota North Stars, April 11, 1981 at Minnesota. Boston had 3 shorthand goals, Minnesota 1. Minnesota won 6-3.

**Most Shorthand Goals, One Team, One Game:**
3 — Boston Bruins, April 11, 1981, at Minnesota. Minnesota won 6-3.
— NY Islanders, April 17, 1983, at NY Rangers. NY Rangers won 7-6.

**Most Shorthand Goals, Both Teams, One Period:**
3 — Toronto Maple Leafs, Detroit Red Wings, April 5, 1947, at Toronto, first period. Toronto scored two shorthand goals; Detroit one. Toronto won 6-1.

**Fastest Two Goals, Both Teams:**
5 Seconds — Pittsburgh Penguins, Buffalo Sabres at Buffalo, April 14, 1979. Gilbert Perreault scored for Buffalo at 12:59 and Jim Hamilton for Pittsburgh at 13:04 of first period. Pittsburgh won 4-3 and best-of-three PR 2-1.

**Fastest Two Goals, One Team:**
5 Seconds — Detroit Red Wings at Detroit, April 11, 1965, against Chicago. Norm Ullman scored at 17:35 and 17:40, 2nd period. Detroit won 4-2. Chicago won best-of-seven SF 4-3.

**Fastest Three Goals, Both Teams:**
21 Seconds — Edmonton Oilers, Chicago Blackhawks at Edmonton, May 7, 1985. Behn Wilson scored for Chicago at 19:22 of third period, Jari Kurri at 19:36 and Glenn Anderson at 19:43 for Edmonton. Edmonton won 7-3 and best-of-seven CF 4-2.

**Fastest Three Goals, One Team:**
23 Seconds — Toronto Maple Leafs at Toronto, April 12, 1979, against Atlanta Flames. Darryl Sittler scored at 4:04 of first period and again at 4:16 and Ron Ellis at 4:27. Leafs won 7-4 and best-of-three PR 2-0.

**Fastest Four Goals, Both Teams:**
1 Minute, 33 Seconds — Philadelphia Flyers, Toronto Maple Leafs at Philadelphia, April 20, 1976. Don Saleski of Philadelphia scored at 10:04 of second period; Bob Neely, Toronto, 10:42; Gary Dornhoefer, Philadelphia, 11:24; and Don Saleski, 11:37. Philadelphia won 7-1 and best-of-seven QF series 4-3.

**Fastest Four Goals, One Team:**
2 Minutes, 35 Seconds — Montreal Canadiens at Montreal, March 30, 1944, against Toronto. Toe Blake scored at 7:58 of third period and again at 8:37; Maurice Richard, 9:17; Ray Getliffe, 10:33. Montreal won 11-0 and best-of-seven SF 4-0.

**Fastest Five Goals, Both Teams:**
3 Minutes, 6 Seconds — Chicago Blackhawks, Minnesota North Stars, at Chicago April 21, 1985. Keith Brown scored for Chicago at 1:12, second period; Ken Yaremchuk, Chicago, 1:27; Dino Ciccarelli, Minnesota, 2:48. Tony McKegney, Minnesota, 4:07 and Curt Fraser, Chicago, 4:18. Chicago won 6-2 and best-of-seven DF 4-2.

**Fastest Five Goals, One Team:**
3 Minutes, 36 Seconds — Montreal Canadiens at Montreal, March 30, 1944, against Toronto. Toe Blake scored at 7:58 of third period and again at 8:37; Maurice Richard, 9:17; Ray Getliffe, 10:33, and Buddy O'Connor 11:34. Canadiens won 11-0 and best-of-seven SF 4-0.

# Individual Records
## Career

**Most Years in Playoffs:**
20 — Gordie Howe, Detroit, Hartford
— Larry Robinson, Montreal, Los Angeles

**Most Consecutive Years in Playoffs:**
20 — Larry Robinson, Montreal, Los Angeles

**Most Playoff Games:**
227 — Larry Robinson, Montreal, Los Angeles

**Most Points In Playoffs (Career):**
306 — Wayne Gretzky, Edmonton, Los Angeles

**Most Goals In Playoffs (Career):**
95 — Wayne Gretzky, Edmonton, Los Angeles

**Most Game-Winning Goals In Playoffs (Career):**
18 — Maurice Richard, Montreal
— Wayne Gretzky, Edmonton, Los Angeles

**Most Overtime Goals In Playoffs (Career):**
6 — Maurice Richard, Montreal (1 in 1946; 3 in 1951; 1 in 1957; 1 in 1958)

**Most Power-Play Goals In Playoffs (Career):**
35 — Mike Bossy, NY Islanders

**Most Shorthand Goals in Playoffs (Career):**
11 — Mark Messier, Edmonton

**Most Three-Or-More-Goal Games In Playoffs (Career):**
7 — Maurice Richard, Montreal. Four three-goal games; two four-goal games; one five-goal game.
— Wayne Gretzky, Edmonton. Two four-goal games; five three-goal games.
— Jari Kurri, Edmonton. One four-goal game; six three-goal games.

**Most Assists In Playoffs (Career):**
211 — Wayne Gretzky, Edmonton, Los Angeles

**Most Penalty Minutes In Playoffs (Career):**
564 — Dale Hunter, Quebec, Washington

**Most Shutouts In Playoffs (Career):**
15 — Clint Benedict, Ottawa, Mtl. Maroons

**Most Playoff Games Appeared In By A Goaltender (Career):**
132 — Billy Smith, NY Islanders

**Most Minutes Played By A Goaltender (Career):**
7,645 — Billy Smith, NY Islanders

## Single Playoff Year

**Most Points, One Playoff Year:**
47 — Wayne Gretzky, Edmonton, in 1985. 17 goals, 30 assists in 18 games.

**Most Points By A Defenseman, One Playoff Year:**
37 — Paul Coffey, Edmonton, in 1985. 12 goals, 25 assists in 18 games.

**Most Points By A Rookie, One Playoff Year:**
21 — Dino Ciccarelli, Minnesota, in 1981. 14 goals, 7 assists in 19 games.

**Longest Consecutive Point-Scoring Streak, One Playoff Year:**
18 games — Bryan Trottier, NY Islanders, 1981. 11 goals, 18 assists, 29 points.

**Longest Consecutive Point-Scoring Streak, More Than One Playoff Year:**
27 games — Bryan Trottier, NY Islanders, 1980, 1981 and 1982. 7 games in 1980 (3G, 5A, 8PTS), 18 games in 1981 (11G, 18A, 29 PTS), and two games in 1982 (2G, 3A, 5PTS). Total points, 42.

**Most Goals, One Playoff Year:**
19 — Reggie Leach, Philadelphia, 1976. 16 games.
— Jari Kurri, Edmonton, 1985. 18 Games.

**Most Goals By A Defenseman, One Playoff Year:**
12 — Paul Coffey, Edmonton, 1985. 18 games.

**Most Goals By A Rookie, One Playoff Year:**
14 — Dino Ciccarelli, Minnesota, 1981. 19 games.

**Most Game-Winning Goals, One Playoff Year:**
5 — Mike Bossy, NY Islanders, 1983. 19 games.
— Jari Kurri, Edmonton, 1987. 21 games.

— Bobby Smith, Minnesota, 1991. 23 games.

— Mario Lemieux, Pittsburgh, 1992, 15 games.

### Most Overtime Goals, One Playoff Year:

3 — Mel Hill, Boston, 1939. All against NY Rangers in best-of-seven SF, won by Boston 4-3.

— Maurice Richard, Montreal, 1951. 2 against Detroit in best-of-seven SF, won by Montreal 4-2; 1 against Toronto best-of-seven F, won by Toronto 4-1.

### Most Power-Play Goals, One Playoff Year:

9 — Mike Bossy, NY Islanders, 1981. 18 games against Toronto, Edmonton, NY Rangers and Minnesota.

— Cam Neely, Boston, 1991. 19 games against Hartford, Montreal, Pittsburgh.

### Most Shorthand Goals, One Playoff Year:

3 — Derek Sanderson, Boston, 1969. 1 against Toronto in QF, won by Boston 4-0; 2 against Montreal in SF, won by Montreal, 4-2.

— Bill Barber, Philadelphia, 1980. All against Minnesota in SF, won by Philadelphia 4-1.

— Lorne Henning, NY Islanders, 1980. 1 against Boston in QF won by NY Islanders 4-1; 1 against Buffalo in SF, won by NY Islanders 4-2, 1 against Philadelphia in F, won by NY Islanders 4-2.

— Wayne Gretzky, Edmonton, 1983. 2 against Winnipeg in DSF won by Edmonton 3-0; 1 against Calgary in DF, won by Edmonton 4-1.

— Wayne Presley, Chicago, 1989. All against Detroit in DSF won by Chicago 4-2.

### Most Three-Or-More Goal Games, One Playoff Year:

4 — Jari Kurri, Edmonton, 1985. 1 four-goal game, 3 three-goal games.

### Longest Consecutive Goal-Scoring Streak, One Playoff Year:

9 Games — Reggie Leach, Philadelphia, 1976. Streak started April 17 at Toronto and ended May 9 at Montreal. He scored one goal in each of seven games; two in one game; and five in another; a total of 14 goals.

### Most Assists, One Playoff Year:

31 — Wayne Gretzky, Edmonton, 1988. 19 games.

### Most Assists By A Defenseman, One Playoff Year:

25 — Paul Coffey, Edmonton, 1985. 18 games.

### Most Minutes Played By A Goaltender, One Playoff Year:

1,540 — Ron Hextall, Philadelphia, 1987. 26 games.

### Most Wins By A Goaltender, One Playoff Year:

16 — Grant Fuhr, Edmonton, 1988. 19 games.

— Mike Vernon, Calgary, 1989. 22 games.

— Bill Ranford, Edmonton, 1990. 22 games.

### Most Consecutive Wins By A Goaltender, One Playoff Year:

10 — Gerry Cheevers, Boston, 1970. 2 wins against NY Rangers in QF, won by Boston 4-2; 4 wins against Chicago in SF, won by Boston 4-0; and 4 wins against St. Louis in F, won by Boston 4-0.

### Most Shutouts, One Playoff Year:

4 — Clint Benedict, Mtl. Maroons, 1926. 8 games.

— Clint Benedict, Mtl. Maroons, 1928. 9 games.

— Dave Kerr, NY Rangers, 1937. 9 games.

— Frank McCool, Toronto, 1945. 13 games.

— Terry Sawchuk, Detroit, 1952. 8 games.

— Bernie Parent, Philadelphia, 1975. 17 games

— Ken Dryden, Montreal, 1977. 14 games.

**Most Consecutive Shutouts:**
3 — Clint Benedict, Mtl. Maroons, 1926. Benedict shut out Ottawa 1-0, Mar. 27; he then shut out Victoria twice, 3-0, Mar. 30; 3-0, Apr. 1. Mtl. Maroons won NHL F vs. Ottawa 2 goals to 1 and won the best-of-five F vs. Victoria 3-1.
— Frank McCool, Toronto, 1945. McCool shut out Detroit 1-0, April 6; 2-0, April 8; 1-0, April 12, Toronto won the best-of-seven F 4-3.

**Longest Shutout Sequence:**
248 Minutes, 32 Seconds — Norm Smith, Detroit, 1936. In best-of-five SF, Smith shut out Mtl. Maroons 1-0, March 24, in 116:30 overtime; shut out Maroons 3-0 in second game, March 26; and was scored against at 12:02 of first period, March 29, by Gus Marker. Detroit won SF 3-0.

## One-Series Records

**Most Points In Final Series:**
13 — Wayne Gretzky, Edmonton, in 1988, 4 games plus suspended game vs. Boston. 3 goals, 10 assists.

**Most Goals In Final Series:**
9 — Babe Dye, Toronto, in 1922, 5 games vs. Van. Millionaires.

**Most Assists In Final Series:**
10 —Wayne Gretzky, Edmonton, in 1988, 4 games plus suspended game vs. Boston.

**Most Points In One Series (Other Than Final):**
19 — Rick Middleton, Boston, in 1983 DF, 7 games vs. Buffalo. 5 goals, 14 assists.

**Most Goals In One Series (Other Than Final):**
12 — Jari Kurri, Edmonton, in 1985 CF, 6 games vs. Chicago.

**Most Assists In One Series (Other Than Final):**
14 — Rick Middleton, Boston, in 1983 DF, 7 games vs. Buffalo.
— Wayne Gretzky, Edmonton, in 1985 CF, 6 games vs. Chicago.

**Most Game-Winning Goals, One Playoff Series:**
4 — Mike Bossy, NY Islanders, 1983, CF vs. Boston, won by NY Islanders 4-2.

**Most Overtime Goals, One Playoff Series:**
3 — Mel Hill, Boston, 1939, SF vs. NY Rangers, won by Boston 4-3. Hill scored at 59:25 overtime March 21 for a 2–1 win; at 8:24, March 23 for a 3-2 win; and at 48:00, April 2 for a 2-1 win.

**Most Power-Play Goals, One Playoff Series:**
6 — Chris Kontos, Los Angeles, 1989, DSF vs. Edmonton, won by Los Angeles 4-3.

**Most Three-Or-More Goal Games, One Playoff Series:**
3 — Jari Kurri, Edmonton 1985, CF vs. Chicago won by Edmonton 4-2. Kurri scored 3 G May 7 at Edmonton in 7-3 win, 3 G May 14 in 10-5 win and 4 G May 16 at Chicago in 8-2 win.

**Most Shorthand Goals, One Playoff Series:**
3 — Bill Barber, Philadelphia, 1980, SF vs. Minnesota, won by Philadelphia 4-1.
— Wayne Presley, Chicago, 1989, DSF vs. Detroit, won by Chicago 4-2.

## Single Playoff Game Records

**Most Points, One Game:**
8 — Patrik Sundstrom, New Jersey, April 22, 1988 at New Jersey during 10-4 win over Washington. Sundstrom had 3 goals, 5 assists.
— Mario Lemieux, Pittsburgh, April 25, 1989 at Pittsburgh during 10-7 win over Philadelphia. Lemieux had 5 goals, 3 assists.

**Most Points By A Defenseman, One Game:**
6 — Paul Coffey, Edmonton, May 14, 1985 at Edmonton. 1 goal, 5 assists. Edmonton won 10-5.

**Most Goals, One Game:**
5 — Newsy Lalonde, Montreal, March 1, 1919, at Montreal. Final score: Montreal 6, Ottawa 3.
— Maurice Richard, Montreal, March 23, 1944, at Montreal. Final score: Montreal 5, Toronto 1.
— Darryl Sittler, Toronto, April 22, 1976, at Toronto. Final score: Toronto 8, Philadelphia 5.
— Reggie Leach, Philadelphia, May 6, 1976, at Philadelphia. Final score: Philadelphia 6, Boston 3.
— Mario Lemieux, Pittsburgh, April 25, 1989 at Pittsburgh. Final score: Pittsburgh 10, Philadelphia 7.

**Most Goals By A Defenseman, One Game:**
3 — Bobby Orr, Boston, April 11, 1971 at Montreal. Final score: Boston 5, Montreal 2.
— Dick Redmond, Chicago, April 4, 1973 at Chicago. Final score: Chicago 7, St. Louis 1.
— Denis Potvin, NY Islanders, April 17, 1981 at New York. Final score: NY Islanders 6, Edmonton 3.
— Paul Reinhart, Calgary, April 14, 1983 at Edmonton. Final score: Edmonton 6, Calgary 3.
— Paul Reinhart, Calgary, April 8, 1984 at Vancouver. Final score: Calgary 5, Vancouver 1.
— Doug Halward, Vancouver, April 7, 1984 at Vancouver. Final score: Vancouver 7, Calgary 0.

**Most Penalty Minutes, One Game:**
42 — Dave Schultz, Philadelphia, April 22, 1976, at Toronto. One minor, 2 majors, 1 10-minute misconduct and 2 game-misconducts. Final score: Toronto 8, Philadelphia 5.

**Most Penalties, One Game:**
8 — Forbes Kennedy, Toronto, April 2, 1969, at Boston. Four minors, 2 majors, 1 10-minute misconduct, 1 game misconduct. Final score: Boston 10, Toronto 0.
— Kim Clackson, Pittsburgh, April 14, 1980, at Boston. Five minors, 2 majors, 1 10-minute misconduct. Final score: Boston 6, Pittsburgh 2

**Most Penalties, One Period and Most Penalty Minutes, One Period:**
6 Penalties; 39 Minutes — Ed Hospodar, NY Rangers, April 9, 1981 at Los Angeles, first period. Two minors, 1 major, 1 10-minute misconduct, 2 game misconducts. Final score: Los Angeles 5, NY Rangers 4.

**Fastest Two Goals:**
5 Seconds — Norm Ullman, Detroit, at Detroit, April 11, 1965, vs. Chicago and goaltender Glenn Hall. Ullman scored at 17:35 and 17:40 of second period. Detroit won 4-2.

**Fastest Goal From Start Of Game:**
6 Seconds — Don Kozak, Los Angeles, April 17, 1977, at Los Angeles vs. Boston and goaltender Gerry Cheevers. Los Angeles won 7-4.

**Fastest Two Goals From Start Of Game:**
1 Minute, 8 Seconds — Dick Duff, Toronto, April 9, 1963 at Toronto vs. Detroit and goaltender Terry Sawchuk. Duff scored at 49 seconds and 1:08. Final score: Toronto 4, Detroit 2.

**Fastest Two Goals From Start Of Period:**
35 Seconds — Pat LaFontaine, NY Islanders, May 19, 1984 at Edmonton vs. goaltender Andy Moog. LaFontaine scored at 13 and 35 seconds of third period. Final score: Edmonton 5, NY Islanders 2.

# Early Playoff Records
## 1893-1918
### Team Records

**Most Goals, Both Teams, One Game:**
25 — Ottawa Silver Seven, Dawson City at Ottawa, Jan. 16, 1905. Ottawa 23, Dawson City 2. Ottawa won best-of-three series 2-0.

**Most Goals, One Team, One Game:**

23 — Ottawa Silver Seven at Ottawa, Jan. 16, 1905. Ottawa defeated Dawson City 23-2.

**Most Goals, Both Teams, Best-Of-Three Series:**

42 — Ottawa Silver Seven, Queen's University at Ottawa, 1906. Ottawa defeated Queen's 16-7, Feb. 27, and 12-7, Feb. 28.

**Most Goals, One Team, Best-Of-Three Series:**

32 — Ottawa Silver Seven in 1905 at Ottawa. Defeated Dawson City 9-2, Jan. 13, and 23-2, Jan. 16.

**Most Goals, Both Teams, Best-Of-Five Series:**

39 — Toronto Arenas, Vancouver Millionaires at Toronto, 1918. Toronto won 5-3, Mar. 20; 6-3, Mar. 26; 2-1, Mar. 30. Vancouver won 6-4, Mar. 23, and 8-1, Mar. 28. Toronto scored 18 goals; Vancouver 21.

**Most Goals, One Team, Best-Of-Five Series:**

26 — Vancouver Millionaires in 1915 at Vancouver. Defeated Ottawa Senators 6-2, Mar. 22; 8-3, Mar. 24; and 12-3, Mar. 26.

## Individual Records

**Most Goals in Playoffs**

63 — Frank McGee, Ottawa Silver Seven, in 22 playoff games. Seven goals in four games, 1903; 21 goals in eight games, 1904; 18 goals in four games, 1905; 17 goals in six games, 1906.

**Most Goals, One Playoff Series:**

15 — Frank McGee, Ottawa Silver Seven, in two games in 1905 at Ottawa. Scored one goal, Jan. 13, in 9-2 victory over Dawson City and 14 goals, Jan. 16, in 23-2 victory.

**Most Goals, One Playoff Game:**

14 — Frank McGee, Ottawa Silver Seven, Jan. 16, 1905 at Ottawa in 23-2 victory over Dawson City.

**Fastest Three Goals:**

40 Seconds — Marty Walsh, Ottawa Senators, at Ottawa, March 16, 1911, at 3:00, 3:10 and 3:40 of third period. Ottawa defeated Port Arthur 13-4.

# Index

**A**

Abel, Sid, 94, 106, 110, 113, 117, 118, 141, 159
Aberdeen, Earl of, 11, 12
Aberdeen, Lady, 12
Adams Division, 174, 193, 198-99, 236
Adams, Jack, 77, 79, 95, 107, 112, 118, 124-26, 138, 141-42
Adams, Weston, 106
All-Montreal team, 37, 38
Allan Cup, 114
Allen, Keith, 159
Amateur Hockey Association, 9
American Division, of NHL, 63-66, 69, 70, 73, 74, 76, 78, 83
American Hockey League, 72, 91
American Olympic team, 199
Amonte, Tony, 238
Anderson, Glenn, 218, 236
Anderson, Lorne, 115
Angotti, Lou, 204, 208
Apps, Syl, 83, 86, 89, 93, 94, 95, 96, 102, 105
Arbour, Al, 167, 180, 228-29
Arena Cup, 31
Armstrong, George, 143, 146-47, 164, 227
Armstrong, Neil, 171
Art Ross Trophy, 120, 139, 142, 148, 151, 159, 175, 193, 208, 219, 231, 237

Ashbee, Barry, 171
Ashley, George, 158
Ashley, John, 151, 153, 155, 163
Atlanta Flames, 174
    join NHL, 166
Aubut, Marcel, 217
Aurie, Larry, 79

**B**

Babando, Pete, 108, 111, 112
Backstrom, Ralph, 150, 152
Bailey, Bob, 130
Bailey, Irvine (Ace), 75-76
Bain, Danny, 7, 20, 22-23
Balfour, Murray, 135, 138, 139
Ballard, Harold, 152, 183, 185, 227, 243
Balon, Dave, 144, 148
Barilko, Bill, 114
Barkley, Doug, 150
Barlow, Billy, 11, 12, 13
Barrasso, Tom, 204, 224, 234, 240
Barry, Marty, 79, 84
Bassen, Hank, 138, 150
Bathgate, Andy, 124, 134, 139, 144, 145
Bauer, Bobby, 85, 91
Baun, Bob, 146, 147
Beck, Barry, 186, 214-15
Belfour, Ed, 233, 240
Beliveau, Jean, 112-13, 117, 119, 121,

125-26, 128, 131-32, 137, 148-49, 152, 159, 163, 241-42, 244
Bell, Gordie, 125
Bellows, Brian, 233
Benedict, Clint, 45, 47, 49, 56, 61, 62, 68
Bentley, Doug, 96, 98, 102, 107
Bentley, Max, 102, 104, 105
Berenson, Gordon (Red), 157
Berezan, Perry, 212
Bergeron, Michel, 210, 217, 218, 223
Berlin, Ont., 38-39. see also Kitchener, Ont.
Berry, Bob, 199, 208
Berube, Craig, 236
Bibeault, Paul, 98, 104
Bladon, Tom, 183
Blair, Wren, 156
Blake, Hector (Toe), 13, 80, 99, 100, 102, 105, 124, 126, 134, 136, 138, 140, 142, 149, 154, 156
Bodnar, Gus, 98, 101, 105
Boll, Frank (Buzz), 81
Bonin, Marcel, 132, 134
Bossy, Mike, 186, 190, 192, 195-99, 201, 202, 223
Boston Bruins, 63-65, 75, 174, 198
    as Cup winners, 67, 89, 93, 161, 166
Bouchard, Butch, 115, 244
Bouchard, Dan, 171
Bouchard, Pierre, 181
Boucher, Billy, 58, 59, 65, 66, 67
Boucher, Frank, 51, 65, 66, 67, 78, 83, 92, 98, 102
Boucher, George, 112
Bourque, Phil, 240
Bourque, Ray, 234, 239
Bower, Johnny, 133, 136, 137, 139-42, 145, 148, 153-54, 242
Bowie, Russell, 18
Bowman, Scotty, 154, 160, 164, 167-68, 177, 180, 193, 194, 211, 215, 240, 241, 243-44
Bowness, Rick, 239
Boyle, Colonel Joe, 28
Brandon, Man., 27, 32
Brewer, Carl, 147, 149
Bridgman, Mel, 179, 183
Brimsek, Frank, 88, 89, 93, 94, 103-104, 109
Brink, Milt, 83

Broadbent, Harry (Punch), 49, 50, 51, 56
Broda, Walter (Turk), 83, 87, 91, 92, 95, 102, 105, 107-10, 112-114, 116
Brodeur, Richard, 201
Brooks, Herb, 199, 218, 223
Brophy, Fred, 3, 31
Brophy, John, 214, 215, 219-20
Broten, Aaron, 221
Broten, Neal, 233
Brown, A., 23
Brown, Adam, 97
Brown, Arnie, 144
Bruneteau, Modere (Mud), 80, 101
Bucyk, Johnny, 129, 153, 165
Buffalo Sabres, 174, 198
    join NHL, 162
Buffey, Vern, 148, 149, 153
Bullard, Mike, 219
Bure, Pavel, 231
Burnett, Red, 115
Burns, Pat, 223, 225
Bush, Eddie, 94
Byng, Lady, 78

**C**

Cain, Herb, 98
Calder Trophy, 83, 100, 112, 125, 137, 140, 142, 147, 151, 193, 231, 233
Calder, Frank, 45, 60, 61, 64, 70, 72, 76, 80, 81, 89, 95, 96, 103
Calgary Flames, 198
    as Cup winners, 226
Calgary Tigers, 52, 55, 57-58, 59, 61
Calgary, Alta., xii
California Seals, 174, 181
Campbell, Clarence, 4, 83-84, 103, 106, 110, 122, 124, 133, 135, 138, 142, 144, 147, 171, 208, 241
Canada Cup, 183, 235-36
Canadian Amateur Hockey League, 18, 24, 26
Canadian Division, of NHL, 63, 64, 66, 69, 70, 72, 74, 76
Canadian Hockey Association, 37, 38
Canadian Olympic team, 60, 63
Canadian Society Hockey Dinner, 241
Carpenter, Doug, 208, 227
Carr, Lorne, 86, 95, 104
Carson, Bill, 67
Carson, Jimmy, 222, 224

Cashman, Wayne, 170
Cattarinich, Joe, 51
Central Professional Hockey League, 141-42, 197
Chabot, Lorne, 65, 75, 78, 80, 93
Chadwick, Bill, 95
Chadwick, Ed, 133
Chambers, Dave, 232
Champoux, Bob, 145
Chartraw, Rick, 191
Cheevers, Gerry, 166, 167, 184, 187, 188
Chelios, Chris, 225, 229, 231, 238
Cherry, Don, 184, 187, 188, 190, 193, 233
Chevrier, Alain, 224
Chicago Black Hawks (Blackhawks after 1985), xii, 63, 64, 69, 72, 77, 174, 198
   as Cup winners, 76-77, 87, 139
Chicoutimi, Que., 59, 62
Chittick, Fred, 13, 14
Clancy, Francis (King), xiv, 51, 56, 70, 79, 81, 83, 85, 108
Clapper, Aubrey (Dit), 69, 78, 83-84, 102
Clarence Campbell Award, 186
Clarence Campbell Conference, 174, 198-99
Clarke, Bobby, 169, 172, 173, 176, 178, 183, 208, 232
Cleghorn, Sprague, 51, 54, 57
Clement, Bill, 177
Cleveland Barons, 181, 189
Cobalt, Ont., 36, 37, 38, 39
Coffey, Paul, 192, 197, 205, 207, 210, 211, 218
Collins, Bill, 144
Colorado Rockies, 181, 189, 193, 198, 202
Colville, Matthew (Mac), 96
Colville, Neil, 84, 96
Conacher, Charlie, 73, 78, 83, 109, 112
Conacher, Lionel, 77, 85
Conacher, Roy, 104, 107
Conn Smythe Trophy, 149, 151, 156, 159, 161, 163, 165, 169, 173, 177, 181, 184, 189, 197, 201, 204, 208, 214, 222, 226, 231, 234, 240
Connell, Alex, 62, 64, 66
Connors, Harry, 67
Cook, Bill, 75, 78-79, 83

Cook, Fred (Bun), 83
Cook, Lloyd, 51
Cooke, Jack Kent, 187
Corbeau, Bert, 47
Cornwall, Ont., 34
Corson, Shane, 217
Cote, Alain, 217
Cournoyer, Yvan, 148, 149, 153, 168, 169, 170, 241-42
Courtnall, Russ, 239
Couture, Billy, 44, 54-55, 57, 59, 64
Cowley, Bill, 80, 93, 96
Craven, Murray, 237
Creamer, Pierre, 219
Creighton, Don, 130
Crisp, Terry, 218-19, 226, 232
Crozier, Roger, 145, 147, 150, 151, 167-68, 177
Crutchfield, Nelson, 78-79
Cude, Wilf, 76, 79
Curry, Floyd, 121
Cusick, Fred, 127

**D**
Dandurand, Leo, xii, 51, 54-55, 57
Darragh, Harold, 47
Darragh, Jack, 49, 50, 51
Davidson, Bob, 89, 95, 101, 104
Davidson, John, 190, 191
Dawson City Nuggets, 27-29
Dawson City, Yukon, 5, 27-8
Day, Clarence (Hap), 72, 73, 79, 95, 98, 105, 106, 109, 112, 115, 227
DeBrusk, Louie, 236
Dejordy, Denis, 152
Delvecchio, Alex, 138, 145, 169
Demers, Jacques, 204-5, 213, 214, 215-16, 218, 221, 223, 232
Denneny, Corbett, 46, 49, 51-52, 53, 54-55, 56
Desjardins, Gerry, 177
Detroit Cougars, 63, 67, 73
Detroit Falcons, 74
Detroit Olympia, 74
Detroit Red Wings, 75, 80, 174, 192, 198, 201, 231
   as Cup winners, 81, 84, 97, 111, 117, 121, 124
Dewsbury, Al, 112
Dey's Arena, Ottawa, 32, 52
Dickens, Ernie, 105

Dineen, Kevin, 237
Dionne, Marcel, 182, 190, 192, 193, 227
Doak, Gary, 184
Doraty, Ken, 74
Dornhoefer, Gary, 176
Douglas, Kent, 142, 148
Drillon, Gordie, 86, 89, 94, 95
Drinkwater, Graham, 17, 19-20
Druce, John, 229
Dryden, Ken, 163-64, 168-69, 177, 181-85, 205, 213, 241-42
Dudley, Rick, 227
Duff, Dick, 134, 141, 143, 144, 149
Dumart, Woody (Porky), 85, 91, 118
Duncan, Art, 72
Dupont, Andre, 172, 173
Durham, Lloyd, 109
Durnan, Bill, 98, 100, 103, 105, 107, 108, 109, 111
Dutton, Mervyn (Red), 59, 84, 86, 96, 99, 103
Dwyer, Bill, 61, 77
Dye, Cecil (Babe), 53

E

Eagleson, Alan, 182, 231, 235
Eastern Canada Hockey League, 31, 32, 34-35, 37
Edmonton Eskimos, 52, 55, 56-57
Edmonton Journal, 199
Edmonton Oilers, 185, 198
    as Cup winners, 207-8, 210, 218, 221-22, 230
    join NHL, 193
Edmonton, Alta., 5, 35, 38, 62
Edwards, Don, 183
Ehman, Gerry, 133
Esposito, Phil, 144, 154, 157-59, 162-63, 165-66, 168, 170, 173, 175, 186, 196, 199, 223-24, 227, 242
Esposito, Tony, 159, 168-69, 175, 187, 203
Evans, Jack, 204
Ezinicki, Bill, 105

F

Fairbairn, Bill, 165
Faulkner, Alex, 143
Favell, Doug, 154, 157
Federal League, 26, 31, 33, 34

Fedorov, Sergei, 231
Ferguson, John, 144, 149, 153, 158, 164, 182, 185, 204, 223
Fetisov, Viacheslav, 226
Findlay, J. A., 20
Flaman, Fern, 130
Fletcher, Cliff, 166, 236
Fleury, Theoren, 225
Foligno, Mike, 225
Fontinato, Lou, 125, 131, 139, 142
Foran, William, 33, 42-43, 72, 102
Forrest, Albert, 29
Foyston, Frank, 47
Francis, Emile, 104, 147, 171
Francis, Ron, 239
Fraser, Kerry, 217
French Connection Line, 176
Friday, Bill, 150
Frycer, Miroslav, 219-20
Ftorek, Robbie, 227
Fuhr, Grant, 207, 212, 231-32, 236

G

Gadsby, Bill, 123, 135, 146, 159
Gagnon, Johnny, 71, 82
Gainey, Bob, 184, 191, 229, 232
Gallinger, Don, 103, 106
Gallivan, Danny, 208
Galt, Ont., 5, 38, 39
Gardiner, Charlie (Chuck), 71, 76-77, 78
Gardner, Cal, 109, 127
Gare, Danny, 178
Gartner, Mike, 234
Garvin, Ted, 169
Gee, George, 111
Gelinas, Martin, 222, 230
Gelineau, Jack, 109
Geoffrion, Bernie (Boom Boom), 82, 112-13, 116, 119, 121, 123-24, 128, 131, 134, 137-38, 150-51, 166
Gerard, Eddie, 51, 56, 57, 63, 65-66
Giacomin, Ed, 151, 170
Gilbert, Gilles, 170, 172-73, 190
Gilbert, Rod, 140, 151, 165, 168, 171
Gillies, Clark, xiv
Gillis, Paul, 217
Gilmour, Doug, 226, 236
Gilmour, H. L., 30
Gingras, Tony, 19, 20
Giroux, E., 30

Godleski, Vin, 221
Godynyuk, Alexander, 236
Goldham, Bob, 95, 105, 112, 123
Goldup, Hank, 92
Goodenow, Bob, 235
Goodfellow, Ebbie, 76, 112
Goodman, Paul, 87
Goring, Robert (Butch), 198, 210, 215
Gorman, Tommy, 77, 103
Gosselin, Mario, 216
Gottselig, Johnny, 71
Goyette, Phil, 129, 136, 144, 151, 167
Gracie, Bob, 73
Graves, Adam, 229, 238
Green, Norman, 232, 233
Green, Red, 60
Green, Ted, 155, 159, 162
Gretzky, Wayne, 189, 192-93, 196,
    199, 202-3, 204-5, 207-211, 215,
    218-19, 222, 224, 227-28, 230, 232,
    236
    traded to Los Angeles Kings, 222-23
Griffis, Si, 42
Grosso, Don, 94
Grundman, Irving, 189
Guidolin, Armand (Bep), 167
Gund, George and Gordon, 189

**H**

Hadfield, Vic, 163
Haileybury, Ont., 36, 37, 38, 39
Hainsworth, George, 66, 67, 78, 79, 83,
    93
Halifax Crescents, 22
Halifax, N.S., 5
Hall, Glenn, 124, 125, 138, 140, 142,
    148, 152, 154, 156, 164, 243
Hall, Joe, 47-48
Hamilton Tigers, 60, 61
Hamilton, Jackie, 97
Hamilton, Ont., 46, 232
Hanlon, Glen, 216
Harkness, Ned, 169
Harris, Billy, 188
Harris, Ron, 168, 170
Hart Trophy, 120, 140, 151, 159
Hartford Whalers, 185, 192, 198
    join NHL, 193
Harvey, Doug, 121, 125, 133, 134, 135,
    136, 139, 141, 156, 227, 242
Harwood, Mel, 95

Hawerchuk, Dale, 192, 231
Hawood, Greg, 222
Hay, Bill, 135
Hayward, Brian, 217
Hebenton, Andy, 128
Hedberg, Anders, 189
Henderson, John, 123
Henderson, Paul, 144, 167
Henning, Lorne, 210
Henry, (Sugar) Jim, 112, 117, 118, 119,
    123
Henry, Gordon (Red), 119
Hern, Riley, 35
Hershey Bears, 119
Hewitson, Bobby, 71
Hewitt, Bill, 19
Hewitt, Foster, 19, 73
Hewitt, W. A., 18-19, 70
Hextall, Bryan, 85, 92, 94
Hextall, Ron, 215, 216, 218, 219, 224-25
Hicke, Bill, 137, 138
Hickey, Pat, 193
Hill, Mel, 88, 89
Hitchman, Lionel, 54, 56
Hockey Hall of Fame, xiv, 4, 31, 77
*Hockey Night in Canada*, 73
Hodge, Charlie, 123, 144, 149
Hodge, Ken, 154, 170
Holmes, Harry, 45, 61, 93
Horeck, Pete, 109
Horner, Red, 75, 79, 81, 84, 87, 91-92
Horton, Tim, 123, 141, 169
Horvath, Bronco, 135
Hospodar, Ed, 217
Houle, Rejean, 188, 191
Housley, Phil, 231
Houston Aeros, 169
Houston Astros, 202
Howe, Gordie, 104, 106-7, 110, 113,
    115-18, 120, 126, 128, 131, 138,
    142-44, 157, 163, 169, 192, 223,
    227, 241
Howe, Mark, 169, 192
Howe, Marty, 169, 192
Howe, Syd, 77, 79, 95, 98, 104, 157
Howell, Harry, 124-25, 151
Hrudey, Kelly, 216, 228
Hughes, Pat, 207
Hull, Bobby, 132-33, 135, 138-39, 141,
    143, 148-52, 157, 163, 167, 192,
    241

Hull, Brett, 224, 228, 232
Hull, Dennis, 171
Hunter, Dale, 201, 206, 220

**I**

Ilitch, Mike, 202, 221
Imlach, George (Punch), 131, 133-36, 138-39, 149, 153-54, 158, 162, 179, 187, 193
Imperatore, Arthur, 189
International Professional League, 21-22
Ion, Mickey, 44
Irvin, Dick, 70-73, 92, 96, 103-105, 113-114, 118-19, 121, 123-24
Irvine, George, 44
Irvine, Ted, 158
Ivan, Tommy, 108

**J**

Jackson, Harvey (Busher), 73, 74, 83
Jagr, Jaromir, 231, 239, 240
James Norris Trophy, 120, 142, 159, 190
Janney, Craig, 237
Jarvis, Doug, 219
Jeffrey, Larry, 145
Jenkins, Roger, 77
Jennings, Bill, 153
Johnson, Bob, 219, 232, 236, 240
Johnson, Tom, 167
Joliat, Aurel, 54, 57, 59, 70, 82
Jones, Terry, 199

**K**

Kansas City Scouts, 174, 181
Karakas, Mike, 83, 86-87, 99
Kearns, Doc, 26
Keeling, Butch, 67
Keenan, Mike, 208, 213, 223, 231, 233
Kelly, Bob, 177
Kelly, Leonard (Red), xiv, 106, 117-18, 120, 135, 140, 147-48, 150, 156, 159-60, 167, 170, 179, 241-43
Kendall, George, 40
Kennedy, Forbes, 158
Kennedy, George, 40
Kennedy, Ted, 97, 100, 105-6, 108, 110, 114, 123, 127
Kenora Thistles, 5, 32-34
Keon, Dave, 137, 141, 142, 143, 145, 148

Kerr, Dave, 76, 84, 86, 91
Kerr, Tim, 209
Kid Line, 73, 79, 83
Kilander, Ken, xii
Kilcoursie, Lord, 7, 8
Kilrea, Hec, 83
Kitchener (Berlin), Ont., 38, 39, 85
Klima, Petr, 211
Klingbeil, Ernie, 83
Klukay, Joe, 108
Koharski, Don, 220-21
Kraut Line, 85, 89, 90-91, 94, 102, 103
Krushelnyski, Mike, 222
Krutov, Vladimir, 226
Kucera, Frantisek, 240
Kurri, Jari, 209, 218, 236
Kyle, Gus, 109

**L**

Labine, Leo, 116
Lach, Elmer, 99, 100, 119
Lady Byng Trophy, 78, 100, 120, 142, 151
Laflamme, Gerry, 64
Lafleur, Guy, xiii, 164, 175-76, 178, 181-82, 184-86, 188-90, 192, 202, 208, 210, 223, 227, 241, 244
LaFontaine, Pat, 204, 216, 228, 236
LaForge, Bill, 208
Lalonde, Edouard (Newsy), 34, 37, 44, 47, 54, 180
Lambert, Yvon, 190
Langelle, Pete, 95
Langlois, Albert (Junior), 133
Langway, Rod, 229
Laperriere, Jacques, 148
Lapointe, Guy, 181
Laprairie, Benjamin (Bun), 83
Larionov, Igor, 226
Larmer, Steve, 239
Larochelle, Wildor, 70
Larocque, Michel (Bunny), 170, 182
Larose, Claude, 244
Larouche, Pierre, 186
Lawton, Brian, 204
Laycoe, Hal, 122, 159, 162
*Le Canada*, 58
Leach, Reg, 180, 181, 183
Leduc, Albert, 70
Lee, Peter, 186
Leeman, Gary, 236

Leetch, Brian, 237
Lefley, Chuck, 168
Lehman, Hugh, 46, 93
Lemaire, Jacques, 156, 184, 191, 206, 210
Lemieux, Claude, 213, 225-26
Lemieux, Mario, xiv, 192, 208, 219, 223, 225, 228, 234-35, 237, 238-40, 243
Lepine, Alfred, (Pit), 70
Lesueur, Percy, 31, 32
Leswick, Tony, 117, 121, 242
Levesque, Paul, 241
Levinsky, Alex (Hawk), 75, 86
Lewicki, Danny, 107
Lewis, Gord, 14
Ley, Rick, 227, 229
Lichtenhein, Sam, 46
Lindbergh, Pelle, 211
Lindros, Eric, 227, 235, 236
Lindsay, Bert, 42
Lindsay, Ted, 106, 109-10, 113, 117, 120, 123-24, 126, 137, 147, 150, 167, 168
Linseman, Ken, 207
Liscombe, Carl, 95, 101
Litzenberger, Ed, 138, 142
Liut, Mike, 205
Livingstone, Eddie, 43, 45, 47
Loob, Hakan, 219
Los Angeles Forum, 155
Los Angeles Kings, 174, 198
    join NHL, 149
Loughlin, Clem, 77
Lowe, Kevin, 207, 222, 239
Luce, Don, 178
Lumley, Harry, 101, 108, 112, 126, 133
Lund, Pentti, 111
Lynn, Vic, 105, 118
Lysiak, Tom, 203
Lytle, Andy, 93

**M**

MacDonald, Parker, 145, 199
MacInnis, Al, 226
MacKay, Mickey, 42, 46
Mackell, Fleming, 130
MacLeish, Rick, 173, 176, 183
MacNeil, Al, 162, 164
Macoun, Jamie, 214, 236
MacTavish, Craig, 233

Madison Square Garden, 65
Mahoney, Bill, 204
Mahovlich, Frank, 127, 133, 136, 141, 142, 144, 145, 163, 244
Mahovlich, Pete, 181, 186
Makarov, Sergei, 226
Maki, Chico, 168
Maki, Wayne, 159, 162
Malone, Joe (Phantom), 40, 41, 45, 55
Maloney, Dan, 208
Maloney, Dave, 191
Manderville, Kent, 236
Maniago, Cesare, 150
Manitoba Hockey Association, 15, 34
Mantha, Sylvio, 70, 80
Maple Leaf Gardens, 68, 72, 76
March, Harold (Mush), 76
Marcotte, Don, 189
Maritime Professional League, 40
Marotte, Gilles, 154
Marsh, Lou, 50, 53, 54, 69
Marshall, Bert, 179, 199
Marshall, Don, 123, 136, 137, 143, 144, 151
Martin, Alex, 15
Martin, Clare, 109
Martin, Pit, 154
Martin, Richard, 176
Mason, Bob, 216
Masson, Charlie, 33
Matheson, Godfrey, 99-100
Mazur, Eddie, 119
McArthur, Dalt, 138
McCammon, Bob, 219
McCauley, John, 206
McClelland, Kevin, 207
McCool, Frank, 100-101, 102
McCourt, Owen (Bud), 33
McDonald, Lanny, 188, 193, 212, 226
McDonald, Wilfrid (Bucko), 79, 95
McDougall, Bob, 19, 20
McDougall, Hartland, 15
McFarlane, Brian, 167, 168, 171
McGee, Frank (One-Eyed), 25, 26, 27, 29, 30, 31, 32, 39
McGimsie, Billy, 29
McGregor, Bruce, 138-39, 143, 170
McInnis, Paul, 221
McIntyre, Jack, 118
McKenney, Don, 144
McLaughlin, Major Frederic, 83, 85, 88, 99-100

McLea, Ernie, 17
McLean, Hugh, 113
McMullen, John, 202
McNab, Max, 108
McNall, Bruce, 219, 222-23
McNeil, Gerry, 109, 111, 114, 115, 119, 121
McNeill, Billy, 135
McSorley, Marty, 222
Meehan, Gerry, 164, 215
Meeker, Howie, 104, 105, 143
Melnyk, Jerry, 136
Meloche, Gilles, 209
Memorial Cup, 114
Merritt, Whitey, 15, 17
Messier, Mark, 192, 207, 208, 217, 230, 231-32, 236-38
Metz, Don, 95
Metz, Nick, 94, 95
Middleton, Rick, 189, 190, 222
Mikita, Stan, 135, 139, 141, 148, 150, 151, 156-57
Milbury, Mike, 227, 234
Miller, Joe, 66
Miner, John, 222
Minnesota North Stars, 198
   absorb Cleveland Barons, 189
   join NHL, 149, 154
Mogilny, Alexandr, 226
Mohns, Doug, 149
Moller, Randy, 206
Molson Breweries of Canada, 189
Moncton, N.B., 40
Mondou, Pierre, 70
Montagnards (Federal League), 34
Montreal Amateur Athletic Association, 9-10, 11-12, 14
Montreal Canadiens, xiii, 37, 39-40, 43-48, 57-60, 63-64, 68, 82, 174, 198
   as Cup winners, 45, 59, 70-1, 99, 103, 119, 126, 129, 131, 134, 136, 149, 151, 156, 159, 163-4, 169, 181, 184, 188-9, 191, 214
Montreal Crystals, 11, 13
Montreal Forum, 59, 71, 82, 105
*Montreal Gazette*, 11, 13
*Montreal Herald*, 18
Montreal Maroons, 59, 61-65, 77, 80-81, 85, 88
   as Cup winners, 79

Montreal Shamrocks, 18, 20, 22-23, 35, 37, 38
Montreal Victorias, 9-10, 11, 14, 16-18, 19-20, 24-25, 26, 35
Montreal Wanderers, xii, 5, 26-27, 31-35, 37-39, 41, 42, 45-46
   as Cup winners, 32, 34
Moog, Andy, 197, 239
Moore, A. E., 30
Moore, Alfie, 87
Moore, Dickie, 121-21, 124, 130, 131-32, 138, 144
Moran, Amby, 52
Morenz, Howie, 57, 59, 60, 64, 69, 70, 71, 77-78, 80, 82
Morris, Bernie, 45, 59
Morrison, Don, 112
Morrow, Ken, 206
Mortson, Gus, 106
Mosdell, Ken, 104, 116, 121
Mosienko, Bill, 100, 102, 115
Mount Royal Arena, 54
Mowers, Johnny, 97
Muckler, Ed, 227, 236
Mullen, Joey, 224, 238
Mummery, Harry, 544
Munro, Dunc, 63
Murdoch, Bob, 218, 227
Murdoch, Don, 232
Murphy, Joe, 214, 229-30
Murphy, Ron, 124, 158-59
Murray, Bryan, 232
Myers, Bob, 201
Mylnikov, Sergei, 226

N

Naslund, Mats, 217
National Hockey Association, 37-38, 39, 40-41, 43, 45, 47
National Hockey League, 3, 47, 103-104
   expansion and franchise shifts, 61, 63, 149-50, 154, 162, 166, 174, 181, 192-93, 202, 227-28, 232
   expulsions and suspensions, 54, 60, 64, 75, 106, 122, 158, 194, 208, 215, 221, 225, 231-32
   formation, 45
   players' strikes, 60, 61, 237
   playoff format, 51, 63-64, 66, 68-69, 74, 96, 154, 163, 164, 174-75, 185-

86, 198-200, 215
  structure, 51, 63, 75, 88, 174, 192-93, 198-9
Nattress, Ric, 236
Neale, Harry, 208, 211
Neeley, Cam, 234
Neilson, Roger, 201, 227
Nelson, Frank, 18
Nesterenko, Eric, 148, 149
Nevin, Bob, 141, 144
New Glasgow, N.S., 5, 32
New Jersey Devils, 202
  Schoenfeld dispute, 220-21
New Liskeard, Ont., 36
New Westminster, B.C., 40
New York Americans, 61, 63, 67, 68, 77, 81, 82, 84, 86, 89, 91, 96
New York Islanders, xiii, xiv, 174, 198
  as Cup winners, 196, 197-98, 201, 204
  join NHL, 166-67
New York Rangers, 27, 63, 64, 69, 174, 198
  as Cup winners, 66, 75, 84, 92
NHL Players' Association, 127, 181-82, 231
  collective bargaining with NHL, 235
  players' strike, 237
Nicholls, Bernie, 236
Nicholson, William (Big Bill), 24, 38
Nieuwendyk, Joe, 219
Nighbor, Frank, 42, 44, 49, 55
Nilsson, Kent, 218
Nilsson,, Ulf, 189, 190
Noble, Reg, 53
Norris Division, 174, 193, 198-99, 236
Norris, Jack, 154
Norris, Jim, 81, 97, 118, 132
Norris, Marguerite, 124
Northcott, Lawrence (Baldy), 78, 79
Nykoluk, Mike, 208
Nystrom, Bob, 195, 196, 209

**O**

O'Brien Trophy, 88
O'Brien, Ambrose, 36-38, 40
O'Brien, M. J., 36-38, 40
O'Meara, Baz, 54
O'Neill, Brian, 221
O'Reilly, Terry, 215, 222, 225
Oakland Seals. see also California Seals
  join NHL, 149

Oates, Adam, 211, 237
Olmstead, Bert, 125
Olympic Games, 60, 63, 199
Ontario Hockey Association, 9, 26
Ontario Professional League, 34, 38, 39
Orr, Bobby, 151, 154, 158-61, 163, 165-66, 170, 172-73, 175, 182, 189-90, 205, 211
Ottawa Capitals, 17, 19, 25
*Ottawa Citizen*, 14, 19
Ottawa Senators (1993), 232, 235, 236
Ottawa Senators (until 1934)
  as Cup winners, 35, 39, 50, 51, 56, 64
Ottawa Silver Seven, xi, 25-26, 27, 29-30, 31-32, 109
Ottawa Victorias, 33, 34
Ottawa, Ont., 11, 12, 23
Otto, Joel, 224

**P**

Pacific Coast Hockey League, 39-40, 41, 42, 43, 44, 46, 50, 52, 55, 57
Paddock, John, 195
Page, Pierre, 223, 232
Paiement, Wilf, 193
Palmateer, Mike, 188
Palmer, Bud, 126
Pappin, Jim, 152
Parent, Bernie, 154, 163, 171-73, 176-77, 179, 204
Parise, Jean-Paul, 175
Park, Brad, 165, 170, 180, 188, 203, 211
Patrick Division, 174, 193, 198-99
Patrick, Frank, 37, 39-40, 42, 46, 60
Patrick, James, 228
Patrick, Lester, 27, 31, 32, 37, 39-40, 42, 46, 60-61, 63, 65-66, 79, 85, 92, 102
Patrick, Lynn, 85, 94, 112, 116, 117, 118
Patrick, Murray (Muzz), 85, 92, 124, 141
Pavelich, Marty, 123
Pavelich, Matt, 171
Payne, Steve, 198
Pederson, Carl, 4
Peeters, Pete, 195, 196, 203
Penney, Steve, 205
Perreault, Gilbert, 176, 214
Perron, Jean, 210, 223

Peters, Jimmy, 109
Petit, Michel, 236
Philadelphia Flyers, 174, 198
    as Cup winners, 173, 177
    join NHL, 149, 154
Philadelphia Quakers, 70, 71
Philadelphia, Pa., 63
Phillips, Tom, 29
Pietrangelo, Frank, 233-34
Pilote, Pierre, 142, 148
Pilous, Rudy, 144
Pitre, Didier, 44
Pittsburgh Penguins, 174, 198
    as Cup winners, 234, 240
    join NHL, 149
Pittsburgh Yellow Jackets, 61, 62, 63,
    65, 69
Plager, Bob, 238
Plamondon, Gerry, 108
Plante, Jacques, 119, 121, 123, 125,
    129, 130, 134, 135, 137, 140, 144,
    150, 158, 160, 163, 211
Playfair, Larry, 225
Pleau, Larry, 227
Pocklington, Peter, 207, 222, 230
Poile, Bud, 105, 159, 162
Pollock, Sam, 147, 184, 189
Pony Line, 102
Port Arthur, Ont., 39
Port Hope, Ont., 39
Portland Rosebuds, 42
Potvin, Denis, 190, 194, 195, 197, 241
Poulin, Dave, 210
Powers, Eddie, 140, 142
Pratt, Walter (Babe), 84, 101, 106
Prentice, Dean, 124
Preston, Rich, 203
Priakin, Sergei, 223, 226
Primeau, Joe, 73, 83, 112, 114-15, 124
Prince Albert, Sask., 39
Prince of Wales Conference, 174, 198-99
Prince of Wales Trophy, 88, 125, 182
Probert, Bob, 232
Production Line, 106, 107, 109
Pronovost, Andre, 126, 130, 139
Propp, Brian, 195, 225
Provost, Claude, 134, 148
Prystai, Metro, 112
Pulford, Bob, 136, 141, 145, 154, 167
Pulford, E. H., 30
Punch Line, 100, 106

Q
Quackenbush, Bill, 109, 117
Quebec Aces, 113
Quebec Bulldogs, 37, 38, 39, 41-41, 45
Quebec Nordiques, 185, 198, 235
    join NHL, 193
Quebec Senior Hockey League, 113,
    117
Quebec, Que., 3, 11, 12-13
Queen's University, 5, 14, 20, 31
Quenneville, Joel, 193
Querrie, Charlie, 52, 53
Quilty, Johnny, 104
Quinn, Jim, 235
Quinn, Pat, 157-59, 208, 215
Quintal, Stephane, 237

R
Raleigh, Don, 111
Ramsey, Craig, 215
Ranford, Bill, 236
Rat Portage Thistles, 25-26, 29-30; see
    also Kenora Thistles
Rat Portage, Ont., 5, 25-26
Ratelle, Jean, 165, 180
Reardon, Ken, 104, 108, 111
Reardon, Terry, 103
Reaume, Marc, 135
Reay, Billy, 104, 144, 155
Redmond, Craig, 222-23
Reese, Jeff, 236
Regina Capitals, 52-55, 57
Reibel, Earl (Dutch), 121
Reise, Leo, 110-111
Renfrew Millionaires, 37, 38, 39, 46
Renfrew, Ont., 36, 40
Resch, Chico, 188, 190, 217
Rice, Steven, 236
Richard, Henri, xiii, 125, 128, 136, 140,
    144, 149, 151, 153, 163-64, 169
Richard, Maurice (Rocket), 96, 98-101,
    103-105, 110, 113-114, 116-17,
    119-126, 128-32, 136-38, 144, 150,
    175, 180, 208, 223, 241
Rideau Hall Rebels, 6, 8
riots in Montreal, 122, 208
Risebrough, Doug, 212, 232
Rivers, Gus, 69
Roach, John Ross, 53, 73
Robert, René, 176
Robertson, Earl, 84

Robinson, Larry, 188, 189, 191, 213, 229
Robitaille, Luc, 215
Rochefort, Leon, 144
Rodden, Mike, 80
Roenick, Jeremy, 224, 238, 239
Rolfe, Dale, 171
Rollins, Al, 112, 113, 116, 120, 122
Romnes, Doc, 87
Ronson, Len, 144
Rooney, Steve, 209
Ross, Art, 32-33, 35, 41, 58, 59, 88, 97-98, 102
Ross, P. D., 8, 72, 102
Rousseau, Bobby, 140, 148, 150, 156, 165-66
Roy, Patrick, 212, 213, 214
Ruel, Claude, 157, 197
Russell, Ernie, 38
Ryan, Tim, 167, 168-69

**S**

Saleski, Don, 179
Salming, Borje, 179
Samuelsson, Ulf, 234
San Jose Sharks, 237
Sanderson, Derek, 158, 161, 167
Saskatoon Crescents, 61
Saskatoon Sheiks, 52, 54
Sather, Glen, 227
Sator, Ted, 211, 215, 225, 227
Sauve, Bob, 203
Savard, Andre, 219
Savard, Denis, 229, 231
Savard, Ernie, 80
Sawchuk, Terry, 112, 113, 116-18, 120-21, 124, 127, 129, 138, 141, 145, 147, 152, 154, 156, 242
Schaefer, Paul, 83
Schinkel, Ken, 167
Schmautz, Bobby, 184, 188
Schmidt, Milt, 85, 90-91, 104, 129, 139, 142, 151, 154
Schock, Ron, 156
Schoenfeld, Jim, 211, 220-21
Schriner, Sweeney, 83, 94, 95, 104
Schultz, Dave, 171, 181, 196
Seattle Metropolitans, 42, 44-45, 46, 47, 50, 57, 60
Seibert, Earl, 86
Seiling, Rod, 144

Selke, Frank, 68, 103, 114, 131, 144, 147
Semenko, Dave, 207
Shack, Eddie, 131, 135, 143
Shero, Fred, 173, 189
Shibicky, Alex, 96
Shore, Eddie, 62, 64, 67, 74, 75-76, 81, 91
Shutt, Steve, 181
Simmer, Charlie, 190
Simmons, Don, 127, 128, 129, 130, 133, 141
Sinden, Harry, 151, 161, 190
Sittler, Darryl, 179-80, 182, 193
Skinner, Alf, 46
Skinner, Jimmy, 124, 169
Skov, Glen, 132, 133
Skrudland, Brian, 213
Sloan, Tod, 114, 125-26
Smeaton, Cooper, 102
Smith, (Chicago, recent, in Cup finals), 239
Smith, Ag, 84
Smith, Alf, 32, 33-34
Smith, Billy, 183, 190, 195, 204
Smith, Bobby, 189
Smith, Floyd, 177, 227
Smith, Gary, 168
Smith, Harry, xii, 30, 32
Smith, Kate, 173, 175, 181, 187
Smith, Mike, 223
Smith, Neil, 227, 234
Smith, Norm, 79, 80, 83
Smith, Sid, 108, 114
Smith, Steve, 212, 218, 239
Smiths Falls, 5, 31
Smythe Division, 174, 192, 198-99
Smythe, Conn, 63, 70, 72, 80, 84, 91, 92, 95, 99, 105, 106-107, 108, 114-16
Smythe, Stafford, 129, 156, 158
Snider, Ed, 235
Soviet Union, 144, 165, 167
Spectrum (Philadelphia), 155
Spokane Canaries, 44, 45
Springfield Indians, 91
St. Louis Blues, 174, 198
    join NHL, 149, 154
St. Louis Eagles, 77, 80
St. Patrick's Day riot, 122, 208
Stanfield, Fred, 154, 160

Staniowski, Ed, 178
Stanley of Preston, Lord Frederick
    Arthur, xv, 4, 6, 7-8, 10, 11, 34-37
Stanley, Algernon, 6, 7
Stanley, Allan, 109, 136
Stanley, Arthur, 6, 7
Stanley, Barney, 42
Stanowski, Wally, 106, 107
Starikov, Sergei, 226
Stasiuk, Vic, 138, 159
Stastny, Anton, 201
Stastny, Marian, 201
Stastny, Peter, 192, 193-94, 201, 216
Staszak, Ray, 211
Stellick, Gord, 227
Stemkowski, Pete, 165, 170
Stevens, Kevin, 237
Stevens, Scott, 232
Stewart, Bill, 85, 87-88
Stewart, Gaye, 102, 105, 112
Stewart, Nels, 62-63, 66, 91
Stewart, Ron, 187
Stickle, Leon, 195
Storey, Roy Alvin (Red), 133
Strachan, Jimmy, 59
Sudbury Wolves, 60
Sullivan, George (Red), 141
Sullivan, Jim, 221
Sundin, Mats, 226-27
Sundstrom, Patrik, 220
Suomi, Al, 83
Suter, Gary, 236
Sutter, Brent, 220
Sutter, Brian, 238
Sutter, Duane, 195
Sweetland, John, 8, 10
Sydney, N.S., 5, 41

**T**

Talbot, Jean-Guy, 167
Tampa Bay Lightning, 232, 235, 236
Taylor, Billy, 94, 95, 104, 106
Taylor, Dave, 190
Taylor, Fred (Cyclone), 37, 46
Team Canada, 144, 167, 236
Temiskaming Mines League, 36
Thomas, Cy, 105
Thomas, Wayne, 178
Thompson, Cecil (Tiny), 66, 67, 81, 88
Thompson, Cliff, 122
Thompson, Paul, 76, 86

Thompson, Percy, 61
Thoms, Bill, 75
Tikkanen, Esa, 229, 233
Timgren, Ray, 108, 109
Timmins brothers, 36, 37
Tkaczuk, Walt, 165
Tobin, Bill, 105
Tonelli, John, 196, 199, 212
Toppazzini, Jerry, 130
Toronto Arenas, 45, 46
Toronto Blueshirts, 40, 41-42, 43-44, 45
Toronto Maple Leafs, 174, 198
    as Cup winners, 53, 73, 95, 101,
    105, 107, 109, 114-15, 141, 143,
    146-47, 154
Toronto Maple Leafs (1908), 34
Toronto Marlboros, 26, 29
Toronto St. Patricks, 50-54, 58, 60, 63
*Toronto Star*, 19, 30, 50-51, 53, 54, 58,
    60, 70, 93
Toronto Tecumsehs, 40
*Toronto Telegram*, 14
Toronto Wellingtons (Iron Dukes), 23-
    24
Torrey, Bill, 166-67, 196
Tremblay, Gilles, 143, 144, 150
Tremblay, Jean-Claude, 135
Tremblay, Mario, 188, 215
Tremblay, Rejean, 226
Tretiak, Vladislav, 241, 242
Trihey, Harry, 18
Triple Crown Line, 190
Trois-Rivieres, Que., 29
Trottier, Bryan, xiv, 186, 190, 192, 197,
    231
Trottier, Dave, 83
Turgeon, Pierre, 236-37

**U**

Udvari, Frank, 141
Ullman, Norm, 143, 145, 148

**V**

Vachon, Rogatien (Rogie), 151, 153,
    159, 183, 219
Vadnais, Carol, 191
Vaive, Rick, 212
Van Hellemond, Andy, 191
Vancouver Canucks, 174, 198
    join NHL, 162
Vancouver Maroons, 55-58, 60, 61

Vancouver Millionaires, 40, 42, 44, 46, 47, 50, 51, 52-53, 55
Verbeek, Pat, 237
Vernon, Mike, 224
Vezina Trophy, 62, 78, 88, 100, 107, 125, 137, 140, 142, 144, 147, 177, 182
Vezina, Georges, 43, 45, 59, 60, 62, 93
Victoria Cougars, 60-61
Victoria Rink, Montreal, 11, 17
Victoria, B.C., 40, 41-42, 55, 57, 62
Voss, Carl

**W**

Walker, Jack, 44, 61
Walker, Squib, 107
Walsh, Marty, 39
Walter, Lou, 109
Wamsley, Rick, 236
Wares, Eddie, 94
Warwick, Grant, 94
Washington Capitals, 189, 193, 198
    join NHL, 174
Wasnie, Nick, 70
Waterloo, Ont., 14
Watson, Bryan, 150
Watson, Harry, 60, 104, 108, 114
Watson, Joe, 179
Watson, Phil, 94, 99, 124, 125, 128, 130, 139, 140.142
Watt, Tom, 199, 204, 210, 232
Webster, Tom, 227, 238
Weiland, Ralph (Cooney), 69, 89, 91
Wensink, John, 184
Wentworth, Cy, 71, 79
Western Canada Hockey League, 52, 55, 57, 60-61, 62, 63
Westmount, Que., 25, 26
Westwick, Harvey (Rat), 32, 33-34
Wharram, Ken, 148, 149, 152
Williams, Dave (Tiger), 182, 188, 194
Wilson, Cully, 59
Wilson, Johnny, 159
*Winnipeg Free Press*, 15-16
Winnipeg Jets, 185, 189, 193, 198, 202
Winnipeg Maple Leafs, 34
Winnipeg Rowing Club, 26
*Winnipeg Tribune*, 23
Winnipeg Victorias, 15, 16, 19-20, 22-23
World Hockey Association, 167, 169, 185, 189, 193

Worsley, Lorne (Gump), 125, 128, 130, 140, 144, 148, 149, 151, 154
Worters, Roy (Shrimp), 93
Wregget, Ken, 212, 225

**Y**

Young, Doug, 76
Young, Howie, 138
Young, Weldy, 11-12, 28
Yukon Territory, 5, 27-28
Yzerman, Steve, 221, 231

**Z**

Ziegler, John, 185, 189, 215, 221, 227, 232, 236, 237